Ethics and HRD

*New Perspectives in Organizational Learning,
Performance, and Change*
Jerry W. Gilley, Series Editor

Ethics and HRD
by Tim Hatcher

High Impact Learning
by Robert O. Brinkerhoff and Anne M. Apking

Transforming Work
by Patricia Boverie and Michael Kroth

*Philosophy and Practice of Organizational Learning,
Performance, and Change*
by Jerry W. Gilley, Peter Dean, and Laura Bierema

*Assessing the Financial Benefits of Human Resource
Development*
by Richard A. Swanson

The Manager as Change Agent
by Jerry W. Gilley, Scott A. Quatro, Erik Hoekstra,
Doug D. Whittle, and Ann Maycunich

Ethics and HRD

A New Approach to Leading Responsible
Organizations

New Perspectives in Organizational Learning,
Performance, and Change

Tim Hatcher

BASIC
BOOKS

A Member of the Perseus Books Group

Many of the designations used by manufacturers and sellers to distinguish their products are claimed as trademarks. Where those designations appear in this book and Basic Books was aware of a trademark claim, the designations have been printed in initial capital letters.

Copyright © 2002 by Tim Hatcher
Previously published by Perseus Publishing
Published by Basic Books

Library of Congress Control Number: 2002105976
ISBN 0-7382-0564-8

Basic Books is a member of the Perseus Books Group.

Find us on the World Wide Web at http://www.basicbooks.com

Books published by Basic Books are available at special discounts for bulk purchases in the U.S. by corporations, institutions, and other organizations. For more information, please contact the Special Markets Department at the Perseus Books Group, 11 Cambridge Center, Cambridge, MA 02142, or call (617) 252–5298 or (800) 255-1514, or e-mail special.markets@perseusbooks.com

Text design by Tonya Hahn
Set in 10.5-point Minion by the Perseus Books Group

First printing, July, 2002

Publisher's Note

Organizations are living systems, in a constant state of dynamic evolution. *New Perspectives in Organizational Learning, Performance, and Change* is designed to showcase the most current theory and practice in human resource and organizational development, exploring all aspects of the field—from performance management to adult learning to corporate culture. Integrating cutting-edge research and innovative management practice, this library of titles will serve as an essential resource for human resource professionals, educators, students, and managers in all types of organizations.

The series editorial board includes leading academics and practitioners whose insights are shaping the theory and application of human resource development and organizational design.

Series Editor
Jerry W. Gilley, Colorado State University

Editorial Board

This book is dedicated to
Linda Hatcher, my life's companion.

FEBRUARY, 2002 TIM HATCHER

Contents

Part 1 ■ The Need for Ethical HRD

Part 2 ■ Mapping the Territory: The Conceptual and Practical Framework of Ethical HRD

Part 3 ■ Contemporary Issues Influencing Societies, Organizations, and HRD

List of Figures and Tables

Preface and Acknowledgments

Warning: There will be times when the ideas, suggestions, and observations you read herein may seem peculiar, even bizarre, especially for a book in a series on organizational learning, performance, and change. What you are about to read may or may not be controversial depending on your point of view, and might *prime facie* seem prejudiced, biased, and opinionated, again, based upon your point of view.

For the prejudices, opinions, strong beliefs, and passions that support the content of this book I offer no academic hedges, no protective disclaimers. And I offer no apologies. You may find it tempting to dismiss the ideas you encounter here as exaggerations of a self-obsessed "baby boomer" or lunacy in such a consumer-based economy. Or, you may think them simply unrealistic in today's bottom-line business climate. But, you may also find a resonance with your experiences with organizations and communities and the people in them, and your true, heart-felt attitudes toward organizations as ethical and responsible places. Before dismissing what your intellect says is fantasy, consult your heart. Do not be lulled into that complacent and all too comfortable place where we always seek a quick fix, a "silver bullet" for our complex organizational and societal problems. Instead, acknowledge that tiny yet nagging voice of conscience that you recognize as simply the right thing to do. And doing the "right thing" cannot, *must not* be taken lightly.

I am grateful to those who came before; whose works are represented here and who influenced my thinking and being—for laying the groundwork for new ideas. I also acknowledge the scholars and practitioners of the Academy of Human Resource Development, without whose support, challenge, and encouragement this book would have not been possible. My gratitude goes also to the staff at Perseus Publishing, especially to Nick Philipson, for his leadership in the New Perspectives in Organizational Learning, Performance, and Change series and to Arlinda Shtuni for her helpful editing. To Jerry Gilley goes credit for the vision of the series and encouragement for me to continue writing. Finally, thanks to Reid Bates for his thoughtful review of my words and thoughts.

Part 1

The Need for Ethical HRD

Introduction and Overview

Doing good is not easy. It is not always obvious or enjoyable. It can even be painful. Being ethical, moral, and caring about people and the environment is daunting in a world filled with conflict and hatred on a global scale, where hundreds of species and entire cultures teeter on the brink of destruction, where new surveillance technologies deprive us of our privacy and our humanity, where corporations dump people like garbage and are more powerful than governments, and where commerce is hell-bent on unchecked economic expansion. Although not all organizations are irresponsible, it seems we have come to the point where we *must* have people and organizations that do the right thing more often than the alternative, organizations and leaders that are moral, ethical, and socially responsible.

The time to act is already upon us. We can no longer afford to be complacent. The price of our complacency may at first seem negligible. Paying out a little money under the table to do business in China isn't such a big deal—almost everybody does it. Reporting a small trickle of industrial wastes into an already polluted stream is only going to stir up trouble for the company, isn't it? And what about the results of that needs assessment being used to justify a lay-off? It's not the human resource development (HRD) department's fault; they were only doing their job. Cutting a few people or dumping a little waste doesn't really create much of a problem for society or the environment. Companies and the people in them do this sort of thing every day, and are still successful; but for how long?

There is growing evidence that companies without a moral compass will be left adrift in a sea of organizations charting an ethical course. Recent reports from the Business for Social Responsibility, the Conference Board, *Fortune* magazine, Arthur Little, Ltd., and other leading business research organizations reveal:

3

- Employees are turning their backs on employers with no sense of moral responsibility. Ethical issues are becoming crucial in the recruitment process. Companies with tarnished reputations face problems in recruiting top talent.
- A total of eighty-five of the London Stock Exchange (FTSE) 100 (UK's Dow) top companies have a code of ethics. And even though many observers see such statements as mere rhetoric, companies that focus on ethics actually do better. A 1999 survey showed that companies with codes of ethics outperformed those with none. Even the stock market is getting into the act. Two indices, the Dow Jones Group Sustainability Index and the FTSE4Good index show that listed companies outperform others on an average of over 35 percent.
- Companies with good reputations enhance their brand image. The proportion of corporate value obtained from intangible assets like reputation rose over 50 percent from 1981 to 1998.
- Customer loyalty is enhanced. A recent study found that almost 100 percent of the population wants companies to focus on more than profit and over 50 percent of the respondents said they form an impression of a company based on its social responsiveness, or lack thereof.
- Assets in socially screened investment portfolios rose by almost 40 percent between 1999 and 2001. A total of 33 percent of stock analysts consider that environmental issues affect the value of investments.
- Ethical companies enhance their productivity and improve the quality of their products and services. They also expend fewer resources on regulatory oversight.
- Companies with environmental management systems substantially reduce their operating costs. Operational efficiencies are enhanced through reductions in material wastes and energy consumption.
- Even MBAs, young Turks taught well to count beans, are getting into the socially responsible act. A survey of graduate programs in the United States, Asia, Europe, and the Americas by the Aspen Institute reveals a growing dedication to the inclusion of social and environmental issues in MBA programs.

Less than stellar behavior associated with organizations and their leaders accounts for losses of almost $3 trillion a year in the United States alone (Estes, 1996), and worldwide, the figure may be triple. But the true costs of unethical and immoral corporate activity remains hidden behind the drawn faces of frustrated and dejected employees, abused and gun-shy communities, and ecosystems reeling from overuse and undermanagement.

Unethical companies suffer financial losses not only as a result of fines and other legal costs but also as a result of a disintegrating reputation. And it's not just bad behaviors we know about. It's not just an *Exxon-Valdez* or a Union Carbide Bhopol, but financial giants like Salomon Brothers and Prudential and standard-bearers like Texaco, Shell, and Enron. These and other companies suffer losses not so much from fines, but the loss of trust from the investment community and the public. A company that is not trusted by employees, customers, suppliers, communities, and other stakeholders will suffer in the long run.

Once a company turns its back on ethics, there is literally no place to hide. Companies quickly learn that bad behavior they thought was hidden in one obscure location or through complex regulations or accounting procedures is suddenly all over the Internet one day and the day after their CEO is sweating bullets on CNN. The unsavory saga of Kenneth Lay and Enron had just unfolded as this book went to press.

It is easy to point the finger of blame at leadership. Managers, CEOs, and CFOs who call the shots are to blame, not engineers, technicians, clerks, or lowly trainers. But are our leaders solely responsible? Can we relinquish responsibility to top management so easily? Human resource development professionals are just as guilty and the profession of HRD is as culpable as any CEO or top manager. HRD professionals have been complicit in helping to create organizations and workplaces that do little to enhance the human spirit or protect the environment. The knowledge we help to build is used for myriad reasons; some enhance us whereas others are questionable in terms of their outcomes. HRD changes attitudes as well. Some are changed to emancipate people; some are changed to make people more acquiescent. And performance is improved for economic gain alone at the expense of society and the environment. Is it right for us to provide training in organizations that rob us of our spirit? Is it right for us to improve the performance of companies that destroy the environment or ruin an indigenous culture? Issues concerning ethics and social responsibility are all around us, all the time. Great thinkers, philosophers, scholars, and philanthropists toil night and day to solve our moral dilemmas. But within HRD who is doing anything about ethics and social responsibility? Who is "minding the store"?

It was never my intention to *comprehensively* explore ethics, corporate social responsibility, environmentalism, or HRD. That is beyond the scope of this book. I do believe, however, that the time has come to introduce some new and different ideas about the role of HRD in creating ethical and sustainable workplaces and to introduce concepts and strategies that hopefully will inform, inspire change, or at least stimulate dialogue. With new and different information we are better equipped to articulate our personal views and defend them. But most important, an opportunity exists for HRD professionals to gain a new philosophical perspective that allows for critical examination of our own thinking and attitudes and to create a new possibility for the future of the field of HRD.

Underlying Assumptions

It is important for the consumers of the ideas offered here to understand the underlying assumptions. These assumptions are important for us to better understand a particular point of view. If openness is maintained in the interpretation of the ideas and strategies herein, a broader and more holistic view of what human resource development can accomplish and an appreciation and awareness of the immediacy of changes needed in HRD research and practice can be realized.

One of the primary assumptions that sets the tone for this book is the belief that humans are social beings that strive for membership in orderly social structures and to feel "alive" by contributing to others (human and nonhuman entities such as plants and animals) and to society. We are philanthropic and volunteer our time, energies, and skills; most of us care about the planet; and we empathize with people who are less fortunate. We are also values-driven and with few exceptions strive to do what we believe is the right thing most of the time. We attempt to transfer these innately human desires to our organizations. But as much as we desire meaningful, humane, and inspiring workplaces, many of our organizations fall short.

Because organizations are not artificial entities, but are simply groups of *people*, they seek order out of chaos and to feel "alive." They accomplish this by accommodating economic and social norms that prescribe corporate culture, processes, and outcomes. Unfortunately, too few of us work in "alive," responsible, and humane organizations dedicated to individual success, much less social and environmental success. Many of us work in organizations that exhibit more "dead" than alive tendencies; inert organizations that strive only to feed the coffers of a handful of stockholders or, worse, to meet the capricious demands of Wall Street or Fleet Street. But are our organizations really the mindless automatons they appear to be? Are they not more reflective of the collective mind-sets of employees and leaders?

The extent to which an organization is aware of its outcomes to people, cultures, society, and the environment is a direct result of leadership and whether key employees exhibit ethical and socially responsible behaviors. But too few business leaders behave as if they have any sensibilities or competencies in establishing or maintaining socially responsible and ethical organizations. Leaders pressured to achieve financial results at any cost typically place the ends before the means. Business becomes a sort of survival of the fittest where eat or be eaten is the predominate code of ethics, the same law of the jungle that street gangs use. Leaders must work hard to keep business and their own souls separated and to ensure that a company's goals are met, goals that typically do not include simply doing the right thing. Yet "our obsession for the economic is not something that can be managed apart from or in parallel with our spiritual sensibilities" (Dalla Costa, 1998, p. 60).

With globalization, high-speed technological changes, wildly fluctuating economies, a changing workforce, an unstable environmental climate, and erratic politics, corporate ethics and social responsibility are needed more now than ever before. The general absence of ethical and responsible leadership has created an opportunity for human resource development professionals to transform themselves from the handmaidens of management to become leaders in ethics and social and environmental responsibility. The field of HRD can take the lead in developing ethical and socially responsive workplaces and human resource development professionals can become the *conscience* of our organizations, a conscience that is most assuredly needed.

Another assumption is that research and practice in HRD is not based on a theoretical framework that addresses the important issues of ethics and social responsibility. With a few exceptions, namely Richard Swanson's recent addition of an ethical "rug" underneath his three-legged stool (see p. 8 for an explanation of HRD theoretical foundations), and Roger Kaufman and his colleagues' work in addressing societal issues in strategic planning for HRD (see Chapter 4 on theory and research in CSR), little has been accomplished in developing theoretical foundations for HRD that provide a framework where ethics and social responsibility are consistently and adequately addressed. In other words, HRD's research and practice is couched primarily within whatever discipline is most prevalent instead of which foundations will lead us to more ethical, responsible, and sustainable ends. Currently, economics is the primary foundation on which much research and practice in HRD is based (Hatcher, 2000b). Using economics as a theoretical base for HRD research and practice seems limiting and precludes the kinds of outcomes that sustain the environment and us.

Another problem with HRD research and practice as it is currently being carried out is that much of it is based on a rational scientific model left over from the seventeenth century. For example, the large majority of HRD-related

---

Theoretical Foundations of Human Resource Development

Being a multidisciplinary field, the underlying theoretical foundation of HRD is derived from multiple theories and disciplines. Several disciplines or theories have been identified as contributing to the knowledge base of HRD, namely education, general systems theory, economics, psychology, sociology, and organizational behavior (Hatcher, 2000b). Other disciplines such as anthropology and management have also been mentioned (Chalofsky and Lincoln, 1983). Jacobs (1990) indicated five bodies of knowledge: education, systems theory, economics, psychology, and organizational behavior. Passmore (1996), reflecting on the work of Swanson, said there are three disciplinary bases: economics, general systems theory, and psychology. Swanson (1999) recently added ethics as the rug underneath his three-legged stool of HRD theories that include general systems theory, economics, and psychology. Jacobs (1990), Swanson (1999), Passmore (1996), and Hatcher (2000b) concluded that although various bodies of knowledge had influenced HRD, it should focus on economic, psychological, systems theory, social benefits, and ethics.

---

published research is descriptive, using survey-based measures. Although qualitative research such as ethnographies and case studies are gaining some ground, by and large HRD research is still stuck in a seventeenth-century rut. But there is hope. Survey-based research, if well done and well intentioned, can add real value. On the other hand, much current research and practice in HRD is being forced into a model that does little to enhance our abilities to add value to anything but a financial statement or supporting academic tenure. Do not assume that adding financial value to companies or being awarded tenure is bad. It would be unadvisable to be so naive. But there is no good reason why we shouldn't strongly question why we can't also add value to humanity, community, society, and the ecosystem, especially when they are in such need of our help. As my friend and colleague Neal Chalofsky recently asked in a conference workshop on spirituality in HRD, "What if we took HRD out of the organizational context?" What if we removed the constraints of the corporation and organization? What would HRD look like then?

Why must we be so focused, so myopically intent on return on a monetary investment when we can also show how what we do can improve how individuals treat one another, what we do to the cultures our companies impact, how we affect the communities we rely upon, and how we impact the environment that we all must share? Maybe one of the reasons we are so focused on the bottom line is that we don't realize there is more than one bottom line.

Kaufman (1997) said we have two bottom lines: a conventional one of short-term profits and a progressive one of value added to society. Elkington (1998) suggested a triple bottom line focusing on economic prosperity, environmental quality, and social justice. Although they are innovative and important, these approaches fall short when trying to address the overt relationship, the obvious correlation between profit and environmental and social principles. They also fail to address the important and growing role that HRD plays in this relationship.

It is axiomatic that without profit, without financial support almost all other organizational efforts appear moot or at least live precarious lives. Certainly, without finances organizations have a difficult time positively influencing the environment or society or anything else, for that matter. But organizations that are blind to shifting societal needs can also suffer financially. The U.S. tobacco industry's failure to read a changing cultural dynamic negatively impacted their bottom line. Seeing profit, the environment, and society as three separate and *unequal* entities keeps companies from addressing problems in a holistic manner, and begs for isolated, limited, and ineffective interventions. Narrow views distort the true interdependent and symbiotic relationship that exists between the environment, society, and profit, that when one gains in strength the others are also impacted.

Organizations that fail to understand the cause and effect side of being ethical and environmentally and socially responsible are more and more subject to scrutiny by a demanding and increasingly aware public, technology-savvy special interest groups, and caring and sometimes radical consumers looking for a bargain while insisting on corporate citizenship. Enron is a good example of a successful company that suffered because of improprieties in accounting and leadership that caused a free fall in its reputation. This lack of understanding of our interdependency requires a more inclusive approach to ethics and social responsibility.

Another important inference is that we are facing a paradox that human resource development should be vital to the examination of corporate social and environmental responsibility but that to date has made few contributions. It is not delivering what it could deliver to organizations, to society, and the environment. The task facing us is difficult: to *prove* that HRD should be central to the creation of ethical and responsible organizations but with little more than atheoretical evidence. To date, HRD's contribution to ethics and the social responsibility of our organizations appears trivial, particularly as compared to other disciplines such as sociology. But its concerns are not tangential to ethics or social or environmental responsibility—they are essential. The assumption is that we can and should address this paradox by providing realistic and meaningful solutions through learning and performance improvement processes.

The final assumption is that even though most professionals would agree that HRD has some ethical, social, and environmental responsibilities, shifting our focus to them is not an overly popular or readily accepted position, and those who hold such beliefs are in a small minority. I will address the minority issue first, the validity issue second, and finish by addressing detractors and critics who hold different and opposing viewpoints.

Based on seminal research into the role of transformational values in American life, P. H. Ray and S. R. Anderson (2000) discovered the existence and emergence of a large group of people they call "cultural creatives." Estimated at over 50 million strong in the United States and an estimated 80 to 90 million more in Europe, cultural creatives possess values and beliefs that make them especially sensitive to humanitarian, spiritual, and environmental needs. These beliefs include spiritual transformation, ecological sustainability, the value and worth of relationships and feminine points of view, and "disaffection with the large institutions of modern life, including both left and right in politics, and rejection of materialism and status display" (P. H. Ray and S. R. Anderson, 2000, p. 4). These millions of people make up the leading edge of most of the positive cultural and environmental changes currently taking place and have a significant influence on society and the environment. Since it would be hard to consider 150 million people as a minority, we are certainly not alone.

Whether HRD should become more involved in ethics and social responsibility is best answered by adding an additional assumption. The assumption is that the consciousness of humanity is in flux and in response HRD must assume a more responsive position. My research and publications on the role of HRD in enhancing social and environmental responsibility and the research and theories of Ken Wilber, Clare Graves, and D. Beck and C. Cowen on developing a point of view or theory of the universe that includes integrating spirituality, values, business, politics, and science provide empirical and conceptual support for this assumption.

The profession of HRD espouses to develop people and enhance organizations and thus *inherently* has a responsibility to the *receivers* of an organization's output. This holds true, whether a positive output is desired, as in the case of a skilled workforce, or a negative output, as in pollution. Yet this prime edict, this inherently vital purpose of the profession to address the true outcomes of our actions beyond the factory gates or boardroom walls has been all but ignored.

FIGURE 1.1   Social Responsibility Performance Outcomes Model

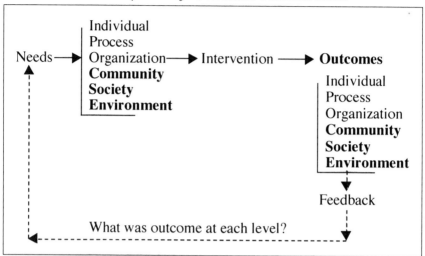

SOURCE: T. G. Hatcher (2000a). The social responsibility performance outcomes model: building socially responsible companies through performance improvement outcomes. *Performance Improvement 39*, 21. Reprinted by permission of the International Society for Performance Improvement.

Research suggests that because the stated purpose of HRD is to enhance the strategic initiatives of an organization, it is directly and obviously linked to the outcomes of the implementation of corporate strategies (Hatcher, 1998, 1999, 2000a, 2000b, 2001; Kaufman, 1992). The implication is that the more involved HRD is in establishing strategy for an organization the more such goals might reflect humane and environmentally sustainable objectives. This is especially true when HRD professionals apply conceptual models such as the Social Responsibility Performance Outcomes Model illustrated in Figure 1.1 (Hatcher, 2000a). This planning and performance improvement model was designed to help the HRD professional enhance individual, process, and organizational levels of performance, and also to focus on desired outcomes external to the organization that include societal and environmental levels of performance. This stakeholder model systematically addresses the impact of HRD methods such as a needs assessment and interventions such as training beyond people, processes, and organizations to include their impact on society, communities, and the environment.

Models such as this reflect the changing nature of work, the search for meaning in work, and HRD's changing role in that transition. The notion that HRD is not separated from, but is part of the overall fabric of business, society, and our psyches, and that what we do and how we view reality has an impact at all levels. This should be readily recognized as *systems thinking*. But it is more than just seeing how parts are interrelated and the extent to which they are interdependent; it is part of a larger, more holistic, integrative assumption, and a broader, more inclusive theory, what Wilber (2000) calls a *theory of everything*.

Based on leading research into human consciousness and values by Graves (1970), refined by Beck and Cowan's (1995) *Spiral Dynamics,* and finally consolidated in Wilber's *Theory of Everything* (2000), a conclusion is drawn that we are at a transition point in our journey as humans in the cosmos. We have reached a terminus of one worldview and are ensnared in the transition to another.

In getting to this point we have achieved success in basic survival, we have found some sense of harmony and security, have experienced and appreciated the power of magic and mystical forces in our lives, have sought purpose and to bring truth and order to our existence, and pursue prosperity through scientific achievement and material gains. But now the ground is shifting. We are being shaken into another reality, another "wave of existence" that reflects the need for us to move beyond the material, the scientific, and the economic, but toward what?

First, we can embrace environmental sensitivity, dialogue, relationships, human potential, human rights, liberation theology, Gaia, feminism, diversity, community, caring, and spirit. Then we move into integrative, natural, holistic, "grand unification," and mystical flow-states (Wilber, 2000). Without the belief that we *progress,* that we *evolve* into these successive levels of consciousness, we are destined to "remain victims of a global 'autoimmune disease'" (Wilber, 2000, p. 14), where various beliefs and worldviews are constantly in conflict with one another and continually fight to establish supremacy. As these words were being written, such a conflict, a war of ideologies, was being waged. We are witness to the destruction wielded by terrorists professing one of Islam's dogmas, the *Jihad,* a false holy war with the ideology of the West, with deeds that will forever be immortalized as barbaric. So, whether you are a corporate crusader, a fanatical consumer, a critic of all things transcendent, a warmonger, a religious fanatic, noncommittal to just about anything, or a "cultural creative," this noble intent should be acknowledged and your worldviews scrutinized to be more ethical and responsible. The hope is that even the most rabid critics still have a touch of social conscience and altruism somewhere in their heart.

Turning now to the critics who are at this point no doubt geared up with their denunciations, allow me to address a few of their more obvious criticisms. One response may be that we are having a hard enough time coping with an ever-changing corporate climate, responding to executive demands and volatile and capricious markets; that as much as we might like to have squeaky-clean ethics and help society and the environment, even if we could, it is just not part of our mission as a field of study and practice. We are *human* resource development, with many foibles for sure, but human nonetheless. We simply cannot expect ethical perfection and are not responsible for what happens to our cultures and our ecosystems. To try and add an additional focus on things as ambiguous as society or ubiquitous as the environment to our responsibilities would stifle whatever minimal improvements we may be making to performance and learning in our organizations. In response to this reluctance to address social and environmental ills, it should be obvious to all but the most uninformed that however much we may want to relinquish our responsibility, we cannot help but influence society and the environment. Thus, we need to acknowledge our responsibility and get on with the work of better integrating HRD with ethics and social responsibility.

The next response from the critics is that if we choose a narrow role for HRD as primarily enhancing corporate strategies and if those strategies are within the rules of the game and limits of the law, then inherently HRD is socially responsible. This response tries to defuse the conflict between social responsibility and the role of HRD by assuming that as long as a company is legally upright then it is responsible, and thus as a corporate function HRD is adding to that responsibility. But what about HRD in organizations that meet the letter of the law yet creates products or offers services that cause pain to people, society, or the environment, or have the potential to destroy? How can we justify our position as developers of humans and the creation of a caring and sustainable profession if we are complicit in helping organizations harm humanity and the environment?

This "head in the sand" response suggests that if our organizations relinquish their social responsibility by ignoring ethical, social, and environmental problems, the problems will just go away. It also suggests that organizations are *separate from,* not *part of* society or the environment, but more business *and* society than business *in* society. Business *and* society permits business to be seen as a set of independent variables with little or no legitimacy or responsibility to an external society. Business *in* society, on the other hand, views business as a subsidiary of society, "created to serve economic functions in an institutional division of labor that, if left to operate unimpeded, results in societal stability and well-being" (Wood, 1991b, p. 67). To illustrate the recklessness of the business *and* society model, one need look no further than the many social and environmental problems that consistently impact our organizations and HRD professionals. Ignoring problems only exacerbates their severity and tenure; they do not go away.

Another critical point of view suggests that HRD is still a fledgling field of study; that because in its infancy HRD as a profession is not capable of nor should be expected to address ethical, social, and environmental problems with anything but the most elementary outcomes. To respond, address the question of whether HRD is a collection of skills, a profession, or an occupation. If we espouse to be a *profession* we must understand that a profession is different from a collection of skills or an occupation by certain shared characteristics. These characteristics are extensive intellectual knowledge and the provision of products and services that are important to the organized functioning and enhancement of *society*. Human resource development has recognized collections of competencies[1] that identify extensive intellectual knowledge. But what we have yet to acknowledge or resolve is our fundamental responsibility to society. We need to critically assess certain taken-for-granted worldviews in which HRD is embedded, to enhance the likelihood that as individuals and as a profession we will act consciously and take a leadership role on issues of social responsibility and environmental stewardship. This is the true test of a profession.

There are no doubt other disapproving opinions by people with arguments that are well thought out and well intentioned, arguments that I have not considered. Silencing the critics is not my objective. Frankly, if there were no critics, there wouldn't be much to say to begin with.

There has never been a better and more significant time than now to critically assess where we stand as professionals and leaders, to make a conscious decision to bring ethics and social and environmental responsibility to the forefront. What we should no longer accept is acquiescence and apathy. We cannot continue along the same path, a path that has led us to what many believe is the brink of disaster. But instead of such a "gloom and doom" scenario, a more positive view suggests that we have a *choice*. We can choose to embrace ethics and social and environmental responsibility, or live with the consequences. The problem is the true nature of such consequences is a mystery. History paints a dismal picture every time we have chosen to turn our backs on ethics and social responsibility. There is value in these lessons but only if we choose to recognize and learn from them. Faced with a dilemma, a crisis, or a conflicting situation provides us with an opportunity to learn. Learning begins with the need to change and change is stimulated by new ideas. This book presents new ideas that are designed to stimulate changes in the way we treat one another and our relationships with organizations, communities, cultures, societies, and the environment.

But this book is about more than learning and change. It is about *vision* for leadership in organizations. A vision of a future that we want to be a part of, that is safe, nurturing, and full of hope and security. A vision of leadership in organizations that recognizes, nurtures, and is responsible to all stakeholders, including employees, families, communities, the environment, society, and, of course, stockholders. Vision that gives leaders and managers a way to sidestep the current course of indifference toward humanity and our environment that many of our organizations seem to be on, and proceed down a *new* path. Rupert Sheldrake, one of the world's foremost biologists, said, "If we are to enter the new millennium with any hope for the future, we need to recover a new vision of human nature and of our relationship to the living earth" (Sheldrake, 1991, p. 210).

A new way of seeing organizations will not be the easier, softer way. It requires a retooling of current popular beliefs about leadership in and management of human resources, a new way of thinking and acting. Even though some people may see it as too different or impossible to accomplish, it is doable and rational. To build sustainable organizations, we need new tools and methods, but we also need inspiration. Inspiration comes from a personal desire to do things in a different way, and knowledge that organizations can be managed and led differently, more humanely, more responsibly, without compromising economic vitality. This book provides a beginning. It cajoles us to ask new and tough questions and to seek creative solutions to our moral dilemmas. It provides a number of answers, but most important, it offers the means for leaders and others who find themselves part of almost any kind of organization to find inspiration.

Overview of the Book

To meet challenges we must understand what pressures us to behave in ways that are not sustainable, that do not ensure the future will be as bright as the present, and that cause us to act in ways that disregard our ethics and values. We need to become aware of how globalization and technology, development and economics have shaped and continue to shape what the HRD profession may become in the future. Chapters 1 and 2 and Chapters 6 through 9 address these issues and their impact on HRD. But it is not enough to simply be aware; we must arm ourselves with knowledge. Basing our journey on theory is a wise and prudent way to be well grounded in recognized concepts. These concepts are described and discussed in Chapter 3. To know where we need to go, we must appreciate where we have been and where we are now. Chapter 4 does this by reviewing theory and research in ethics, social responsibility, and leadership. Although concepts and theory keep us scholarly, we must also recognize and appreciate how concepts work in practice. Chapter 5 addresses this need by discussing the practice of ethical leadership and social responsibility. Finally, contemporary opinions about the role of HRD have left the field basically impotent in fixing problems in ethics and social responsibility. One reason that HRD has had such little impact is its focus and its goals. Chapter 10 discusses several current imperatives designed to enhance ethics and social responsibility and shows why HRD is in a position to accomplish these imperatives.

In conclusion, opportunities now exist for HRD to assume leadership in enhancing ethical and socially responsible organizations. Possibilities sometimes become probabilities. And what is probable in the end becomes tangible only through *action*. But we must not act on impulse or emotion alone. We must act on *knowledge* and *understanding* to enable us as individuals and as part of a profession to add value beyond the instrumental. We need to view our organizations as part of the greater whole and understand their role in either building a better future or helping to destroy any chance that we might have for one.

This book was written with the passionate belief that we have come to a crossroads of values and beliefs and we must make tough decisions about the future of our world. There is no guarantee that we will make the right decisions. Sadly, history provides too many appalling illustrations of our questionable decisionmaking abilities. If we indeed desire a better world we must engage in active dialogue and learning. This book facilitates that dialogue and the chance to learn.

Note

1. See Pat McLagan's 1989 HRD competencies report published by ASTD and Bill Rothwell's ASTD Competencies studies published in 1999.

What is Driving the Need for Ethical HRD?

Why are some organizations successful and others fail? Why are some companies ethical and socially responsible, but others continue to treat people, cultures, communities, and the environment poorly? Companies and organizations are able to act and react effectively and ethically, and not because they are more technically savvy or have richer experiences with globalization or possess more sophisticated costs controls. It is because they are capable of successfully responding to a wide variety of changes. Change is not a reaction to external pressures, although such pressures certainly exist and companies do sometimes react posthaste, or because they possess the internal tools to do so. Successful change comes as a result of a deep devotion to underlying core values and guiding principles. A good example is Southwest Airlines' belief in its people. The September 11, 2001, terrorist attacks in the United States resulted in the cancellation of all air travel. Most major airlines laid off hundreds of thousands of employees, but Southwest refused to lay off its employees. This core value suggests that it is no coincidence that Southwest was one of only three major airlines reporting profits in the third quarter of 2001.

Organizations also change because of commitment, vision, beliefs, mental models, knowledge and learning, culture and shared underlying assumptions, significant critical events, and changing systems and structures. The catalyst that brings together these change ingredients by providing a focal point for change is *people*. Organizations generally do not change via mechanical or instrumental means alone; they change through transformations in the thoughts, actions, attitudes, and values of people. Organizations can update their technology, build modern structures, or even implement the latest and greatest processes. But without people buying into and getting behind and believing in change efforts, success will be tenuous at best. Almost all change models in use today include addressing a major condition of change as the commitment of all stakeholders to its success.

The "people" function, the primary entity that deals with changing people in organizations through learning and performance, is human resource development. HRD seeks to change people's knowledge, behavior, and attitudes to enhance work-related systems and to respond to the need for change. Changes such as implementation of new technology that impacts work-related systems typically result in HRD reacting by offering a training program, doing a needs assessment, or other activity or intervention common to many HRD professionals. Some scholars and practitioners believe that how HRD reacts to the need for change as a field of research and practice is based on the competence of its professionals. However, people also act and react to external stresses, pressures, and cues, what behavioral psychologists call stimuli based on their culture, values, ethics, and social responsibility. So our ability to change work-related systems and react to pressures and forces does not rely only on competence but also on values and ethics.

Organizations are constantly bombarded by myriad change forces. Economic, logistic, strategic, societal, psychological, technological, environmental, and other forces constantly impact organizational stakeholders and their ability to learn and to perform. Like the parable of the frog that failed to recognize slow changes in its environment and thus did not jump out of the water as it slowly boiled, some forces do not readily reveal their importance to or impact on organizations and people. Instead, they are patient. They lay in wait like a predator, striking only when an organization and its people are least prepared. Sometimes forces of change happen quickly, without warning or insight, what Morris Massey labeled a "significant critical event"; sometimes they happen slowly, silently, and are imperceptible.

The power and unexpected nature of forces both internal and external to organizations typically cause organizational and HRD leaders in particular to react and raise defenses in a self-protective gesture. Unfortunately, reacting always lags behind the need to change and thus all too often fails to adequately respond to the cause of the change or to "fix" the problem. The likely result is that the work-related system and people within it suffer, or worse, they fail. To avoid being blindsided by these change forces, organizations must be protective by nurturing people and processes that are ethical and possess values supportive of sustainability. Because it is easy for ethics to be subordinated to pressures exerted by powerful global influences, there is a critical need for morally strong and unambiguously ethical leadership at all organizational levels.

Certain forces are easier to deal with than others. Some pressures and problems are within the control and influence of leaders and their organizations and some are not. However, simply because an issue is beyond our immediate influence does not mean we should ignore it. Additionally, what may be outside our influence today, or seen as a secondary responsibility, may someday become a primary responsibility. For example, not long ago quality was the responsibility of an inspector; quality was inspected into the product or service with marginal results. Over time consumer demands, competition, improved processes, and quality programs such as total quality management and internationally recognized certifications like ISO 9000 shifted the responsibility of quality from the quality control department to all employees. The lesson here is that even though people in today's organizations may view social responsibility, sustainable behaviors, and ethical organizational outcomes as somehow outside their accountability, as secondary goals to those of economics, they still need to be aware of and be proactive in addressing the issues impacting their organizations' ability to act ethically and responsibly. Whether or not individuals within organizations consciously acknowledge their personal ethical responsibilities, these powerful forces nonetheless have social, environmental, and ethical implications for all of us, from the boardroom to the broom closet.

The change factors that impact an organization's ethics and social responsiveness and drive the need for ethical and sustainable organizations are too numerous and varied to discuss with equal attention or to do them any real justice here. However, issues recognized as providing many of the pressures on today's organizations include globalization and technology. These issues require discussion from a skeptic's point of view, questioning the status quo while seeking a balance between economic, human, and environmental needs. For example, business and HRD professionals in Western societies have generally viewed globalization strictly from an economic point of view if they understand its influence at all. However, ignoring globalization or seeing it myopically as an economic issue greatly limits our worldview and our actions. We need to critically assess how globalization affects the environment and its genuine impact, both positive and negative, on people and cultures. Globalization and technology are discussed in light of how they force companies to react to their pressures and by how they impact developing ethical and responsible organizations.

Before proceeding, it is important to understand that I will discuss these factors in greater detail in later chapters. Chapter 6 offers a detailed discussion of the pros and cons of globalization, and in Chapter 7 I present theories of a technological and a knowledge-based society.

Globalization

Globalization is an ambiguous idea. Not everyone agrees on its definition or that it is a reality. There is no overwhelming consensus about its meaning among scholars or practitioners. Some believe globalization to be a "myth" (Rugman, 2001), whereas others believe it is the vehicle for a freer, more open and democratic society (Friedman, 2000). Regardless of whether the world is more integrated or free now than before, there is certainly a perception among many people in business, industry, and HRD that it is, and it is this perception rather than any empirical reality that drives our actions (Salt, Cervero, and Herod, 2000). Instead of a focus on the extent of globalization, the assumption is that business and HRD leaders perceive its expansion. This perception leads to a more focused discussion on the nature of globalization, and how business and HRD is and should be reacting to it. These discussions are presented here and in more detail in Chapter 6.

The ability of companies to trade goods and services across cultures and governments has been around for a long time. Globalization is not new. What is new is its meteoric growth within the final quarter of the twentieth century and the early beginnings of the twenty-first century. Trade is the key component of globalization. Trade is what regulations like the North American Free Trade Agreement (NAFTA) are all about and it is what multinational organizations (MNOs) that support it thrive on. Freewheeling, free-market globalization based on the "free flow of goods, capital, and people made possible by the dismantling of global trade-and-investment barriers contributed to a boom in trade, which swelled from 18% of global economic output in 1990 to 26% in 2000" (Engardio and Miller, 2001, p. 35). Globalization lowered prices on consumer goods, enabled companies to boost productivity through lowered overhead, and opened up the world to previously untapped talent pools, what many refer to as free-market capitalism.

Capitalism thrives on freedom. It is generally unsuccessful in communistic, dictatorial, or undemocratic regimes. Dictators and despots find the whole idea of free trade abhorrent. Globalization encourages the spread of democracy and with it beliefs in human rights and the organizations dedicated to protecting them. Additionally, some developing nations have benefited from the need for cheap yet skilled workers that globalization creates. Indonesia and India responded to this need by developing specific educational infrastructures responsive to high skill labor needs in the computer industry. It remains unknown to what extent this focus on developing a few highly skilled workers in the midst of abject poverty has had, whether there has been much impact on the overall quality of life in these and other developing nations. On the other hand, many people benefit from global markets, people who without globalization would no doubt suffer lives of hopelessness. Burbules and Torres (2000) said that globalization adds a peculiar form of liberal democracy that brings with it the expansion of human rights, a higher standard of living, and occasions for travel and for enriching contacts with other cultures.

However, all is not right with the world, especially a globalized one. What some see as growth in democracy, production, revenues, and consumption, others experience as growth in waste, environmental and cultural destruction, and disparity between rich and poor (Dalla Costa, 1998). And because it affects employment-related skills and knowledge, globalization touches vocational and occupational education and corporate training and development.

Environmental degradation is one of the harshest criticisms levied against globalization. Although industrial society is creating economic wealth, it is simultaneously creating an environmental deficit. And it is doing this not as a consequence of a failure of modern society but as a success. Hawken (1993) is passionate in his criticism of globalization as a cause of environmental destruction:

> Quite simply, our business practices are destroying life on earth. Given current corporate practices, not one wildlife reserve, wilderness, or indigenous culture will survive the global market economy. We know that every natural system on the planet is disintegrating. The land, water, air, and sea have been functionally transformed from life-supporting systems into repositories for waste. There is no polite way to say that business is destroying the world. (p. 3)

Because Earth is the ultimate basis of resources and capital, the continuous flow of economic pursuits required for global markets can be sustained only if business recognizes that such economic activity must operate as a part of Earth's biosphere and ecosystems. The environment is a finite resource, not a commodity to be exploited. Without it, no business, whether local or global, can take place.

Of course, like most conflicts, the relationship between globalization and the environment is not crystal clear. In fact, the opposing view is that globalization has actually increased our awareness and appreciation of the environment and that even cultures that court dirty industries will benefit in the long run, not only from their economic presence but also from the learning that results from the inevitable regulatory and community-based responses to the effects of pollution or increased wastes. Companies that understand that environmental regulations are in fact not prohibitively expensive and that being "green" means less waste and more profit are growing at an exponential pace. Even companies that in the past were consistent violators of laws that protect the environment such as Dow Chemical and Monsanto are today seen more as environmental stewards whose CEOs wave a "green means money" banner.

Globalization as a change agent has made such a significant impact on the environment that it affects all related systems, including work and employment. Globalization influences vocational and occupational education and corporate training and development through its effect on the composition of work, the control of livelihoods, the skill and knowledge requirements of careers, and the social mobility of work and workers. Job seekers, employers, education and training suppliers, and the needs of society are in a constant "dance" with one another. Globalization and the economy and employers create demand for skills, education and training supplies the skills and knowledge, and people and cultures generate the social demand for skills and knowledge (Little, 2000). Employers move jobs around the globe seeking low-price, qualified, and skilled labor, while workers mobilize themselves and their families in search of jobs. In response, governments create infrastructures to entice employers to a country or region to satisfy a specific skill or knowledge need. Figuring out who is leading in this dance at any given time is a complex task that has implications for people, organizations, society, and the profession of HRD.

Globalization is responsible for a number of occupational shifts, including the steady decline of traditionally well-paying manufacturing jobs in the West, an increase in lower-paying jobs in the service sector, a rise in some professional and technical jobs, simultaneous increases in the upper and lower levels of the occupational structure (Morrow and Torres, 2000), and a mobilizing of access to livelihoods and employment. International trade is changing the character of labor.

Production of labor-intensive goods predominantly in developing countries in the Southern Hemisphere raised the demand for an unskilled but literate labor force. Some types of skill-intensive jobs have also increased, especially those associated with information technologies. The software industry in India, for example, has created new types of jobs for a relatively small number of younger and well-qualified people. Yet qualifications do not guarantee employment. The economic and social demands for qualifications do not always correspond. Many current occupations require little or no formal education or qualifications. Agriculture, an occupation of millions worldwide, does not require qualifications even though many farmers are highly educated and qualified for other careers. Many people possess qualifications and education yet fail to find jobs that they believed their qualifications and education would yield (Little, 2000). This dislocation of labor and the skills and knowledge to support it are part of a larger educational system dedicated to economic development versus education for social change. Scholars, educators, social commentators, and even a few HRD professionals believe that education should be more about effecting needed social change and emancipating the human spirit than about enhancing corporate profit. Globalization has the capacity if not the propensity to dampen any possibility that education might have to enhance society or effect real social change.

As jobs in the high-tech sector become scarce in some regions of the world, as global organizations exert more power over decisions made by governments, including regulations that impact education, and as business sees knowledge and skills as a competitive advantage, education as a business is attracting more and more corporate influence. According to the watchdog group Fairness and Accuracy in Reporting, almost 8 million children are force-fed a diet of 80 percent commercials, sports, weather, features, and profiles and a scant 20 percent recent political, economic, social, and cultural stories through programs like Channel One, an in-school news and advertising TV channel wired into 12,000 U.S. classrooms daily. M. W. Apple added:

> Students, in essence, are sold as a captive audience to corporations, since by law, these students must be in schools. The United States is one of the first nations in the world to consciously allow its youth to be sold as commodities to those many corporations willing to pay the high price of advertising on Channel One to get a guaranteed captive audience [Channel One can charge advertising rates as high as $195,000 per thirty-second ad]. Thus, not only are schools transformed into market commodities but so too are our children. (2000, p. 63)

There is compelling evidence through years of research that a well-crafted advertisement can persuade children that a product is desirable, but if they understand the persuasive purpose of advertising then they are capable of resisting its appeal. But not everyone is convinced. When the Swedes assumed the presidency of the European Union in 2001 they pushed for the rest of Europe to comply with their rules, which ban all television advertising targeted at children under the age of twelve, and although no rules were forthcoming there were serious discussions on the topic among EU members.

Although issues related to globalization such as workforce development and education and environmental degradation may at first appear structural or instrumental, they primarily concern people's values, morals, and ethics.

Environmental degradation caused by construction and operation of an oil refinery in a developing country may appear a less moral than economic issue except when one takes into account the impact the refinery, with its technology, wastes, and Western infrastructure, has on indigenous and uneducated peoples displaced without their consent and with little real understanding about what is happening to them. Attempting to ban advertising from public education reflects not a financial or corporate interest but a belief that children are adversely affected by a constant bombardment of advertisements even when there may be research to the contrary.

Until now people have lived within their own ethnic, national, or cultural boundaries that gave them a sense of definition, belonging, and place. Globalization is causing these boundaries to blur, such that cultural or national group membership may become unclear or completely lost. Wishard (1997) added, "While cultural and national boundaries still exist, they no longer form a relevant psychological boundary. So the issue facing each of us is: With whom do I identify? Who is my group? Indeed, do I have a group any longer?" (p. 20). A more pertinent question may be: To what extent are we being merged into one larger group and how do we adjust to it if we are?

The idea that globalization necessarily decreases or homogenizes cultural diversity is not a foregone conclusion. Debates abound on the validity of cultural homogenization supposedly brought about by globalization. The way we conceptualize culture dictates the extent we believe globalization can affect it. If we believe that culture is bounded by place, that culture is dependent on fixity of location for us to construct meaning, then globalization has the capacity to shift and mediate culture. If, on the other hand, we believe that culture is more fluid, that there is a "traveling culture," and through television, radio, the Internet, and tourism culture is mobile yet remains essentially unimpeded by the increase in global trade, then globalization can actually add value to culture. But lest we become laissez-faire about globalization, we must not take this cultural stability for granted.

Cultural degradation caused by uncontrolled corporatization, what some call colonialism, happens on an all too regular basis. In Alaska, for example, the impact of globalization has recently hit home in a 1,000-year-old Inuit-based native culture where people used to have a transcendent sense of identity with nature. Today, instead of gathering around a woodstove to hear tales of polar bear hunts from their elders, the tribe's children gather around Panasonic TVs to hear tales of Barney or Pokémon. But not all cultures are bending to the tide of Americanization or even modernity. In fact, some cultures are learning to resist the tide of globalization. The Bruderhof, an Amish-like religious community, rejects much of the modern world, at the same time engaging in global commerce. Not holding private property, the Bruderhof, who originated in Germany and now live in nine communities on three continents, earn a collective living through several businesses. They have a successful toy company, a publishing house, a company that manufactures equipment for people with disabilities, and Danthonia Designs, a handcrafted sign company. Although they use a blend of Japanese and American management techniques in their diverse business interests, their overriding philosophy is nonviolence, love of neighbors and enemies, and sexual purity.

Although many critics of globalization would prefer that it simply disappear or be transformed into something less ubiquitous and less intrusive on cultural permanence, it appears that globalization is here to stay, owing to a growing global economic dependency and that thus far it has failed to completely homogenize, Disneyize, McDonaldize, or Walmartize the world.

> Getting rid of the existing world economy would require some painful structural readjustments. Export industries would have to be shrunk . . . prices of some products would rise dramatically and those who buy such products would find themselves with much reduced real incomes. In a very real sense the global economy has become physically embodied in our ports, airports, and telecommunications systems. But most important, it is embodied in our mind-sets. (Thurow, 1996, p. 119)

Although the cultural degradation debate is far from settled and the impact of globalization on cultures remains an issue that requires examination, there is no doubt that one of the reasons that globalization is occurring at such a breakneck pace is the growing influence of the corporation.

Corporatization

Because large corporations are now some of the most powerful institutions on the planet, they have spread their influence over a wide swath of cultures, communities, industries, governments, and locales. There is a growing sense that the role of government has shrunk, caused by an emergent consolidation of power and influence in the private sector. To effect environmental protections or to ensure the future of an indigenous culture, one does not petition a senator or picket No. 10 Downing Street, you have to write to Jack Welch (recently retired CEO of GE) or boycott Royal Dutch Shell. Power now rests not with government but with large multinational companies.

Multinationals with profits as their beacon call control globalization, not governments that typically seek to protect citizens. With blinders on ensuring a continuous and unwavering focus on the bottom line, global companies have tended to ignore all but the most economically important clients. Thus, globalization does not necessarily advance the poorest or the weakest people in society. Globalization as a result of corporatization is not the rising tide it was once thought to be and certainly falls short in lifting all boats at the same time and equally as high.

Corporations are not mere economic instruments but are ubiquitous and dominant forces that impact society and cultures in diverse and complex ways. We should acknowledge this penchant for power and the participation of HRD in helping corporations achieve it. Understanding instead of justifying or rationalizing corporate power better enables us to witness the full range of issues that comes with such authority. Viewing the recent trust litigation against Microsoft, the Enron scandal, or the continuing social and health issues associated with the tobacco industry in terms of the role of HRD gives us unique insights into corporate power and responsibility and sheds light on the character and tenure of our involvement.

Now that corporations have become one of the most dominant focal points of global human activity, the actions and values exhorted by corporations exact a far greater toll and can distort both the culture of business and the wider society and the ecosystem. Supporting this control is the perception that because business is rational, then all other human perceptions and perspectives are questionable (Dalla Costa, 1998). If nonbusiness activities such as life and politics, society and culture, and human values and beliefs like morality are messy and subjective, then business is tidy and objective. Moving away from economic rationality toward a real soul searching of how much power and influence we really want a Kentucky Fried Chicken or a British Petroleum (BP) to have over our own and our children's lives as employees and as citizens may give us the freedom to realize that economic rationality keeps us from the truth. Economic rationality is how we rationalize a price fixing, a bribery, a harmful drug recall, or the illegal release of a toxic substance. We don't blame a person or the company, we blame the economics.

Corporate power exhorted through multinational giants like Enron is a common picture of globalization out of control. Yet the idea that the leviathans of business are getting bigger may not be the reality that many think it is. The proportion of American output coming from big companies rose gradually from 22 percent in 1918 to 33 percent in 1970, but it did not change between then and 1990. (Surely, given the arrival of thousands of small dot.coms, it must have fallen since. "The U.S. Labor Department reported in 2000 that almost 70 percent of all new jobs were created in small companies.) And in Germany, Japan, and Britain, the proportions all fell pretty dramatically between 1970 and 1990" (Micklethwait and Wooldridge, 2000, p. 101). Giant companies do not have free rein; they are not unimpeded in their pursuit of profits, as some may have us believe. They do business not in isolation but open to scrutiny by other businesses, local governments, and nongovernmental organizations (NGOs). Visit any multinational organization and you'll see international nongovernmental agencies such as the International Labor Organization (ILO) circling, monitoring their every move.

It is not absolutely clear what the outcomes of corporate power will be. It may result in a spreading of riches, an equality of peoples and cultures and the dissemination of democratic ideals. Or it may corrupt governments, foul the environment beyond recovery, or force once-proud cultures into the shadows of modernity. At this critical juncture in our history, in which the most important human goal seems to be to find meaning and recapture the sanctity of life, "we must decide whether the power to govern will be in the hands of living people or will reside with corporate entities driven by a different agenda" (Korten, 1995, p. 68). To accomplish this goal, there is an immediate need for us to be liberated from the illusion that corporations are free from human accountability. They are not.

Whether it is viewed as "winning at poker on the deck of the *Titanic*," the savior of poverty and pestilence in developing countries, or merely a blip on the screen of Gaia's evolution, there is no doubt that globalization is a vital and multifaceted force to be reckoned with. Friedman said:

> Under the globalization system you will find both clashes of civilization and the homogenization of civilizations, both environmental disasters and amazing environmental rescues, both the triumph of liberal, free-market capitalism and a backlash against it, both the durability of nation-states and the rise of enormously powerful nonstate actors. (2000, p. xxi)

Globalization and corporate power would be little more than rhetoric without the data gathering, information dissemination, and communication-enhancing capabilities of technology. Technology is a tool of globalization, the primary instrument that enables the internationalization of organizations and people.

Technology

Technology, a word with multiple meanings and divergent contexts and applications, is a contradiction, a paradox. It is simultaneously simple and complex, definite and ambiguous, and limiting and ubiquitous. It can mean a means to an end as in "The answer to our health problems is in medical technology." Or, technology can be an archetype or a concept, one of humankinds' great ideas. But no matter how it is used there is no doubt that technology is a powerful construct in the lives of hundreds of millions of inhabitants of the Western world and in an increasing number of people in developing nations.

Based on the root words *techne,* the Greek word for art, and *logos,* Greek for *word, technology* is the art of applied science. Art implies human creativity and skills with an aesthetic and even spiritual basis, yet our contemporary concept of technology is aligned more with scientific problem solving, communications, and the cold dissemination of information in support of rational economics than with some inspirational goal. By reflecting on how we currently characterize technology we become more aware of its potential and the extent that we are addressing such potential—both good and bad.

Describing technology with some specificity determines its application and evolution. For example, "advanced" technology has a different connotation than *technology* alone. Technology is an activity that applies the principles of science and mechanics to the solution of problems. It includes tools, resources, processes, people, and systems. Its goal is to accomplish tasks and provide an advantage to humans within a specific social, economic, or environmental context. Technology may be viewed simply as a tool, as industrialization, or as novelty (McOmber, 1999).

As a tool, technology becomes an architect of culture, where culture is dependent on its existence. Technology may also be defined in terms of its coexistence with industrialization. We recognize entire cultures based on their technical sophistication; that technology is the product of a specific historical time and place. Technology as novelty implies that whatever is new is technology and that new technologies are always displacing the old. This constant replacement forces reorganization of social structures, values, and priorities (McOmber, 1999). Sadly, this approach forces us to focus on the new at the expense of learning from and applying lessons of the past. Not so long ago we believed that computers would replace paper, only to discover they created a previously unheard-of demand for paper. Just so, we currently believe that technology will address many of our educational and training needs. Novelty also tends to create labels for cultures or subcultures such as the "Bronze Age" or "the information age." Movement from one "age" to another celebrates the new higher form of technology at the expense of the old. For example, how much information or value could be transferred from the "Bronze Age" to the "information age"? Although technology today is viewed as advanced or "high," some people believe that the unique approach of *appropriate* technology should be its next "age."

Advanced technology means new, newer, or recent. Talking about "high" technology or "high-tech" industries, we are interested in technology that makes an economic, social, or ecological impact through constant research and development of products or services. These products or services include but are not limited to advanced computing, advanced materials with engineered properties, biotechnology, microelectronics, and medical devices.

Advanced technologies, due in part to their newness and novelty, sometimes produce unintended consequences. For example, personal computers were designed with ease of manufacture in mind, not human interface; thus, they cause many unintended health problems for workers. When people are ignored in consideration of technology the end result is often not a pretty sight. We expend vast resources to try to solve complex problems, or worse, we cover them up or ignore them in hopes they will go away. The science of ergonomics is a response to the unintended consequences of technology. Because of these unintended consequences of advanced or high technology, a healthier definition and use of technology is "*appropriate*" technology.

Based on the early work of British economist E. F. Schumacher, the concept of appropriate technology, which he called "intermediate technology," takes all stakeholders of the technology into account with an emphasis on the environment. Schumacher suggested that we make things smaller (Schumacher, 1973), and do things simpler and cheaper through "low cost technologies" that would alleviate environmental destruction (Schumacher, 1979). Appropriate technologies take all stakeholders and especially the environment into consideration; they also meet the needs of the task being carried out by being effective and reliable, address the user by being safe and easy to use, and consider the values of the context in which they are used (organizational mission, culture, ethics, beliefs). Considering these points creates a picture of technology that is more than a tool, more than a means to an end, and more than an economic device.

Technology enables our organizations to be successful through innovations and by driving down the costs of doing business. But technology comes at a price. In the environmental and medical fields questions are arising about ethics and to what extent we have the right to manipulate nature. Ethical questions about technology also apply to business. The emerging field of biometrics promises to make privacy as we know it a thing of the past, forever changing the relationship between employees and employers. Technology thus challenges our ethics and what we consider valuable.

Summary and Conclusions

There is little doubt about the enormous influence that globalization and technology are having on people, organizations, communities, and the environment. Discussion from a divergent and dissenting viewpoint was required to expose their circuitous and multifaceted nature. Acknowledging that such powerful influencers affect our abilities to develop ethical and responsible organizations is the first step toward sustainable change. Questioning the status quo is a healthy exercise when coupled with an intellectual serving of facts and divergent viewpoints.

Although not all of the many and varied influences on people and organizations were discussed, the effect of globalization and technology were highlighted as having probable impact on developing ethical and responsible organizations and as a prologue to establishing a conceptual framework and discussing the research and practice of ethics and social responsibility. These "big picture" issues set the foundation for possible explanations of organizational behaviors and an understanding of why organizations and people respond to ethics and social responsibility in the way that they do.

Human resource development professionals have limited opportunities to manipulate or influence ubiquitous globalization and technology. Yet these forces are overwhelming the field of HRD. We have the option to assume a subjugated posture, allowing external forces to determine individual and organizational outcomes. Or we can choose to better understand the true nature of such forces and how they impact us. Armed with this knowledge, we can make better decisions about the humane use of technology, what globalization really means within an enterprise, and how we can influence it. Knowledge gives us power to be flexible in the content and context of analyses, the design and implementation of interventions, and how and when to evaluate.

Understanding that the outcomes of HRD are constrained by external forces is a beginning step in creating processes and a profession dedicated to sustainable outcomes. But simply knowing there are powerful forces to reckon with is not enough. A firm foundation is required on which to undergird our research, develop our concepts, and base our decisions. The next chapter introduces new concepts and theories as a foundation for a more sustainable profession.

Part 2

Mapping the Territory: The Conceptual and Practical Framework of Ethical HRD

The Conceptual Framework

Concepts are ideas that help to explain theory. Theory helps to explain what a phenomenon is and how it functions. Theoretical and conceptual foundations explain what the underlying theories or concepts of a phenomenon are, how they work together, and how they support the phenomenon under investigation. A theoretical framework for building ethical and responsible organizations through human resources is based on a synthesis of the following elements: the essential nature of values and ethics in HRD, the impact of worldviews on people and leaders in organizations, and the role of values-based leadership in developing ethical and responsible organizations.

Although values and ethics have always been an ancillary part of HRD, there is a pressing need for values and ethics to move beyond this secondary role and become the focal point for HRD research and practice. Viewing HRD more as an ethical imperative than a simple organizational function with ethics as one initiative causes us to shift our thinking beyond the instrumental to include more holistic and value-laden issues such as those posed by society, the environment, and human rights.

Values, Beliefs, and Ethics in HRD

Values are an exclusively human characteristic. They are enduring beliefs that specific modes of conduct are preferable to an opposite or converse mode (Rokeach, 1973). A thing has value if we appreciate it, approve of it, or prefer it. Values are related to interests, pleasures, likes, desires, obligations, wants, needs, and attractions and are a primary determinant for behavior. Generally speaking, we act on what we value within the constraints of mores and laws.

Enabling individuals and organizations toward ethical and socially responsible behaviors requires an understanding of values and what they mean to us as people and as members of organizations and society.

Although it may appear that Homo sapiens have some common values, there are in fact few values that are considered universal, that cut across all cultures and religions. Other cultures, groups, or individuals interpret concepts such as peace, compassion, and justice differently. Thus, although values may be an intimate part of us as individuals and as part of a particular culture or organization, they are varied, complex, hard to define, and even harder to agree on across cultures.

To the extent that the relationship between values and behaviors rings true, what conclusions can we draw from the fact that annual losses due to corporate corruption equates to almost 13 million jobs in North America alone, and roughly two-thirds of America's largest companies have been involved in some form of illegal activity (Dalla Costa, 1998)? What is the cause of such bad behavior? Are corporate pressures so great that people are forced to check their values at the company door or factory gate? Or are we socializing bad behaviors by rewarding "being a team player," "collegiality," and "not making waves" more than doing the right thing? Whatever the reasons for corporate bad behavior, there is little doubt that people's values play a pivotal role. Intimate relationships exist between values and actions and between corporate problems and behaviors. We see problems, including those related to our companies, in light of one or more values. For example, if equality is not recognized as a value, then inequality is not a problem. And if HRD leadership is not compassionate, then interventions will most likely not be caring and considerate of the people involved.

Values are a critical part of HRD research and practice. They are both explicit and implicit in common models of practice. In addition, research in HRD includes an indirect focus on values in two ways. First, the *AHRD Standards on Ethics and Integrity* (see Appendix A) includes statements that identify values of the profession of HRD. For example, the general principles speak to HRD professionals being "honest, fair, and respectful of others . . . [and] understand that a healthy economy, healthy organizations, and a healthy ecosystem are intricately interconnected" (Russ-Eft, Burns, Dean, Hatcher, Otte, and Preskill, 1999, pp. 2–3). Second, the theoretical foundations of HRD include ethics and psychology, both of which are value-laden (the other recognized and value-laden theoretical foundations are sociology, economics, and general systems theory). Codes of ethics and theoretical foundations suggest that values should be at the heart of all professional HRD endeavors such as consulting, teaching, and conducting research.

Reviews of practitioner-based literature such as *Training, Training and Development,* and *Performance Improvement,* empirically based literature in *Human Resource Development Quarterly, Human Resource Development International,* and *Performance Improvement Quarterly,* and conference proceedings of the Academy of Human Resource Development, the American Society of Training and Development, and the International Society for Performance Improvement from 1990 to 2001 revealed a dearth of research and publications on values and beliefs in HRD. Although empirical research that identifies the beliefs and values of HRD professionals is limited, preliminary results of research found that HRD professionals felt economics was currently the most influential theoretical foundation.

This single-mindedness is institutionalized by a focus on performance versus learning or meaning (Hatcher, 2000b; Bates, Chen, and Hatcher, 2002). Research also shows that values play a major role in leaders' decisions (Rokeach, 1973). Thus, even when we inherently know that values are important we tend to isolate them from our research and practice.

Ethical problems abound in the conduct of business. We are bombarded with controversies around bribery and mismanagement of funds, discrimination and human rights violations, waste mismanagement, gender and diversity discrimination, pollution and environmental destruction, and plagiarism, copyright, and controversy with ownership of intellectual property. Confronting concerns such as these means confronting ethical issues. Developing solutions to these dilemmas requires more than application of a code or a decision flow chart, an e-mail, a meeting or two, or other cursory responses. It requires that we view ethics not only from a business point of view but also from a philosophical standpoint. Our responses should come from a foundation of understanding what is right and what is good, not simply what is expedient and instrumental or financially justifiable. It requires an understanding of our research and practice in light of our moral and ethical philosophy.

Analyzing ethical dilemmas systematically and in meaningful ways is difficult since ways of viewing ethics are multidimensional. Shrader-Frechette (1998) added that although we are technically competent we are tragically incompetent in ethical thinking and decisionmaking. We can fix an ailing heart or repair a space shuttle miles above Earth, but still have great difficulties making judgments about personal, environmental, and social good. Ethical theories can help our decisionmaking because they provide a "vantage point—a perspective—regarding the purposes and processes of ethical decision making" (Dean, 1993, p. 15), and serve to clarify interconnections between principles, hypotheses, and concepts.

Theoretical Approaches to Ethics

Philosophies and theories can be overly complex and abstract and thus incompatible with day-to-day practice of HRD. Indeed, there are a number of theoretical perspectives available, but only those potentially most meaningful and valid for HRD will be discussed here. The intent of the following descriptions of ethical theories is not to wax poetic about philosophy or to "sell" one idea over another at this point, but simply to illustrate a few points of view that might help us better understand ethics and provide information to make better ethical decisions.

Ethical theories provide a basis for mutual understanding and dialogue by providing a common language for us to communicate, discuss, and evaluate ethical issues. It is also important to recognize and understand these theories because they may be partly responsible for some of the ethical dilemmas we face. The business ethicist Des Jardins (1993) suggested that these theories might even be part of the problem, that people have been misled by these theories.

The position that ethics is contextual, that ethical values are a matter of mere opinion or personal feeling relative to a time, culture, and religion (Des Jardins, 1993), and that no single moral standard, no universal ethic exists that is applicable to all people at all times is known as ethical relativism. Ethics is relative to the age, the place, and the circumstances in which it is found. It is in no sense absolute (Donaldson and Werhane, 1988). The ethical relativist takes the stance that trying to find the "right" or "true" answer to questions of ethics and social responsibility is a waste of time because it is all a matter of opinion and context.

The ethical absolutist, on the other hand, believes that there are "true" and "right" universal moral rules that are applicable in any context. Absolutism makes codes of ethics possible. But it also supports intolerance, colonialism, and forcing alien values on native cultures. The problem with both these ethical viewpoints is that they are extremes, and extremes do little to help us make better decisions or behave ethically. In fact, they "trivialize the subject of ethics" (Ruggiero, 1997, p. 68). So there are really no right or wrong positions to take. Where a profession like HRD falls on a spectrum of absolutism on one end and relativism on the other may influence the establishment of ethical norms and behaviors for the field.

Theoretical normative ethics that are pertinent to many HRD and business leaders and scholars and serve as foundations for HRD research and practice include teleological theories, deontological theories, and environmental ethics. Each theory is described and discussed in light of its relevance to research and practice of HRD.

Teleology, from the Greek *telos,* meaning "end" or "goal," is a consequentialist theory. That is, whether an action or practice is right or wrong is a function of its consequences. Consequentialism significantly underlies development of codes of ethics and other regulations. Utilitarianism is an example of teleological or consequentialist theory.

Classic utilitarian theory is the view that one should always choose that which will tend to produce the greatest good for the greatest number. The idea that people seek higher levels of pleasure as the basis for their decisions about right and wrong may seem narcissistic, yet the principle of an inner feeling for humanity, what Ruggiero (1997) called generalized benevolence, that our happiness should not be pursued at the expense of others, emerges from utilitarian thought. Maximizing the overall good by seeking behaviors that tend to capitalize on positive consequences is ethically right.

The idea of maximizing the common good underlies much of current business activity, including HRD. But utilitarianism is not without its problems. For example, how do we measure what is "good"? How would we know if we are "maximizing the overall good"? And what happens when we are forced to quantify, somehow measure good? If people, organizations, or communities have conflicting desires or preferences in terms of what they consider good, how will we resolve this conflict?

Moreover, how can we measure the good inherent in such an ethical environment? Under corporate pressures we are often compelled to substitute some quantifiable factor such as numbers of discrimination claims or harassment lawsuits or occurrences of whistle blowing for the idea of being ethical or being *good.* These factors might be indirect indicators of an ethical climate but they are surely tangential to a nurturing and safe work environment and do not give us a complete picture of what it means to have an ethical workplace.

Theories that rival teleology are known as deontological, or nonconsequentialist views of ethics. The Greek term *deon* means "duty" or "to bind." A deontologist believes that moral rightness takes precedence over an action's consequences, that we have a moral duty to do what we believe to be intrinsically right. Since we have little control over the consequences of our actions, the moral nature of the act in question is more important than the outcomes. It means acting on principle rather than consequences (Des Jardins, 1993). Associated with Immanuel Kant's (1724–1804) categorical imperative, deontology helps to establish principles that are unbiased and capable of being universalized. We do not determine what is ethical based on whether these universal principles are rational, or accepted by all actors (Des Jardins, 1993).

Much of what we espouse in HRD is principles-based. That is, the implementation of interventions, analyses, evaluation, and most all HRD-related activities in an organization are simply not possible without basic principles such as respect for others, integrity, trust, and the notion of community. And we are ethically obligated to treat people as rational and self-sufficient beings, not as some commodity or economic resource to be used and discarded; to recognize people's rights and potential, and help them in realizing this potential (Maclagan, 1998). Deontology is an ethical theory that places human principles before culture or religion. Yet principles that are strictly human-centered limit us. They constrain the need for us to view our ethical behaviors in broader, more holistic terms to include the environment as part of our ethical and moral fabric, to move beyond human-centered anthropocentric ethics.

Environmental ethics focus on environmental and ecological controversies that threaten our planet and humanity and raise questions about what we value, to whom or what we grant moral status, and about the kind of world we want to sustain. These are fundamentally questions of ethics. They enjoin us to acknowledge and appreciate the relationship between our environment and ourselves and to understand that whatever we do to the environment we do to ourselves.

Because environmental issues are complex they require multidisciplinary solutions that transcend simple "quick-fix" technical approaches to include those of economics, sociology, psychology, anthropology, law, and, of course, ethics. Although most environmental issues require application of technology, it is almost "impossible to find an environmental issue that does not raise basic questions of value" (Des Jardins, 1993, p. 5). Through an understanding of environmental ethics, a systematic account of the moral relations between people and the environment (Des Jardins, 1993), we are able to see and appreciate our world and thus act in a more responsible manner.

The development of environmental ethics gives us an opportunity to distinguish between utilitarian theories that place humans at the center of the universe and biocentric theories that place us as a part of the environment. It allows us to address the question of whether we should destroy a species for utilitarian good or protect the species because it has as much inherent value as we do. When we place equal worth on other species, plants and animals, the oceans, and sentient beings for nonutilitarian reasons we shift our value structure away from humanism toward holism, away from "speciesism" toward Gaia—the idea that Earth itself is a living entity worthy of our value.

Valuing the environment equal to humankind is the radical viewpoint of environmental ethics. It is an extreme view that may limit our ability to accept and apply theory in our everyday endeavors. A more moderate general systems view with which HRD professionals should be acquainted is that we are part of the greater scheme of things and that we ought to value all life, but not necessarily place any or all life *above* ours. Valuing does not necessarily mean developing a hierarchy. Systems thinking helps to bridge the gap between the bottom-line nature of business and a broader and more all-encompassing worldview of HRD and its role not only in organizations but also in humanity, ecosystems, and the cosmos.

Not everyone agrees that environmental ethics is needed or is a valid theory of ethics, and its usefulness for business applications is debatable. For the HRD professional, environmental ethics offers an opportunity for us to see ourselves and our actions in light of the larger picture, that we have a responsibility beyond providing an intervention or evaluating a training program.

Ethical issues in HRD can be viewed and resolutions enhanced through the broad teleological/deontological/environmental distinctions in ethical theories. When we seek to avoid harm to individuals or the wider society or produce positive consequences through higher productivity or by enhancing employee benefits, we are viewing ethics through a teleological lens. When an HRD professional makes an ethical decision for or against an action or practice based on teleology, they view the action or practice as moral or immoral because of its consequences or lack of consequences to society (Hatcher and Aragon, 2000a). On the other hand, deontological reasoning holds that an act or practice should be judged as right or wrong because of some feature intrinsic to the act or practice. In other words, what makes an act or practice morally justifiable is the act or practice itself, not its consequences. And when we consider the impact that our activities have on the environment and make decisions based on the consideration that the environment has rights versus one of pure economics, we are using values based on environmental ethics.

The few ethical theories discussed here urge us to strike a balance between competing values "based on reflection, personal experience, and insights derived from the relevant experiences of other professionals" (Gellerman, Frankel, and Ladenson, 1990, p. 57), as well as from codes of ethics or standards of conduct developed from such insights. Values and ethics are fundamental conceptual foundations on which to build a profession that strives to do the right thing by creating sustainable and responsible organizations. Without values, without a soul, the profession is subject to whim and fancy of business built solely on financial gain and most times suspicious of the needs of society and the environment. Without our personal and professional values and ethics we remain subservient and subjugated to the values of our organizations, values based primarily on profit. Thus, seeing values and ethics for the authenticity, vitality, and sanctity they give the profession of HRD fully justifies their use as appropriate and true foundations for our research and practice, which results in ethical and responsible organizations that nurture us and sustain the environment.

The Impact of Worldviews on Organizations, Leadership, and HRD

The way we view the world determines how we view organizations and the role of leadership in HRD. Worldviews are our basic mental picture of reality. Organizations and leadership are results of a perspective; both can be viewed from many angles, opposing, similar, restricted, and endless. Because of the many views of what organizations and leadership are and should be, it is hard to find one view that is ubiquitous. Yet worldviews tend to bring us together for common purposes and help us to find common ground. The ability to acknowledge our own view of the world is a mark of contemporary thinking (Paden, 1992).

Worldviews can also prevent us from seeking new possibilities. They can be inflexible, myopic, and protective. We seek to make our view the correct interpretation, and thus to advocate its validity and rightness. We assume our own point of view to be absolute, not as versions of the world alongside others (Paden, 1992). Because of this carving out of worldviews, the rubric of perception has formed a hodgepodge of language-based provinces whose words and meanings are practicable and understandable only to those who share them, and whose interpretations obstruct all others. Because interaction between these provinces is limited, a class system within business and industry with its own specialized language has emerged that limits sharing and understanding. For example, some worldviews enable leaders to see organizations and their roles in them as purely economic with little regard for social and environmental responsibility, whereas other worldviews limit our actions to those imposed by the government.

A constructive way to view the spectrum of organizational worldviews, especially in regard to social and ethical responsibilities of organizations, is to place the various points of view on a continuum. Figure 3.1 illustrates a range of viewpoints concerning the role of organizations in society. For example, at one end of the continuum is a fundamentalist's view that implies that organizations have only financial and legal responsibilities. People espousing this

FIGURE 3.1   Worldview Continuum

Fundamentalism	Social Institutions	Moral Agency	Virtuous Organizations
Financial and legal responsibility only "Business of business is profit."	Social contract exists beyond economics and legalities. Need to accommodate stakeholders' interests.	Moral obligations similar to people. Morality and ethics are part of culture: The "right thing to do."	Organizations that foster the "good society." Obligation to build a "better world."

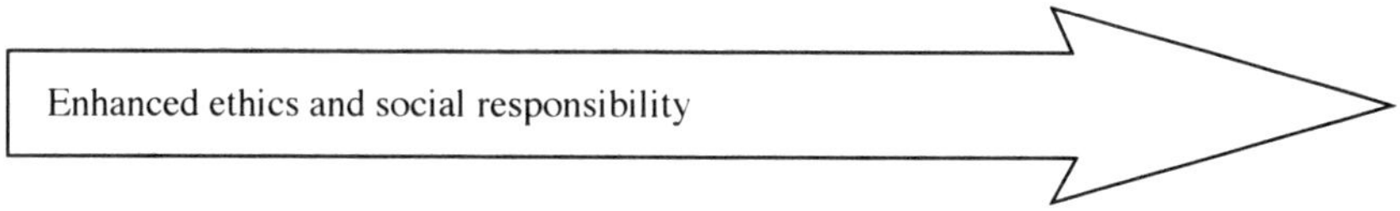

Enhanced ethics and social responsibility

point of view would object to corporate philanthropy. Next is the idea that organizations have moral responsibilities to society much the same as do individuals, what T. Donaldson (1982) called moral agency. Moving toward more ethical and responsible points of view is the notion of social institutions, which implies that a social contract exists between organizations and society. This worldview suggests that organizations are bound to society through a contract similar to legal contracts, where both parties have interests and assume accountability. On the opposite end is the vision that organizations exist to foster the good society and are virtuous—determined to create sustainable organizations dedicated to building a better world.

Worldviews serve as a metatheory (an all-encompassing theory) that describes our reality and serves as a foundation for our day-to-day practice and research. Questioning these presuppositions helps us assess whether they are valid and beneficial or may be hindering our abilities to create a profession that enhances ethical workplaces and builds responsible organizations.

Capitalist economic regimes and the leaders who support them generally assume one point of view to be absolute. But this economically based viewpoint is only one version of the world and should be placed alongside and given equal footing to others. Leaders may assume that since one worldview is widely accepted it is reality and not simply one in many and varied descriptions of reality. In other words, the map is not the territory.

A good example of the need to address worldviews is the recent interest in assessing various perspectives in HRD, namely learning, performance, and spirituality or meaning. A recent HRD conference workshop focused on the inherent tension between these three perspectives and how pervasive performance had become as a result of recent economic growth, especially in the West, and how HRD as a profession's current worldview is skewed more toward performance than meaning (Bates, Hatcher, Holton, and Chalofsky, 2001).

Popular worldviews are seen as so unified and totalitarian that few diverse or cross-cultural perspectives are acknowledged. In a world where diversity in all its various forms is key to organizational success, this limits our ability to develop humane and responsible organizations. Senge (1990) added that new insights in business fail to be used because they conflict with established worldviews.

To navigate the "stormy seas" of global work environments, trade issues, and complex workforce dilemmas with a singular worldview bereft of any comprehension or acknowledgement of other worldviews is a limiting device for organizational creativity, innovation, corporate social responsibility, and the humane and equitable development of human beings. The ability to see and understand our own worldviews and acknowledge others' worldviews is a mark of socially conscious and values-based leadership. "The only course for the leader is to build a vision that followers are able to adopt as their own *because it is their own*" (O'Toole, 1995, p. 10).

Globalization is forcing a new world of social, cultural, and workforce diversity that also sustains pluralistic thinking about how we perceive others who are different from us and have different worldviews. These divergent worldviews offer us the opportunity to make known and even appreciate the limiting and anthropocentric nature of our own worldviews, so common in the West, and the opportunity to modify them.

HRD's Worldviews

Contemporary theory and practice of HRD is embedded within certain worldviews. These worldviews may limit the likelihood that organizations and their leaders will act consciously on issues of humane and equitable treatment and social and environmental responsibility. These limited-horizon worldviews include but are not limited to anthropocentrism, rational scientific assumptions, and logical positivistic approaches; worldviews that limit our responses and decisions to those based almost exclusively on people within economic contexts. Judgments made on the basis of economics force us to make decisions without regard to long-term outcomes, especially in regard to social and environmental impact.

This categorizing of reality implies that we see not only through a particular set of lenses but that we also demarcate what it is we are viewing. The "object" of organizations, leadership, and HRD is defined by different sets of lenses. For example, paradigms, ideas, and theories act as instruments to help us construct what we mean by HRD or leadership. As these change, so too do the "objects" they focus on, as in the case of the shift from an industrial society to a knowledge-based economy and from rational scientific to postmodern thought.

A discussion of common worldviews, namely anthropocentrism and reductionism, helps us understand that the way we view reality has an impact on all our other beliefs. It impacts the way we lead and should also help clarify some of the issues we confront when faced with making decisions about organizational social and environmental sustainability. In addition, a discussion of deep ecology offers us a new and more sustainable worldview.

Anthropocentrism

Anthropocentrism or human-supremism is a worldview that grants moral standing exclusively to humans and considers nonhuman entities and nature as a whole as a means for human ends or human consumption. Of course, being human, it is axiomatic that we are anthropocentric, since we see the world only through our own intellect and conceptual archetypes. Anthropocentrism forces us to view nature in utilitarian terms and enables the continuation of irreparable harm to the environment, which also inevitably threatens human well-being.

Examples of using sentient beings as objects of value to be used and exploited are not new to the human race. For example, speciesism is defined as an ethically indefensible form of discrimination against beings on the basis of their membership in a species other than our own (Singer, 1999).

> Analogous to treatment of slaves, the suffering of a slave was not considered to have the same moral significance. Just as the suffering of nonhumans is considered to have less significance as the suffering of humans (Des Jardins, 1993; Kellert, 1996; Singer, 1999).

Patriarchal oppression is another perspective that assumes that the rights of anything other than humans are at the mercy of patriarchal corporations. "The four basic patriarchal oppressions are rulers over people, men over women, possessors over nonpossessors, and humans over nature" (Berry, 1995, p. 14).

But if we take the opposite view that nature is more important than humans, then we assume a dominance-subordinance continuum that places us in an inferior role to nature. As previously mentioned, this subordinate role is difficult to conceptualize on moral and ethical grounds and has its own human-centered characteristics. The fact is, we depend on nature for our existence and its degradation is also ours. Thus, the anthropocentric worldview is flawed. Yet the converse, the idea that we are most important, is not palpable to our sense as humanists seeking to enhance human rights and equality or as HRD professionals seeking to enhance human learning and performance in an equitable fashion. Is the extension of moral standing to nature too outlandish, so foreign, especially in the West, that we revolt at the notion? Or is our current ethical and moral human-centered viewpoint sufficient to address environmental concerns? The larger question becomes: "On what grounds do we recognize or attribute moral standing?" (Des Jardins, 1993, p. 110). Can animals, plants, rivers, mountains, trees, ecosystems, and Gaia, the living Earth, have moral standing? What would it mean to us in HRD if they did? Would it diminish or enhance us?

Like many ethical issues, to whom or what we grant moral standing is not an "either-or" or "black and white" phenomenon. Rather it falls more into categories of "it depends" and "shades of gray." For example, if we take the position that humans have moral standing because we are different from nonhuman species, a difference based on our ability to think and choose (some call this intellect or psyche), then entities without this capacity cannot be considered moral. If this is true, what do we do about the hundreds of thousands of people who lack the ability to reason, to think, or make choices for themselves? Are the disabled and mentally challenged thus immoral? If we grant moral standing only to rational humans, then we cannot address the rights of future generations. This contradicts the whole idea of sustainability in toto since "it makes little sense to say of people who do not exist that they possess rights or anything else for that matter" (Des Jardins, 1993, p. 110).

The Western beliefs in human uniqueness and spiritual superiority encourage contempt of nature and an overriding desire to control and use it. Eastern beliefs encourage seeing the world as part of a fabric, that all living things, plants, and animals have intrinsic worth. Although these beliefs appear true, the reality is that many of the societies that espouse a more benevolent attitude toward the environment are the same societies that are responsible for much of its current destruction. Modern Pacific Rim countries have been responsible for widespread habitat destruction, damaging harvesting practices, and overexploitation of several wildlife species, especially marine life. The fact is, most Eastern societies demonstrate little respect, compassion, or concern for the environment or for biodiversity. Ironically, it is the Western societies and particularly the United States and some Scandinavian countries that have the most ambitious environmental protections and successful ecosocial movements. Kellert (1996) explained this disparity by saying that the beliefs of Eastern cultures are more eco-sensitive and may be idealized; this is not representative of modern societies, and may possibly be the views of a small, educated elite. His research into the environmental values and beliefs of Eastern versus Western societies revealed that there might not be as much of a disparity between the two belief systems as previously thought.

Anthropocentrism is bits and pieces of systems that can be separated, studied, or appreciated apart from the whole; it is the reduction of an object to its most simplistic components. With anthropocentrism we lose the totality of, the essence of the object, its soul. This reduction of the complex to the simple, known as reductionism, is responsible for the endless quest for efficiency and linear cause-and-effect relationships in business often at the expense of ethics, values, social responsibility, and humanity.

Reductionism

Reductionism and its related philosophy of logical positivism ignore the complexity of life and the fragile balance of ecosystems. It also helps us to maintain organizations that place a premium on control and rationality and demeans our transcendence of the physical to the spiritual. Although reductionism is still the predominant worldview in business and industry, "there are deficiencies in the positivist paradigm when it is used to describe, explain, and predict behavior in organizations" (Marsick, 1990, p. 7). Before we review these deficiencies it will be instructive to define reductionism.

Reductionism is the belief that complex phenomena can be reduced to simpler, more basic processes, which can then be further reduced to the simplest level of explanation. The idea that your favorite pet is simply a collection of molecules or that our beliefs are merely an aggregation of data from our physical senses or that a job can be broken down into separate parts that can then be taught are forms of reductionism. "If a phenomenon is not deemed fully real, we must get down to the reality that is the source or substance of the phenomenon. We take it apart to see what makes it tick, or we retrace the development of the phenomenon to its roots" (R. H. Jones, 2000, p. 13). This search for the real is pervasive both in and out of scientific fields.

> It is not unusual to hear that all that is real is only the physical, the rational, the programmable, or whatever is given primacy. . . . For example, a person is said to be nothing but a body—there are no souls, and our mind is really nothing but

the activity of our brain. . . . Similarly, society is simply the interaction of individuals . . . [and] philosophy is nothing but mental states, which in turn are nothing but neurological events. (R. H. Jones, 2000, p. 14)

The idea that the whole is no more than the sum of its parts, and that the parts alone are what is real has not helped to explain the complexity of life or our constant seeking for meaning in work. The effect has been to undermine our uniqueness and our spirituality by reducing us to lifeless bits and pieces with no spirit, dehumanizing us by explaining away what makes us special.

Reductionism's related philosophy, logical positivism, is a philosophy that emphasizes knowledge based on experience. Logical positivists believe that existence, particularly the language used to express existing things or the way things are, can be reduced to terms of directly observable objects, or sense data. Thus, any statement of fact can be empirically verified. One result has been to define the world in terms of the observable, the physical, and the logical, and to disregard the metaphysical.

Because of its direct influence on the theoretical foundations of HRD, it is important for us to briefly discuss the idea of antireductionism. An antireductionist views the world as an organism or ecologically, seeing wholes rather than bits and pieces. This systems worldview was developed into a general systems theory (GST), which is today a theoretical foundation of HRD (Swanson, 1999; Hatcher, 2000b).

Pioneered by biologists such as von Bertalanffy and German Romantic philosophers like Kant and Goethe, systems thinking concentrates "not on basic building blocks, but on basic principles of organization" (Capra, 1996, p. 30). Its application in HRD is evidenced through practices such as organizational analysis and in research through various qualitative methods, especially those with emergent properties. Marsick (1990) applied systems thinking to training and learning. She said:

A systems thinker might assume that different definitions and assumptions exist and seek to understand why and how training is defined and operationalized differently by stakeholders in various subsystems in the organization. For the systems thinker, variety simply illustrates the multiple views of reality, the multiple levels at which learning takes place, the multiple loci of control of learning in organizations, and the value of identifying ways in which congruence is built among interacting subsystems. (p. 15)

Systems thinking allows us to move beyond the reduction of things into parts and to see the wholes and structures in our organizations, to understand the interconnectedness and interdependence between HRD and individuals, organizations, cultures, communities, society, and the environment.

Yet even with systems thinking, the fact is that anthropocentrism and reductionism exist. Seeing the world in bits and pieces has caused a near-complete manipulation over nature and an overall weakening of the Earth's ecosystem. The way we view our relationship with nature has driven this lust to control our environment. Yet anthropocentrism and reductionism have also brought many medical breakthroughs and life-giving technologies, and created innovative life-enhancing environments in which to live and grow. But if we shift our ideas about our superiority over nature and begin to view all living beings as having moral privileges, then our abilities to make changes in our organizations that result in sustainable changes in our environment becomes more real. A worldview that is receiving growing attention in business and industry is such an ecocentric ethic known as deep ecology.

Deep Ecology

> The whole question of values is crucial to deep ecology . . . whereas the old paradigm is based on anthropocentric (human-centered) values, deep ecology is grounded in ecocentric (earth-centered) values. All living beings are members of ecological communities bound together in a network of interdependencies. When this deep ecological perception becomes part of our daily awareness, a radically new system of ethics emerges. (Capra, 1996, p. 11)

Deep ecology is an ecophilosophy, what Arne Naess, its founder, called an equilibrium of all things in nature that questions the views and attitudes of nature held by Western societies. Deep ecology has profound philosophical implications that transform our understanding of the world in which we live and what it means to be human.

Deep ecology is based on two ultimate norms: self-realization and biocentric equality. Biocentric, meaning a life-centered philosophical orientation, is a value that all natural things—ecosystems and life, including human and landscape—have intrinsic value and the right to exist. An important aspect of this ethic is that this intrinsic value is independent of the usefulness of the nonhuman world for human purposes.

Self-realization in deep ecology is the consciousness of the potentialities of life. Humans realize that when we identify with the universe as part of its rich diversity, we are connected with something greater than our ego, greater than our humanity. According to Naess, self-realization is experiential as well as intellectual; we develop an identity with nature through practice and study

TABLE 3.1 A Comparison of Deep Ecology and Business-Related Worldviews

Nature and the natural environment is a resource for humans to use. Only value of nature is instrumental. Human dominance over nature.	All life/nature has intrinsic, inherent value independent of human usefulness. Humans seek harmony with nature.
Achievement/success through standardization, metrics of excellence based on narrow outcomes.	Richness and diversity (including biodiversity) contribute to overall reality and rejects any single stand of excellence
Consumption is satisfying. Consumerism drives economic and social success.	Consumerism is not satisfying. Life is appreciated as an inherent value rather than adhering to an increasingly higher standard of living. There is a difference between *big* and *great* and *more* and *enough*.
Ample natural reserves are infinite and should be used.	Resources are limited. Earth's supplies are finite and should be conserved and protected.
Scientific policies. Technology as progress and solutions. "Technology will solve our problems."	Appropriate, sustaining, and ecoefficient technologies and scientific policies that sustain conditions for biological and cultural diversity.
Material and economic growth is only means to enhance human potential.	Nature should remain pristine except to satisfy vital human needs.
Maintain *status quo*. "Don't fix it if it isn't broken."	Humans must act now to achieve sustainability. Inaction insures ecological destruction.

SOURCE: Adapted from: Devall, B., and G. Sessions, (1985). *Deep Ecology: Living As If Nature Mattered.* Layton, UT: Peregrine Smith Books, and Sessions, G. (Ed.) (1995). *Deep Ecology for the Twenty-First Century.* Boston and London: Shambhala.

(he was a world-class mountain climber), which helps widen our sense of identification with others, our environment, and the cosmos.

The soul of deep ecology consists of a number of principles about human nature and our relationship with nature. This platform of beliefs and values differs from a traditional business-oriented worldview in fundamental ways. See Table 3.1 for a comparison of deep ecology and traditional business worldviews.

Deep ecology as a worldview has the potential to impact the social responsiveness of the profession of HRD in several ways. First, it broadens our value systems to recognize that in many ways society and industrial environments in particular enslave people, and only in a state of pristine nature does humanity live in a state of absolute fulfillment. It also helps us value our appreciation of our stewardship to nature, moving us to what Frederick (1998) called a "cosmological" definition of human consciousness and purpose. This helps us understand that all environments, organizations, communities, and individuals are subject to the forces of the cosmos and that all of the important issues and questions concerning human meaning and meaning in organizations evolves from these cosmological processes.

For HRD professionals a shift in worldviews gives us the opportunity to change the way we conceive of today's organizations and our relationship to them. One such opportunity is through a finding of meaning as it relates to our work. The search for meaning and purpose underlies most religious and philosophical pursuits. Deep ecology provides us with a way to attach a much deeper meaning to our actions and the actions of organizations. But beyond this organizational responsibility, deep ecology can also provide us a way to seek one of the most fundamental of human needs, the need to better understand our place in the cosmos.

Deep ecological awareness is thus consistent with a spiritual awareness. To embrace an ethic like deep ecology is to ask deeper questions about our worldviews and our way of life. When we connect with the web of life we reestablish our link with something larger than us that transcends our understanding, yet makes us feel more a part of a higher calling than we could ever experience without it. If humans' ultimate goal is to seek spiritual, not economic fulfillment, then the organizations where we spend much of our lives provides the context for this quest. HRD, where we learn, develop, and grow, serves as the means for this spiritual end. Thus, the relationship between deep ecology and HRD may not be as disparate as it might seem. As a way to view the world, deep ecology provides us a lens through which to view a deeper and more transcendent understanding of the interconnectedness of our organizations, the environment, and our place in the cosmos.

Worldviews such as deep ecology and systems thinking give us the capacity to see multiple realities and to experience the interconnectivity between people and the ecosystem. Worldviews can also limit our sight by driving us to constantly seek one right answer or to try and predict and control objective reality. Anthropocentricism and reductionism are examples of limiting ways of viewing reality. In a complicated and increasingly diverse world it is axiomatic that we turn to paradigms that will not limit us or constrain us from solving complex problems or further developing our transcendent nature. Seeking meaning in our work is a recurrent theme throughout our discussions about values, ethics, and worldviews. Work is where HRD happens and is the context in which we apply our values, ethics, and worldviews.

The Meaning of Work

The traditional definition of HRD is the development of people within organizations. More recently, and more suggestive of deep ecology and systems thinking, human resource development was defined within a work-related context (Bates, Hatcher, Holton, and Chalofsky, 2001). Since work is the context in which our worldviews and our values and ethics are realized, it is logical to conclude that HRD functions within the larger rubric of work. This new explanation that HRD happens not only in formal organizations, but also in informal work-related systems and functions, places HRD squarely within the notion of work as a larger system. But what denotes work? Is it toil for some form of payment? Or is it any activity that we engage in to achieve a goal? And what kind of social or psychological role does work play? To respond, we must address the importance of the question of "what does work mean to us?"

Work means different things to different people within different cultures and contexts. For the individual, work may be a primary life interest, a trivial whim, or something in between. Halberstam said, "Work is both a blessing and a curse" (2000, p. 17), and Howard said work "is the major activity through which we shape our ambitions and our talents and, thus, come to know ourselves" (1985, p. 1).

Work is thus both a process and an outcome. One works for the rewards of doing the work and toward some end state or result. *Webster's New World Dictionary* (Neufeldt, 1995) defined work as: "1. Effort extended to do or make something; labor; toil 2. To be employed" (p. 682). This definition implies energy is expended for some valued gain.

Work can also be differentiated from "nonwork" endeavors such as physiological needs, for example, sleep and eating, or nonwork obligations to family or pets; and leisure or discretionary time such as sports or reading (Hatcher, 1993). Harman and Horman (1990) suggested that we work to create, and only incidentally do we work to eat. Additionally, work may be viewed as the fundamental province for learning and for the development of human potential as well as an educative setting for development and maintenance of a democratic and responsible society.

But to what extent do these ideas about work apply only to developed, industrial cultures? Workers in developing countries may view work differently where they find it hard to actualize the transcendent and social ramifications of work as they labor hour after hour in a field of rice or in a sweatshop. Or do they?

The word "work" denotes several contrasting Western ideologies beyond that of simple labor-based employment. On the one hand, work can subjugate individuals to "productive toil," repetitive, tedious, and physically and mentally demanding and demeaning labor that drives out the soul and reduces the human spirit to mere means to a productivity or sustenance-driven end. Conversely, work can be something enjoyable that gives a sense of fulfillment, purpose, and social responsibility and may even provide a means to a reawakening to a "higher calling," "right livelihood," or a spiritual endeavor. The idea of working for a higher calling is common. For example, right livelihood, an Eastern concept attributed to one of the eight Buddhist steps or paths to enlightenment, suggests that work, whether physically tedious or mentally challenging, is "love made visible"; a concept closely related to deep ecology and spirituality in work.

Right livelihood implies that work should be accomplished without harming, depriving, or exploiting people, animals, and the environment. It also encourages us not only to seek livelihoods that avoid killing or harming other beings, such as manufacturing or selling arms, but to consider the consequences of the outcomes of our vocations. For example, people may avoid careers in the nuclear power industry because of safety and environmental hazards associated with nuclear wastes or because of the possibility of nuclear materials getting into the hands of the wrong people.

Right livelihood doesn't necessarily mean that all people working in the defense industry or in nuclear power plants are evil or subversive. What right livelihood suggests is that one first be aware of and acknowledge the inherent harm their occupation may cause and then seek to *balance* that negative outcome with positive ones. For example, a nuclear engineer might mentor a disadvantaged youth or a chemist developing highly toxic materials may be active in her local place of worship.

Work, even mundane work, can be the source of an inner awakening that causes us to realize the spiritual relationship between our inner being (soul) and our occupation. When we view work as something providing intrinsic worth we move it beyond its extrinsic value as a simple job and give it transcendent value. Briskin (1998) made a distinction between work and a job by saying that "when work becomes a job, its intrinsic value vanishes" (p. 143). A job is external, whereas "work is the expression of our soul, our inner being . . . our inner work" (Fox, 1994, p. 5).

The perspective of work as providing higher meaning or right livelihood to individuals and enhancing society moves beyond traditional ideas of work as means of production dedicated solely to enhancing individual gain or corporate profit. Rather, it recharacterizes work as a concept that the workplace is not separate from, but is interdependent with humans, society, and the environment.

Reinterpreting or reconceptualizing the meaning of work as enhancing the individual's physical and spiritual growth, for the organizations' positive performance, and sustaining the society and the ecosystem requires a fundamental change in the way leaders lead and followers follow. Part Two discusses leadership models and ethical leadership in detail, but it is important to start our journey toward a different understanding of the role of leadership by briefly clarifying leadership, based on ethics and values.

Leadership as a Value

We have overlooked the role of ethical leader in seeking to liberate the best in people within organizations when the best in people is directly linked to a sense of higher self, not just making money, selling more of a product or service, or making something faster and better. As has been frequently iterated, ecosystem and social problems are correlated with and attributed at least in part to global economic gain. This relationship should make it clear that leaders in human resources and related fields need to fundamentally reorient themselves to account for the impact that their decisions and their organizations have on economies and the uncertain effect they might have on individuals, society, and the environment. It is clear to most professionals trying to change people and organizations just how difficult instrumental, organizationally oriented change is, much less trying to change a single individual's values. The goal is really not to change unethical behaviors to ethical ones; that is typically beyond our capability and scope. Instead, the goal is to help people in HRD and our clients appreciate and understand the significance of leadership that goes beyond command and control. This can be done through the establishment of an ethical climate and the encouragement of ethical and moral leadership.

Korten (1995) and others posit that managers are subjugated to the power of economics and thus cannot exert independence when making decisions. To the extent that this is true, HRD and its leaders may seldom be in a position to directly impact resources or expend money for societal or environmental outcomes. But they can provide guidance and facilitate organizational analyses, knowledge management, and other activities and processes that include a broader view of organizations than one of pure economics. This takes more than personal competencies and skills; it requires viewing leadership as an ethical and moral issue.

For HRD to truly make a difference, HRD leaders must make better decisions and become agents for positive change. As Pogo, the well-known cartoon character, said, "We have seen the enemy and he is us." HRD leaders and organizational leaders that we influence through our training and development have the responsibility to change and reinterpret strategies to include ethics and sustainability.

Our organizations lack something, something gut-level, fundamental. Their structure, management, processes, and, in many cases, their very existence is being questioned and scrutinized as never before. Could they be less than the benevolent entities that we have been encouraged to believe in? Are they really the confidant that we have come to trust? Could it be that our recent conversion to the religion of margins is not turning out as we had hoped? Corporations, like any other idols, may be welcoming, but in the end are false. But are they the true villains? Are they really to blame for our forlorn and unfulfilled state? Kanungo and Mendonca (1996) said, ". . . as an entity, the business corporation is incapable of doing good or evil in society. Such results must be directly and entirely attributed to the unethical behavior of individuals—workers or managers [leaders] of the corporation" (p. 5). Maclagan (1998) added, "It is individuals who have sufficient discretion to enable ethical deliberation and choice" (p. 106).

With structural and technical changes in organizations and continuing downsizing and layoffs, people are being asked to do more with less help and with less supervision. This "do more with less" syndrome extends to learning and training and to any kind of constructive feedback from management. Couple employee stress caused by having to perform more and better with phenomenal executive compensation packages, and it is not hard to uncover a system based not on any sense of fairness but on power and exploitation. Dalla Costa (1998) added,

> Poorly managed companies are especially prone to moral and legal risk. The pressure to perform, either at unrealistic levels or in the absence of value-added innovations, encourages the cutting of corners and rationalization that leads to impropriety. (p. 154)

In turbulent times, leaders can provide steerage to lead organizations and companies toward sustainable destinations, much like a ship's captain. With the increasing realization that organizations are too powerful, behave in unacceptable ways, are responsible for much of the degradation of the environment, and continue to degrade native cultures around the globe, it is becoming more evident that we do not need more leaders that can strategize or are more efficient, tougher, or consider business as a game. We need ethical, moral, and responsible leadership that can steer both well and good, simultaneously visioning our destination and teaching us how to steer.

Viewing leadership as an ethical imperative has been all but discounted as antithetical to capitalist thought and action, especially under the logical positivistic economically driven worldviews that are so prevalent in today's companies. However, viewing leadership as an ethical and moral obligation gives leaders a true opportunity to create sustainable workplaces and approach human resource development in ways that are fundamentally different from the more traditional ideas of leaders as managers, manipulators, controllers, and maintainers of the organizational status quo.

Leadership as Moral Imperative

The modern concept of leadership is more than management. Leadership has more than instrumental meaning; it has moral and ethical implications. Leading people, organizations, and communities and governments down a moral path predictably leads to ethical dilemmas. The entire concept of leadership necessarily has an underlying foundation of morality for it to create ethical, sustainable, and responsible organizations. Leaders do more than set a course; they challenge people's value systems and raise their consciousness by modeling end values like sustainability that followers are elevated to achieve (J. M. Burns, 1978; Ciulla, 1998).

Leadership is a social responsibility. It is leading for something larger than the leader or his or her followers—a larger cause, an ethical value, mission, ideal, or philosophy that goes beyond profit or self-seeking accolades. If a leader works to transform the values within an organization with some altruistic goal in mind, then real change can happen, what Daly (1977) called "ultimate ends."

When ethics and morality become leadership values, sustainability and positive change is possible. Values guide how leaders treat not only people but all sentient beings. The altruistic leader seeks to do something for others despite what may prove to be great personal risk or loss. The altruistic leader looks externally and develops what Kanungo and Mendonca (1996) call "environmental sensitivity," a sensitivity to all others, stakeholders involved in and impacted by the organization. Drucker (1968) added that leadership

> must realize that it must consider the impact of every business policy and business action on society. It has to consider whether the action is likely to promote

the public good, to advance the basic beliefs of our society, to contribute to its stability, strength and harmony. (p. 461)

As a foundation for ethical and socially responsible organizations and sustainable change, ethical leadership must have a vision. This vision needs to be substantially different from the organizational and professional status quo, that is, substantially different from what is accepted and rewarded or punished. The vision must be idealized and shared by organizational members (Kanungo and Mendonca, 1996). The act of creating an idealized vision necessarily results in a state of profound commitment on the part of the leader who owns the vision. Commitment to an ideal in turn causes a transformation in the leader. Transformation, unlike simple self-development toward an external objective, has an inner-focused, spiritual, and transcendent quality that manifests itself in ethical behaviors and actions. It is hard to act unethically when you are seeking to make a profession or an organization more responsible. People are inspired to follow such leadership in an effort to capture a similar inner transformation. Thus, altruistic leadership is not a solitary endeavor; it is a communal, collective enterprise.

If leadership is social responsibility, then ethical leaders are socially constructive; they move people beyond economic self-interests toward an ideal that benefits others—human and nonhuman. Ray Anderson of Interface, Inc. is a good example of such a leader. His ideal was that Interface would be the world's first sustainable manufacturer. Through continuous training and persistent communication he shared his vision with the entire organization. Interface employees now have the same vision. They own the ideal and continue to transform themselves and Interface. In this example, the leader's will did not subvert, discount, or replace those of his followers. This "partnership ethics" requires leaders to assume less power and empower employees by requiring the leaders to develop equity and moral considerations between the human and nonhuman communities, respect cultural and biodiversity, include women, minorities, and nonhuman nature in the code of ethical accountability, and provide environmentally sound management (Merchant, 2000).

Leaders set the tone in an organization for people to articulate their values—share and compare them, and to be watchful of their behaviors. They convey through word and deed what is acceptable and unacceptable. Unethical leaders' behavior, because their moral compass is nonexistent or temporarily out of service, is capricious. It changes based on immediate needs, wants, and contexts. When they are questioned about suspicious behavior, unethical leaders can hide behind regulations, obscure language, and situational or culturally based ethics. Their rhetoric and actions can become defensive and ambiguous.

Ethical behaviors, on the other hand, are seldom vague. When a leader mutually sets the higher purpose of an organization as "sustainable manufacturing" or "human rights," and employees believe in the ideals, it is painfully obvious when actions fail to support them. The leader becomes the living manifestation of the ideal and the human embodiment of a code of ethics. Ethical and ideals-driven leaders know where unethical behaviors are likely to happen and establish ways to deal with them if and when they do. Ethical leaders understand that peoples' behaviors are less a shift in values than a reaction to organizational and environmental factors. Thus, it is important for leaders to be mindful of and articulate their motives, so that they too are held responsible. Leaders who understand that the external environment has a strong impact on the organization's moral character are responsible for establishing a moral climate that mediates these external influences with the moral fiber of the workforce.

Finally, it is important to recognize that leadership means a certain amount of power, either through position, authority, or specialized knowledge. If leaders are controlling and manipulative and disregard other's feedback and input, they will model this controlling paradigm in their organizational processes and procedures. However, if they are advocates of autonomy and empowerment and respect democratic values, then these sentiments will be evidenced in processes and procedures. But to use processes and procedures to their fullest extent, leaders must also be aware of the inherent tension between organizational ethical rhetoric and ethical processes like codes of ethics, and individual moral tendencies. Leaders can guide people toward acceptance of the organization as a moral entity versus allowing a "herd mentality" in simply complying with rules and regulations. The goal is to build morally accountable communities where people have a sense of personal, organizational, and environmental responsibility, people who can self-consciously make good decisions.

Ethical leaders know that people are susceptible to human foibles and human weaknesses. Being ethical means admitting that we are all human. We can neither escape being human nor can we escape the responsibility that comes with acting human. "To be moral, then, is not a vacation nor a chore. It is to be human" (Dalla Costa, 1998, p. 137). Every one of our organizations and each individual, then, has an inescapable and undeniable social responsibility. It is this accountability and morality that form the foundation for leadership of ethical and responsible organizations.

Summary and Conclusions

This chapter established a theoretical foundation for the ideas, recommendations, and concepts discussed throughout the book. Theory is the source of knowledge and provides us with philosophical underpinnings to better understand new and sometimes even well-worn concepts. Theoretical and conceptual foundations explained what the underlying theories or concepts were, how they worked together, and how they supported the phenomenon under investigation. The guiding theoretical framework for the phenomenon of ethical and responsible HRD discussed in this chapter included the synthesis of three separate but related concepts: the essential nature of values and ethics in HRD, the impact of worldviews on organizations and leadership, and the role of values-based leadership in developing ethical and responsible organizations. These concepts were articulated to help the reader better understand the role of HRD in developing ethical and socially responsible organizations.

Specific concepts and theories that support a proposed new way of thinking about and doing things are typically examined through research. The theories and research that underlie ethics, corporate social responsibility, and leadership are discussed in the next chapter.

Business Ethics, Corporate Social Responsibility, and Leadership: A Review of Theory and Research

In the previous chapter concepts and ideas were introduced that set the stage for a deeper understanding of the relationship between ethics, social responsibility, and leadership. Establishing a conceptual framework is an important first step in understanding. Another important step is examining related theory and research. It is instructive to review research and theory that support the notion that HRD has a leadership role in building ethical and socially responsible organizations.

Theory and Research in Business Ethics

Ethics has always been a part of business. Problems of morals, values, and responsibility are as old as business itself. But ethics as a formal academic field of study and as a research topic is relatively new. Over the past thirty years or so business ethics has become an established academic discipline in the West. Yet with few exceptions, research integrating human resource development and business ethics is more or less nonexistent.

Business ethics is the study of conflict, conflict between economics and values, between competition, commerce, and capitalism, and between morality, integrity, and responsibility. Business ethics is the examination of values and the way values are carried out in work-related systems.

Business ethics research is therefore multidimensional. It focuses on theoretical and methodological issues, ethical activities, behaviors, and sensitivities, institutionalization of ethics in business and professions, and corporate social responsibility.

Theoretic Issues in Business Ethics

Theoretical or conceptual issues in business ethics focus on the use and validity of various philosophical paradigms such as utilitarianism, postmodernism, rationalism, altruism, pluralism, positivism, relativism, and the like. Theoretical or conceptual issues in business ethics also focus on debates about the theoretical bases of research such as normative philosophy versus descriptive social science.

Philosophy and social science have assumed opposing ends of a continuum in business ethics research. Philosophy tends to answer questions about normative (establishing a norm) issues and social science addresses descriptive and empirical issues (the act of describing or a description based on experience or experiment). Rosenthal and Buchholz (2000) described this split as "another manifestation of the fact-value problem that has existed between science and philosophy for several centuries" (p. 399). Using common needs analysis terminology, the descriptive side is about *what is*, and the normative is about *what should be*. To ignore the descriptive aspects of moral behavior is to risk implausible philosophy, and to ignore the normative aspects is to risk amoral social science (Victor and Stephens, 1994).

The lack of integration between descriptive and normative approaches inhibits the ability of research to achieve shared goals of understanding that leads to ethical and responsible organizations. Scholars such as T. Donaldson (1999), Donaldson and Preston (1995), and Jones and Wicks (1999) call for more integration of normative and instrumental approaches to the theoretical development of business ethics. Before we discuss research on activities, behaviors, and sensitivities, methodological issues in business ethics require some attention.

Methodological Issues.   Business ethics research represents a broad spectrum of methodologies. Research methods used represent several categories including general essay, model building, interviews, case studies, surveys, and meta-analyses using extant databases (Collins, 2000). Although publication of conceptual essays has declined somewhat, in 1990 they made up almost 60 percent of all articles published in the *Journal of Business Ethics* (Collins, 2000). On the other hand, interest in empirical research including survey-based and case study method has steadily increased over the past decade.

Ethical Activities, Behaviors, and Sensitivities.   Ethical activities, behaviors, and sensitivities currently make up about half of all business ethics research. Some research on ethical and unethical activities in various contexts presents a positive ethical picture, whereas others indicate that ethical behaviors are declining (Collins, 2000).

A good deal of research has been directed at issues that are ethically sensitive across cultures. For example, Nyaw and Ng (1994) found differences between students from Canada, Hong Kong, Japan, and Taiwan. They found that Taiwanese students were least sensitive toward issues such as sex discrimination. Other studies illustrate a difference between U.S. respondents' ethical sensitivity and the sensitivities of respondents from other nations. For example, Klein (1999) found that U.S. respondents were more ethically sensitive than respondents from Singapore on issues of honesty and integrity, whereas Whitcomb, Erdener, and Li (1998) found differences between U.S. and Chinese respondents on issues concerning bribery. U.S. respondents appear to be more ethically sensitive than respondents from other nations on many attitudes and behaviors (Collins, 2000).

Gender and organizational rank factors are also common variables linked with ethical sensitivities. Most studies indicate that women are more ethically sensitive than men, although both genders tend to believe they are more ethical than the other. No differences between men and women were discovered when it comes to legal issues such as breaking the law, but women appear to be more sensitive to ethical issues around social responsibility and human relations (Smith and Oakley, 1997). Organizational position and rank as well as membership in an occupational group appear to influence ethical sensitivity. Akaah (1996) found that upper-level managers were less tolerant of unethical behaviors than lower-level employees.

Differences between groups concerning ethical sensitivities are a common theme in business ethics research. A significant number of articles compare differences in ethical behaviors across gender, age, and cultural groups. Context and consequences influence the results of many of these ethical sensitivity studies. Personality, nationality, organizational rank, values and ideology, and moral development have also been found to influence how people respond to ethical dilemmas. In addition, research indicates that issues such as the severity and magnitude of consequences and the perceived social consensus that something is right or wrong matter more than other contexts. This appears to hold true across cultures and across organizational position and rank. Responses to ethical dilemmas may be situationally specific and thus not generalizable to other ethical dilemmas (Collins, 2000). The results of these kinds of research are especially important to HRD professionals attempting to establish ethics standards across cultures.

Ethical Decisionmaking

Ethical perceptions and the way people make ethical decisions impacts one's tolerance of unethical behaviors. Because ethical decisionmaking is an important antecedent of ethical behaviors, it has been a frequent topic of research. Ethical decisionmaking theories and models are divided into two camps: normative—or how people or organizations should make decisions in an ethical manner, and descriptive models—how people actually make ethical decisions in situations involving a perceived ethical dilemma. One of the most commonly cited normative models of ethical decisionmaking is Hunt and Vitell's (1986) model. The model starts with the assumption on the part of the decisionmaker that a scenario contains an ethical element. Once this decision is made, several alternatives are available to the actor. Some alternatives are evaluated in terms of deontological norms and others through a teleological path. To make a teleological evaluation requires the actor to consider anticipated consequences for each alternative action. Consequences include the probability of consequences to certain stakeholders actually occurring, the desirability of the consequences to the stakeholders, and the importance the actor places on different stakeholders. The interaction of these three consequences determines the teleological action. In other words, the greater the desirability of the perceived consequences coupled with its importance, the more positive the teleological evaluation is for that action (Cole, Sirgy, and Bird, 2000). The main tenet of this model is that a person's ethical judgment is formed through the combination of two separate moral evaluations—a deontological and a teleological evaluation (Cole, Sirgy, and Bird, 2000). A deontological approach is concerned with whether an action is good in and of itself, whereas teleological evaluation deals with the consequences of the action as opposed to the action itself.

The importance of the stakeholder is a central theme in ethics and corporate social responsibility research as evidenced in the Hunt and Vitell model. The choice of stakeholders and the relative salience determines the outcomes of the decisionmaking process. For example, an HRD practitioner who considers the environment a more important stakeholder than employees will make different decisions when faced with an ethical dilemma than someone who believes the environment is not as important or who does not even consider the environment as a stakeholder.

Some researchers have interpreted differences in ethical decisionmaking with reference to differences in moral development. According to Kohlberg (1958), for example, an individual's moral sophistication impacts the way they make ethical decisions. Moral sophistication progresses through a series of developmental levels in reaching moral maturity. One's moral development evolves and increases over time through three stages from being primarily influenced by externally prescribed rewards and punishment to expectations of acceptable behavior of significant others to internally defined concerns for principle and universal fairness. Rest's (1994) Model of Moral Action, a cognitive development model, distinguishes four major components: the ethical sensitivity that an ethical dilemma exists, prescriptive reasoning that results in a judgment that an ideal solution exists for the specific situation, and ethical motivation that stems from one's intention of whether or not to comply with the ethical judgment. Outcome, the fourth component, is the ethical decision choice.

T. M. Jones's Issue-Contingent Model of ethical decisionmaking expanded on Rest's model by introducing the idea of moral intensity, or the "extent of issue-related moral imperative in a situation" (1991, p. 372).

Models such as Hunt and Vitell, Kohlberg, Rest, and Jones provide a reasonable theoretical basis for ethical decisionmaking. However, researchers continue to modify existing concepts and develop new ones. For example, Gaudine and Thorne (2001) focused on the role of emotion in the ethical decisionmaking process.

Codes of Ethics and Training

An important component of ethical decisionmaking in the workplace involves the use of formal codes of ethics. A code of ethics is a written, distinct, and formal document that consists of moral standards used to guide member, employee, or corporate practice (Schwarz, 2001; Hatcher and Aragon, 2000a, 2000b). Langlois and Schlegelmilch (1990) defined a code of ethics as a statement describing corporate principles, ethics, rules of conduct, codes of practice, or company philosophy concerning responsibility to employees, shareholders, consumers, the environment, or any other aspects of society external to the organization.

The application of codes of ethics has many benefits (see Table 4.1 for a list of applications of codes of ethics identified in the business ethics literature). For example, they can provide guidance in avoiding legal entanglements and enhance and provide a common moral framework to guide practice. Professional codes of ethics provide people in organizations with a standard of

TABLE 4.1 Applications of Formal Codes of Ethics

Provide norms, values, ideals	Promote a common moral framework to guide practice
Consistent normative standards	
	Improve organizational climate and culture
Support organizational goals	
	Professionalize an occupation or field of study
Promote ethical sensitivity and judgment	
Help to socialize people into a corporate culture	Strengthen support for individual ethical courage
Bring people together by enhancing ethical behaviors	Promote trust
	Promote public image
Provide for avoidance of legal consequences	Build corporate reputation
Make explicit the behavior and operating practices that an organization demands	Provide aspirational and punitive bases for behavior
Help create an environment where ethical behaviors are a norm	Collective reminder of responsibilities for organizational members
Serve as an educational tool; serve as a focal point for discussion in training and education	Developing and modifying a code of ethics can be valuable for a profession
Remove ambiguity in organizational contexts	Serve as a beacon that a profession is serious about responsibility and professional conduct

what is right in a particular context, not just what is appreciated, popular, or esteemed; "their legitimacy is that it is 'right'" (Dalla Costa, 1998, p. 123).

Formal codes of ethics and ethics policies and programs provide a means for organizations and professions to institutionalize values and ethics. Some scholars and practitioners have criticized codes of ethics as being pointless and unnecessary whereas others believe that codes are useful and important, especially in unstable organizational contexts and evolving professional organizations. Whether or not scholars and practitioners agree on their validity, codes of ethics are prevalent in most large modern organizations and are growing in frequency and use. The Center for Business Ethics found that over 90 percent of large corporations have a formal code of ethics (Center for Business Ethics, 1992).

Codes of ethics provide people in organizations with a standard of what is right in a particular context, but sometimes people lack the skills and knowledge required to make effective and high-quality ethical decisions. Training provides a means to develop skills and knowledge about ethical codes and encourages ethical behaviors through socialization. However, fully one-fifth to one-third of employees receive no ethics training or education of any sort (Weaver, Trevino, and Cochran, 1999).

Ethics training programs may either improve a person's behaviors (Delaney and Stockell, 1992) or result in a perception of being unethical (Honeycutt, Siguaw, and Hunt, 1995). Ethics codes are typically general in nature and do not provide specific guidance for new or unusual situations. Training is often used to educate employees about ethical behaviors and provide some guidance in ethical decisionmaking. The focus of ethics training is on the internalization of the code's normative intent, reinforcement of ethical decisionmaking, and the avoidance of behavior that may lead to legal liability (Schwarz, 2001).

Human resource development professionals are assuming more responsibility for ethics and ethical development in organizations. Driscoll and Hoffman (1998) found that HR managers must frequently make and carry out decisions with ethical implications and often take the lead in developing and implementing ethics initiatives. Many organizations delegate key leadership roles to HRD management in establishing and maintaining their ethics programs, and a significant number of practitioners are active in areas involving ethics from providing sources of information on ethics and advice to developing and evaluating ethics training programs. More information about the relationship between ethics and the practice of HRD can be found in Chapter 5.

Ethics research as discussed herein focused on theoretical and methodological issues, ethical activities, behaviors and sensitivities, and the institutionalizing of ethics in business and professions through codes of ethics and training. Although it is a relatively new field of study, business ethics research offers a broad and multidimensional base. It is beginning to provide some understanding about how people develop ethical behaviors and how organizations might develop moral frameworks and enhance the ethical behaviors of their employees.

Thus far, the discussion of business ethics' research has been primarily focused on internal organizational ethics. One critical part of the ethics, values, and belief structures of organizations is their relationship with society. The next section addresses theory and research in corporate social responsibility as a vital part of business ethics research.

Theory and Research in Corporate Social Responsibility

Theory and research in corporate social responsibility (CSR) has been the subject of considerable attention and debate within the academic and practitioner communities for several decades. Also known as corporate social performance (CSP), research has been limited almost exclusively to publications within social issues in management (SIM) or business ethics (BE). With the exception of work by Kaufman (Kaufman, 1992, 1997) and his colleagues (Kaufman and Watkins, 2000; Watkins, Leigh, and Kaufman, 2000) and Hatcher (Hatcher, 1999, 2000a, 2000b), publications on CSR in the HRD or training and development literature is limited.

To understand corporate social responsibility as a research construct requires that organizations be conceptualized as having a responsibility beyond making a profit and being accountable not only to stockholders and customers, but to all stakeholders, including employees, communities, societies, and the environment. Further, corporate social responsibility suggests that organizations have a moral obligation to use their resources for the common good as well as obligations to particular groups such as stockholders, consumers, employees, suppliers, creditors, communities, and the environment. This organizational understanding sets the stage for the underlying theories that support CSR theory and research.

Corporate Social Responsibility Theory

Approaches to CSR theory are comprehensive in nature. This comprehensiveness is interpreted as a weakness in the field's ability to establish a solid theoretical base for research and many scholars believe that a firm theoretical foundation in this area is nonexistent (Carroll, 1994). On the other hand, "A single, unifying theory, while allowing for tidy definitions and visible boundaries, stifles the analysis of [CSR] where it happens in the complex and chaotic world of organizations" (Hatcher, 1998, p. 35).

Even though stakeholder theory is commonly referred to in the literature as a foundation for CSR research, several different theories and concepts have been proposed, including legitimacy theory, contingency theory, and transcendental theory (Frederick, 1998; Hatcher, 1999). Frederick (1998) added that the study of CSR has exhausted its primary analytic framework based on stakeholder theory and needs to move to a new paradigmatic level. Although not an exhaustive listing of CSR theory by any means, descriptions of these theories provide a means of comparison and a better understanding of the richness of theory underlying CSR research.

Stakeholder Theory.   Because stakeholder theory is recognized as a primary theoretical foundation of CSR, it is instructive to begin our discussion on theory with its description. There has been much interest in the idea that a person, organization or group, a community, or even society and the environment has a stake in a firm and has been used as a conceptual framework for CSR since its introduction.

Many articles and books have been published on stakeholder theory, with over 100 articles and over a dozen books in the management literature alone (Donaldson and Preston, 1995). Yet the concept is relatively vague, especially as applied within HRD-related literature.

Jones and Wicks (1999) suggest that stakeholder theory is based on four principles: The corporation has different relationships with many constituent groups that affect and are affected by its decisions (Freeman, 1984); the nature of these relationships in terms of processes and outcomes for the firm and its stakeholders is the primary concern of stakeholder theory; legitimate stakeholders have intrinsic value and no interests dominate others (Clarkson, 1995); and its focus is on management decisionmaking (Donaldson and Preston, 1995). Stakeholder theory posits that the values of an organization's stakeholders and their influence on management decisions predict an organization's performance; that when managers pursue interests of multiple stakeholders the firm will achieve higher performance measures (T. Donaldson, 1999).

But the application of stakeholder theory is not without its problems. First, each constituent potentially wants different things from the company. This is especially true in a growing international business environment where an expanded view of stakeholders based on culture, political makeup, socioeconomics, environmental values, and technology have divergent interests in the firm. What is clear, however, is that "Stakeholders' expectations of corporations, and company impacts on stakeholders, make it essential for managers to be intensely aware of the processes and consequences of stakeholder relations" (Wartick and Wood, 1998, p. 16).

Research into stakeholder theory has often been criticized for a lack of rigor and consistency. This lack of consistency can be defined in terms of two recognized and divergent approaches to stakeholder theory—a social scientific, instrumental approach and a normative ethics approach (Jones and Wicks, 1999). The social scientific approach is descriptive in that the theory purports to explain actual behavior.

A different approach specifies what moral obligations organizations and leaders have to stakeholders. This ethics approach is normative and deontological in nature and implies that leaders ought to view the interests of stakeholders as having intrinsic value (Jones and Wicks, 1999).

Debate continues in the scholarly community on the relevance of these two approaches and their possible convergence (Jones and Wicks, 1999). It is beyond the scope of this chapter to delve into the intricacies of this convergence or to summarize the many responses of its detractors. However, it is instructive for HRD professionals to better understand stakeholder theory and its general applicability to the future growth of HRD as a field of study interested in enhancing ethics and social responsibility. Although the application of stakeholder theory in HRD has been limited (Hatcher, 1999, 2000a; Kaufman, 1992), development and appreciation of stakeholder theory is necessary "if we as a society desire a moral and practical organizational response to the spread of intensely competitive global markets" (Jones and Wicks, 1999, p. 219).

Legitimacy Theory.   Theory based on the idea of legitimacy posits that firms operate within a social network made up of corporate and industry-specific culture. Institutional legitimacy implies that behaviors within a company become valuable and thus are ritualized over time. Rituals, because they "gain status beyond their pragmatic value," become legitimate, and "legitimate behaviors persist, even when they lose their pragmatic value" (Beliveau, Cotrill, and O'Neill, 1994, p. 732). This corporate legitimacy also impacts socialization routines such as orientation training and mentoring activities where newcomers attempt to emulate accepted leadership behaviors within a company. It can also become a problem when individual beliefs and behaviors do not correspond with legitimate behaviors in a firm.

Industry-based legitimacy occurs because behavioral patterns within industries tend to be similar, and companies seeking legitimacy emulate these behaviors. Thus, a company that exhibits CSR behaviors may be seeking legitimacy within an industry where norms reflect social responsibility. Conversely, a firm seeking to enhance its social responsibility within an industry bereft of legitimate CSR-related behaviors may be ostracized, or worse, socially or economically shunned, or both.

Contingency Theory.   Similar to stakeholder theory, contingency theory suggests that social issues are a stakeholder and vary considerably over time. The extent to which an organization responds to different social issues enhances CSR. Issue-contingent models provide guidance on how a firm ought to respond to a social issue based on the nature of the issue (Husted, 2000).

Although contingency theory might be defined under the rubric of stakeholder theory, it is instructive to view it as discrete for two reasons: First, stakeholder theory provides an awareness and identity of stakeholders as recipients of CSR independent of the context under which this relationship happens. Second, contingency theory provides a means to determine under which conditions (context) certain strategies, structures, or both would be most appropriate to improve CSR. The "contingency model of corporate social performance argues that strategies and structures properly aligned with social issues will lead to greater social performance" (Husted, 2000, p. 25).

According to Husted (2000), contingency theory is built around identification of the kind of social issue—or the contingency to which an organization responds, the "fit" between the social issue and the firm, and the specific strategies and structures that "fit" each social issue. Identifying social issues as the gap between what companies do or plan on doing and what society expects should be readily understandable to most HRD professionals and other leaders familiar with rudimentary strategic planning and needs assessment methods. Once the gap is identified, then an intervention or "fit" can be identified and implemented. This "fit" between the organization and the social issue may be based on profit maximization or organizational survival, and includes strategies such as routine responses like environmental scanning and social reporting that HRD is routinely responsible for. The primary limitation of this theory is that only stakeholders with a recognized and resolute voice will be acknowledged through some intervention.

Transcendental Theory.   The third and final CSR theory is transcendental theory. Transcendental theory is concerned with human consciousness. Human consciousness is an awareness of us in relation to our existence, our world, and what we believe is reality. This consciousness is a product of our growth from one level of development to another. Levels of development are based on the way we as groups of humans think, feel, and interpret reality. The idea of human consciousness as stages of development is not new, yet its application to business and the environment is limited. This discussion is based in part on the groundbreaking psychological research of Clare Graves (1970) and the research published in *Spiral Dynamics: Mastering Values, Leadership, and Change* (1995) by Beck and Cowan. Additionally, in *A Theory of Everything: An Integral Vision for Business, Politics, Science, and Spirituality* (2000), Ken Wilber stimulated and helped to solidify the ideas around levels of development of human consciousness applicable as a theoretical foundation of CSR.

Stage theories of human development are common. The idea that we move through successive stages in our lives is an accepted concept. But the idea that we move through successive levels of consciousness, that we move from less to more awareness, has not been widely disseminated in business. Akin to Abraham Maslow's hierarchy of needs that progress from basic physical needs such as food and water to self-actualization, levels of consciousness start at a basic survival level and progress through the need to prosper and finally to the level of integration and holism. According to Beck and Cowan (1995) and Wilber (2000), there are eight levels or thinking tiers. For illustrative purposes each level is described and associated with Maslow's hierarchy of needs:

1. *Basic survival.* The level of basic instincts for food, water, warmth, sex, and safety. Distinct individual self is almost nonexistent and humans form groups in order to survive. Maslow's physiological deficiency needs including hunger, thirst, bodily comfort, and safety and security needs.
2. *Magical: Seeking harmony in a mysterious and dangerous world.* Animism among tribes of people. Maslow's belongingness and affiliation needs.
3. *Hero/individual ego.* Individualism emerges. Power associated with humans and mythic creatures. Feudalism and the idea of the "great man" converge. Maslow's esteem needs. Self-confidence, independence.
4. *Order of the arrow: Purpose through truth established by others.* Life is directed by order or code imposed by righteous "other." Law and codes of conduct drive social hierarchies. Religious or mythic organizations abound. Maslow's esteem and ego needs; the need to conform and belong.
5. *Material/scientific/individual.* Objective, mechanistic, scientific rational gains. Life is a machine or a game to be played. Science rules. Maslow's self-actualization/fulfillment needs. Aesthetic needs for symmetry and beauty. Vocation, devotion to something external.
6. *Human spirit/sensitivity.* Human spirit is separated from dogma. Community, relationships, caring for sentient beings. Human potential and social construction of reality. Maslow's self-actualization and potentiality needs. Enlightenment.
7. *Integrative, systems thinking, natural flows.* Knowledge and understanding are more important than power and status. Maslow's self-actualization and beginnings of transcendence needs. Relationships with others and their potential are important.
8. *Holism, unity, universal order.* New spirituality based on theory of everything. One consciousness. Maslow's transcendence needs.

A simplistic view of business is that it is little more than aggregates of humans with various levels of consciousness seeking common goals. To the extent that this is true, an understanding of the different levels of human consciousness and how we move from one level to another may also help us understand at what level business in general, an industry, or a single organization falls. This understanding might also provide insights into why some businesses and leaders are embracing CSR and others are not and thus may help us develop research that enhances business, industry, or a company's social responsibility.

The levels of human development (Beck and Cowen in Wilber, 2000) are described with examples of each level's application to business and to the environment in Table 4.2.

There are two transcendence theories that are the most meaningful to the development of important CSR research. First is the view of transcendence as an expansion of stakeholder theory or spiritual stakeholder. The second theory views deep ecology as a theoretical foundation with spiritual overtones.

The idea that transcendence is an expansion of stakeholder theory or what might be called the spiritual stakeholder requires that we understand that stakeholders have spiritual dimensions and that the relationship between them and organizations is more than economic. The idea of a spiritual stakeholder is attributed to the work of E. F. Schumacher (1977) and more recently Stead and Stead (1996, 2000).

To date, the relationship between organizations and their stakeholders has been strictly one of economics. An organization wanting to address the non-secular needs of its stakeholders is viewed as either not competitive or relegated to the not-for-profit sector. "In the workplace, we have become polarized between managing the outer organization—work processes, organizational objectives, managerial structures—and the inner organization of people—emotional attitude, mental processes, cooperative spirit" (Briskin, 1998, pp. x–xi). The spiritual stakeholder is one who attempts to bridge this gap by a spiritual connection to the firm. This is accomplished through relationships that include "love, joy, exhilaration, peace, patience, kindness, goodness, faithfulness, gentleness, self control, and the like" (Stead and Stead, 2000, p. 235).

The philosophical roots of deep ecology are found in the ecocentric religions and spiritual ways of life of primal peoples around the world, and to Taoism, Saint Francis of Assisi, Spinoza, and Zen Buddhism (Sessions, 1995). These belief systems establish that all life has intrinsic value and that our spirit and the life spirit are connected. Capra (1996) said, "Within the context of deep ecology, the view that values are inherent in all of living nature is grounded in the deep ecological, or spiritual, experience that nature and the self are one" (pp. 11–12). This awareness of our connection with a larger, higher power is both beyond and yet part of the secular world of business and economics. "Ultimately, deep ecological awareness is spiritual or reli-

TABLE 4.2   Levels of Development/Human Consciousness Applied to Business and Environment

Level of Development/Human Consciousness	Business Application	Environmental Application
1. Basic or instinctual survival—Human consciousness is limited to instincts to seek food, water, warmth, sex, shelter, and safety.	International companies in Third World where starvation, disease, and famine are common or a possibility; firms suffering economic or reputation-based collapse or extreme public antipathy in response to unethical behaviors that cause suffering, destruction, and death.	Environment is feared yet totally embraced and part of. Utilitarian in use of nature for survival.
2. Animism and mystic kinship—Human consciousness is based on tribal bonds, ancestral lineage, magic, ritual, and superstition.	An organization with strong, cohesive, almost magical work groups and deep-seated corporate culture that includes rituals, ceremony, symbols, myths, and stories.	Humans' relationship with the environment is awe and respect based on superstition. Nature for transcendent and basic use.
3. Mythic egoism—Human consciousness is based on ego, hero image. Mythical and powerful beings, gods, good and evil forces. Benevolent leaders, feudal systems.	New, entrepreneurial, creative and highly innovative companies. Frontier mentality. Organizations willing to take risks and go against the status quo. Heroic and visionary leadership.	Humans' relationships with the environment are control and conquer. Life is harsh yet nature is magical.
4. Spiritual conformism—Human consciousness is based on conforming to severe, righteous, fundamentalist codes of right and wrong; paternalistic and hierarchical.	Organizations with strong morality and nationalism imposed by leadership or spiritual or religious orientation of workforce. Punitive codes of ethics/morals. Philanthropy based on dogma. Totalitarian and fundamentalist leadership.	Humans separate from nature. Nature is seen strictly in aesthetic or utilitarian terms. Dogma begins to dictate human's anthropocentricism.
5. Rational scientism—Human consciousness is based on logic, rational, and scientific thought. Highly individualistic, seeking truth and meaning through objective science, systems approach. Achievement and materialistic versus secular success oriented. Money and possession is highly valued. Rise of "industrial man" image.	Economic and scientific management and management theory. Structures and systems, psychology and sociology applied to business. Industrial/scientific revolution. Assembly lines. Financial competition creates massive growth of work-related systems. International business. Corporate states emerge in communist-related countries. Ford, Taylor, Mayo, Follett, and Welch. Machine metaphor for business.	Humans dominate nature. Nature is resources/abundant use for economics.

(continues)

TABLE 4.2   *(continued)*

6. *Human potential and community*—Human consciousness is based on growth and potential, ecological sensitivity, and community development. Interdependence with the ecosystem, bio and cultural diversity. Nonsecular, cosmological spirituality. Relations, connections, communication, and dialogue important. International human rights.	Humanistic systems, systems thinking, business as brain metaphor; employees seen less as commodities and more as people; growth of human rights, human resources, and employee education. Employee empowerment; rise of teamwork, work groups, and diversity; environmental movement into business and industry. Organization change management, cooperation, flatter structures, less hierarchy and more values-based and women leadership. Quality movement, employee ownership, sustainable "Green" businesses. Growth of socially responsive companies. Drucker, Knowles, Peters, Senge, Capra, Schumacher, Roddick, and Anderson.	Environment is revered, protected, sustained. Humans are part of the environment/Gaia. Environment not for human use. Animal rights, protection of old growth and rain forest. Care for the earth; ecological sensitivity.
7. *Coalescence and knowledge*—Human consciousness is based on flexibility, naturalness, practicality, knowledge, and competence.	Organizations are synergistic, and coopetition is common. Win-win business environment. Knowledge, learning, self-direction, and self-actualization are more important than economic and instrumental gain. Ethics and social responsibility are status quo. Organizations seek "flow" states as defined by Csikszentmihalyi. Learning organizations (Senge) are common.	Nature is seen as common good. Environment, ethics, social science, and biology are aligned.
8. *Unified theory and consilience[1]*—Human consciousness is based on holistic universal systems, single consciousness, new spirituality.	Organizations are not separate from nature/ecosystem. Holistic approach to industries and communities. Industrial wastes streams are omitted or completely recycled; cogeneration is standard practice; spirituality in workplace is common. Ken Wilber, E.O. Wilson.	Environment and humankind is single unit. No separation of human from Gaian consciousness. True equality of all living things. Nature and humankind share deep ecology.

SOURCES: Adapted from Beck and Cowen (1995), *Spiral Dynamics: Mastering Values, Leadership, and Change.* Cambridge, Mass.: Blackwell Publishers, and K. Wilber (2000), *A Theory of Everything: An Integral Vision for Business, Politics, Science, and Spirituality.* Boston, Mass.: Shambhala.

1. Consilience means that everything in the universe is organized in terms of a few natural laws that make up the principles underlying all learning and knowledge. From Wilson (1998), *Consilience: The Unity of Knowledge.* New York: Alfred A. Knopf.

gious awareness . . . ecological awareness is spiritual in its deepest essence" (Capra, 1996, p. 7). Since deep ecology is concerned more with metaphysics than science, it makes sense that as a theoretical foundation for research it sustains and amplifies the nonsecular and spiritual dimension of CSR.

The extent that transcendental values are acknowledged as theoretical foundations of CSR research remains to be firmly established. Questions of whether we are prepared to acknowledge our yearning for meaning within the confines of research steeped in science and secularism are still unanswered. The quest for meaning is a journey that humanity has intermittently faltered from and variously sought throughout history, but never given up on. To think it could be relinquished, set aside simply for the sake of business or to develop theory for research is ludicrous. However, as we learn to use our research to tell stories about important relationships and explain why things are as they are and seek out meaning, we realize that it is through stories that we find spiritual significance and make spiritual connections (Stead and Stead, 2000). Using research based on spirituality as stories, we can tie the utility of business to its value-creating and secular side.

In the chaotic and messy world of work it is naive to think that myopic approaches will help us answer complex questions about the relationship between business, society, and the environment. Thus, we need diverse and atypical theory that helps us to respond to this chaos and complexity, not theory that neatly places research into comfortable and predictable categories. Although research has tended to follow some trends or common themes, it has also deviated from them and provided a mosaic of approaches to studying CSR and related topics.

Corporate Social Responsibility Research

Research in CSR has followed two general yet related tracks including analyzing the relationship between business and its larger environment, and links between business and society. The latter track is the richest and has tended to focus on the relationship between social and financial and nonfinancial performance.

The Relationship Between Corporate Social Responsibility and Financial Performance. The relationship between CSR and financial performance is mixed. Some studies have found a positive relationship whereas other have found no relationship at all (Pava and Krausz, 1995). One of the reasons for this lack of consistency in research findings, and the suspected lack of theoretical validity in the area of CSR, is the larger question of what motivates CSR research.

Convincing management to take up the CSR banner because "doing good means doing well"; that CSR is not a costly initiative and will in fact help make a company more profitable motivates many researchers to seek a positive relationship between CSR and financial performance. Thus, enlightened self-interest may be an overriding motivation for CSR and financial performance research. Additionally, the conventional idea that corporate social performance can be captured as a single dimension or construct has been questioned by several researchers, including Griffon and Mahon, 1997, and Rowley and Berman, 2000. Indeed, the multidimensional nature of CSR "complicates the process of identifying the boundary conditions of CSR research" (Rowley and Berman, 2000, p. 398), and thus confounds the relationship between the CSR construct and other variables.

In many cases, measures of CSR represent multiple dimensions. Such aggregate measures make it difficult to interpret the meaningfulness of the measure or to compare variables across firms or industries.

One recommendation has been to use measures based on the *Fortune* Reputation Survey or the Domini Social Index (also known as the KLD index) that may allow us to measure a firm's social performance in a general manner, mitigating the limitations of one single variable and providing a way to make comparisons across studies and industries.

A direct relationship between corporate social performance and financial performance has not been firmly established. There may in fact be much more to CSP than whether or not it produces profit or financial gain. Companies as moral agents "must assume the burdens of morality just like people do, and . . . develop something akin to consciences" (T. Donaldson, 1982, p. 18). If companies have consciences, are considered as moral or immoral, then like people they need values and beliefs that support ethical behaviors. And like people, they need a vision of the future that is sustainable. Corporations need vision as well as practice, valid as well as moral foundations on which to build meaningful research.

Relationship Between Corporate Social Responsibility and Nonfinancial Metrics. Assessing CSR with nonfinancial metrics is a response to questions about the validity and utility of financial metrics. The use of nonfinancial metrics emphasizes measuring factors that might be associated with more humane, responsible, and ethical workplaces.

> Ethical responsibilities embrace a range of norms, standards, or expectations of behavior that reflect a concern for what consumers, employees, shareholders,

the community, and other stakeholders regard as fair, right, just, or in keeping with stakeholders' moral rights or legitimate expectations. (Carroll, 2000, p. 36)

Research that addresses corporate social responsibility more in line with ethical and responsible outcomes includes related variables such as social auditing, a quality workforce, corporate reputation, and perceptions of managers, executives, and important stakeholders, to name a few.

Social or corporate responsibility auditing and sharing information with stakeholders is a practice and popular topic for CSR-related research. Research indicates that the key issues reported through social audits include environment, philanthropy, management's goals and philosophy, health, minorities, plant safety, energy, employee development, local community relations, and business conditions, education, product safety, literacy, and financial performance (Marx, 1992–1993).

Scholars have suggested that CSR may provide a competitive advantage to companies by attracting a more qualified workforce. For example, Greening and Turban (2000) reported that corporate social performance and in particular the dimensions of employee relations, treatment of women and minorities, and concern for the environment were most important in explaining organizational attractiveness. Albinger and Freeman (2000) found that corporate social performance was positively related to employer attractiveness for job seekers with high levels of job choice, suggesting advantages to socially responsive companies in their ability to attract qualified employees. These studies suggest there is a relationship between organizations with high levels of CSR and emphases on developing human resources. Additional studies report a relationship between a firm's reputation and employee turnover (Hatcher, 1999) and the relationship between the actions of top management and social performance (Riordan, Gatewood, and Bill, 1997).

Other studies have shown positive relationships between reputation, performance, and social responsibility (Fombrun and Shanley, 1990; Wood, 1995), and led to suggestions that a company's reputation may influence the quality of its workforce (Pfeffer, 1994). The implications of this research are that corporate reputation is to some extent dependent on measures of social responsibility and that both variables are related to the development of a quality workforce.

Corporate social responsibility research has the potential to enhance not only financial performance, but also to support ethical and responsible outcomes related to the workforce. Thus, HRD may be a direct recipient of positive changes in corporate social performance and may also be a determinate of socially responsible behaviors. But many outcomes require the impetus of organizational leaders. The next topic discusses theory and research in leadership.

TABLE 4.3   Differences Between Leadership and Management

	Leadership	*Management*
Roles	Create mutual vision Influence and build relationships Engage and develop followers Provide mentor/model Personal mastery Values-based actions Inspire and stimulate Holistic	Authorize and direct tasks Task-based actions Develop and implement 　mission/objectives/vision Competence—skills and knowledge Direct, supervise, control, and order Mechanistic
Outcomes	Changes based on mutual needs 　and wants Conserve resources Empower followers Transform organization to 　mutual outcomes Expand capacity for human 　potential Focus on ethical and responsible 　behaviors Higher levels of awareness, 　ability, and potential in followers 　and organization	Exchange of value Tasks completed, goals met, 　objectives accomplished Relationship between leader and 　others completed Effectiveness and efficiency Production Use up resources

SOURCE: Adapted from J. C. Rost (1991), *Leadership for the Twenty-First Century.* New York: Praeger.

Theory and Research in Leadership

To better understand the relationship between leadership and ethical and responsible organizations, it is instructive to consider important leadership theories and related research. But before discussing theory and research it is important to better understand what is meant by leadership.

Over two decades ago, J. M. Burns (1978) said that leadership is different from the traits and behaviors of leaders. But in the years since, we still primarily define leadership as the knowledges, skills, abilities, and traits of leaders. Fittingly, we have reduced leadership to slogans, equated it with economic success and manipulating people, confused it with management, and associated it with authority (Barker, 1997). For a summary differentiating leadership and management see Table 4.3.

Some people also relate leadership to an art form, a moral compass, and a vehicle for social good. Many more scholars define leadership in terms of leaders influencing or otherwise getting followers to do what they want them to do rather than a moral, ethical, or principled process for the mutual benefit of leaders, followers, and stakeholders.

This positivistic approach to leadership should come as no surprise. The whole idea of leadership in organizations is based on an industrial paradigm created and maintained as an application of Newtonian science, the goal of which has been to perpetuate feudalism (Barker, 1997). Wheatley (1992) added that "we manage by separating things into parts, we believe that influence occurs as a direct result of force exerted from one person to another, we engage in complex planning for a world that we keep expecting to be predictable, and we search continually for better methods of objectively perceiving the world" (p. 6). Yet with breakthroughs in cognitive sciences, constructivist approaches to learning, qualitative research designs, continuing advances in physics, astronomy, and genetics, new ideas in self-regulating systems (autopoesis) applied to businesses and industries, and a spiritual awakening, it is becoming increasingly clear that the way organizations are led must change. And this change must reflect holism and mutuality.

Leadership definitions have begun to lean more toward noncoercive, participatory, and democratic relationships between leaders and followers. Joanne Ciulla (1998), in her noteworthy book *Ethics, the Heart of Leadership*, offers an insightful observation. Leadership "is also moving people, in both senses of that term. It involves stimulating their emotions, and it involves motivating them . . . not just resolves or manages" (p. 91).

Definitions help us secure regularity for our terms. Defining leadership perpetuates certain paradigms, concepts, and ideas that help us figure out how and what to do when faced with planned changes or unplanned crises. Theorizing about leadership and conducting research on leadership assists us in defining, enhancing, and better understanding leadership as a field of study.

Leadership Theories

Much like the field of HRD, leadership is composed of multiple, largely disparate theoretical frameworks. It is too early in the field's evolution to call these frameworks a paradigm. Paradigms require a primary science, but leadership has none. Being without a comprehensive set of accepted and recognized principles, leadership theory represents a veritable hodgepodge of concepts and theoretical frameworks. Even what is considered theory is questionable. For example, some theorists have lumped much of leadership theory in with metalevel theories that underlie organizations, that is, organization theories such as postmodernism, transaction cost theory, population ecology, and agency theory (L. Donaldson, 1995). Still others categorize leadership theory as a role or behavioral or personal traits level such as situational, life-cycle, contingency, cultural, transactional, transformational, charismatic, and ethical and values or principled-based leadership theories. Several emerging theories such as leader-member exchange, gender-related, and higher levels of consciousness theories are also relevant to issues of ethics and HRD.

Situational, Contingent, and Cultural-Based Leadership.　The most common traits-based leadership theory is situational theory. Situational leadership theory (SLT), popularized by Hersey, Blanchard, and Johnson (2000) and originally published by Hersey and Blanchard (1969) as life-cycle theory, posits that leaders change their behaviors based on follower maturity. This atheoretical model has moderate support for its validity (Blank, Weitzel, and Green, 1990; Goodson, McGee, and Cashman, 1989; Norris and Vecchio, 1992; Yukl and Van Fleet, 1992; Vecchio, 1987), but provides little guidance on how or why certain leader behaviors correspond to follower maturity levels (Yukl, 1989). Although leaders may change their behaviors based on followers' traits, they also posses dominant behavioral tendencies or dispositions.

Unlike situational theory, where leaders' behaviors are flexible, contingency theories imply that leaders' behaviors are much more fixed, consistent, and thus less flexible. Whereas situational theory advocates that leaders change their behaviors based on follower maturity, contingency theory (Fiedler, 1967) suggests that leaders might change a situation to fit their specific leadership style or even vary leaders for certain situations depending on the fit between the leader's style and the situation.

Situational and contingency theories focused on leadership styles, but Schein (1998) considered ways a leader can create, embed, and change a culture that reflects their own philosophy. Linking culture and leadership, however, has received relatively little research attention. Bass and Avolio (1993) considered how the Organizational Description Questionnaire examined the relationship between transformational leadership and organizational culture, and Sharkey (1999), in her study of whether leadership development was a lever for culture change, found that although changes in culture were not documented, changes in a leader's behaviors did predict a change in organizational culture. The assumption was that as leaders change, so too will the perceptions of followers. Using the recent bond trading scandal at Salomon Brothers as a case study, Sims (2000) posited that new leadership is paramount to successful culture change.

The implication of these few publications is that culture change is to some extent dependant on leadership. Conversely and somewhat surprisingly,

Senge (1996) suggested that little change can occur if it is driven from the top; that in developing culture that supports organizational learning, top management buy-in is a poor substitute for real commitment at many levels, and makes such commitment less rather than more likely. The idea that followers play a critical role in the leader-follower exchange is apparent.

Transactional, Transformational, and Charismatic Leadership.   The basic tenet of the previously discussed leadership theories is that leaders lead and followers follow; that leaders basically make followers do what they want them to do and do things they would not otherwise do on their own. One of the most influential thinkers in leadership theory, James MacGregor Burns, suggested that leaders do not make followers do anything. On the contrary, leaders induce followers to act for certain needs and goals of value to both leaders and followers (1978, 1985). Burns divided this leader-follower interaction into two different kinds of leadership: transactional and transformational.

Transactional leadership occurs when there is an overt attempt to exchange incentives, something of value, with someone in return for their support—"in politics, for instance, jobs for votes, or subsidies for campaign contributions" (Keeley, 1998, p. 113). Each party to the exchange understands the controlling, coercive, and reward-oriented base of power, compliance-related attitudes, and what many scholars and practitioners consider basic unethical moral implications inherent in transactional leadership. The transactional leader operates within the existing system to strengthen existing structures, strategies, and culture rather than trying to transform them.

Conversely, transformational leadership is when people engage with each other in such a way that leaders and followers raise one another to higher levels of motivation and morality (J. M. Burns, 1978). Transformational leaders ignore personal, selfish gains and rather seek a greater, common good or purpose. They elevate the interests of all concerned. They empower followers to also seek the common good, to look beyond their own selfish needs, to include the good of the group. Transformational leaders exhibit charisma, use symbols to direct followers' efforts, encourage them to question the status quo, and treat followers differently but equitably based on their needs (Bass and Avolio, 1993).

The majority of published research on transactional leadership has been conducted in conjunction with its converse, transformational leadership. Research has focused on the relationship of either or both forms of leadership to variables such as gender, culture, and other follower dispositions, and contextual factors such as organizational performance. For example, Jung and Avolio (1999) found that people considered individualists generated more ideas with a transactional leader than a transformational one. Maher (1997) discovered that female managers were rated as more transformational than male managers. Based on the assumption that different cultural groups likely have different conceptions of different forms of leadership, Hartog, House, Hanges, and Ruiz-Quintanilla (1999) found that specific attributes of transformational versus transactional leadership were universally endorsed across cultures. Recent metanalytic studies such as Lowe, Kroeck, and Sivasubramaniam (1996) provide overall support for transactional leadership as an organizational performance stimulus.

Transformational leadership research also focuses on the relationship of leadership to individual demographics, culture, and organizational performance. One of the most striking differences between the results of transactional and transformational research is the ability of transformational leadership to profoundly change people, cultures, and in turn organizations. Dess, Picken, and Lyon (1998) supported this idea by reporting that transformational leadership profoundly alters organizational culture and politics, thereby bringing about ongoing change. Sharkey (1999) found in her study of Scandinavian Airline Systems (SAS) that a variety of organizational development activities were influenced by transformational leadership development. Jung and Avolio (1999) found that collectivists (people working in groups) with a transformational leader generated more ideas than with a more transactional-style leader. Druskat (1994) suggested that transformational leadership is a more feminine style of leadership and found female leaders created follower trust. Because transformational leadership suggests the moral dilemma of favorable attribution effects on followers such as generation of confidence in the leader, making followers feel good in the presence of the leader, and the generation of strong feelings of respect and admiration, a separate and equally rich series of studies of charismatic leaders has grown out of transformational leadership.

Charismatic leadership is often viewed as a necessary ingredient of transformational leadership (Bass, 1985). Max Weber (1921), the famous German sociologist, was the first to advance charisma as leadership to account for followers who are emotionally tied to a leader and display loyalty, devotion, and faith in the leader's character, especially in times of crises. Conger and Kanungo (1988) expanded on this view with a model of a charismatic leader that documents their behaviors and hypothesized outcomes.

Because of its connection with transformational leadership, research on charismatic leadership has similarly focused on its relationship with variables like individual demographics, culture, and organizational performance. The metanalytic work of Lowe, Kroeck, and Sivasubramaniam (1996) provides support for charismatic leadership's role in enhancing organizational performance. In a more recent study, Waldman, Ramírez, House, and Puranam (2001) found that charismatic leadership predicted performance (profitability) under conditions of environmental uncertainty.

Theories and Research in Ethical Leadership

Ethical leadership offers scholars and researchers an option to the dominant, conventional leadership paradigms. Researchers like Ciulla, Gini, Conger, Bass, and Solomon insist that leadership is a complex moral relationship between people, based on trust, obligation, commitment, emotion, a shared vision, and a longing to do well by doing good. Ethics and morality, then, are inseparable and lie at the very heart of leadership (Ciulla, 1998).

Differences in researchers' assumptions underlie much of ethical leadership research. On the one hand, these differences have caused controversy and misunderstandings. On the other hand, different assumptions add to the richness and diversity of ethical leadership research and theory. For example, some researchers view ethical leadership as individual behaviors toward a group to achieve a common goal, whereas others see it as related to and/or dependent on followers. "Without the followers' perceptions, acceptance, and attributions, the phenomenon would simply not exist" (Kanungo and Mendonca, 1996, p. 14). However, this cause-and-effect relationship between an ethical leader and follower behaviors is problematic owing to myriad environmental variables such as resources, technology, and economic conditions that could influence outcomes.

Theoretical bases of ethical leadership draw from transformational, charismatic, and servant leadership (normative) theories. One assumption is that a transformational or charismatic leader challenges followers' value systems by raising their consciousness. Of course, charismatic leadership can be good or bad. Servant leadership (Greenleaf, 1977), or leading based on a desire to serve others, has received less research attention than other approaches, yet remains a compelling and recurring theme in ethical leadership theory and research.

Research associated with ethical leadership falls generally into two camps: conceptual research including definitions of ethical and moral leadership and ethical decisionmaking; normative research that attempts to establish relationships between leadership and follower behaviors.

Creation and validation of definitions of ethical leadership are as problematic as definitions of leadership in general. As Burns stated, "Leadership is one of the least understood phenomena on earth" (1978, p. 2). Adding the notion of ethics, values, or morals further complicates the phenomenon.

Attempting to define ethical leadership has ranged from an ascetic construct (H. B. Jones, 1995) to about being in love (Kouzes and Posner, 1992) to an ecological focus (Hatcher, 2000a). H. B. Jones (1995) studied the relationship between ethics and personality, that people are predisposed through socialization toward ethical character and behaviors. An argument is developed that the character traits of an ascetic personality in a leadership position will have valuable and predictable effects on followers and organizations. It is suggested that leader assessments as an advance indicator to identify "habits of conduct" related to ascetic behaviors might alleviate problems when leaders are faced with morally difficult situations.

More sensational, Kouzes and Posner (1992) represent ethical leadership based on one of the most revered yet misunderstood of all human emotions: love. Drawing on transformational and charismatic leadership and research on empathy, compassion, sensitivity, and honesty, the authors build a case for leading with love. Defined in an organizational context as a feeling or caring of deep respect for oneself and others, or valuing and believing in oneself and others, love creates in leaders the desire to empower others to a new level of consciousness (J. M. Burns, 1978). Connectedness is a tenet of ethical leadership and this includes both connectedness in human relationships and human-environment relationships.

There is a growing interest in ecological leadership as ethical leadership (Stead and Stead, 1996; Hatcher, 2000a). Ecological leadership is defined as the ability to influence individuals and organizations to realize a vision of ecological sustainability (Egri and Herman, 2000). These leaders are guided by ecocentric worldviews and seek to change systems that they perceive are threatening the ecosystem's health. Publications abound on the concept of eco-based and environmentally friendly leadership (management), especially in corporate social responsibility and environmental policy literature. However, leadership research focused on ecological sustainability as a leadership process has not received adequate attention (Shrivastava, 1997).

Research regarding environmental leadership has focused on leadership related to environmental outcomes (Anderson and Bateman, 2000; Bansal and Roth, 2000; Portugal and Yukl, 1994), leader styles and values in organizations in the environmental business sector (Egri and Herman, 2000), and the development of new theories of ecoleadership applicable to innovative companies and overall competitive advantage (Shareef, 1991; Dechant and Altman, 1994).

In their study of leadership values and styles, Egri and Herman (2000) found environmental leaders' personal values were ecocentric, open to change, and self-transcendent, and displayed both transformational and transactional behaviors. Shareef (1991) developed a theory of ecoleadership as compared to transformational and transactional styles:

> Ecovision theory sees leaders merging two distinct components: the ecological perspective with emphasis on a holistic relationship between the organization and the environment, and the ability to produce and renew identities that enhance the environmental context in which the organization functions. (Shareef, 1991, p. 52)

Environmental and ethical leadership may be on the leading edge of traditional leadership theory and research, but are by no means the only innovative areas of research or theory. A brief discussion of leader-member exchange (LMX), and Vedic higher states of consciousness theories, to name a few, is required to glimpse into the future of the field.

Other Leadership Theories

Leader-member exchange (LMX) theory was first introduced in the 1970s as an alternative to transactional and transformational leadership (Jordan, 1998). LMX is based on the idea that leaders and followers have unique relationships based on negotiated social transactions. Burns and Otte (1999) offered an approach to LMX as a guide for human resource development leadership.

Vedic higher states of consciousness view leadership from the deepest aspect of life rather than the surface level of behavior (Harung, Heaton, and Alexander, 1995). The primary tenet of Vedic psychology as applied to business is that leaders develop through levels that start with behaviors such as setting strategy to individual traits or characteristics of the leader to a recognition of patterns of cognitive, social, and motivation differences associated with psychological development and finally to personal transformation and development of consciousness (Harung, Heaton, and Alexander, 1995).

Summary and Conclusions

Multiple leadership theories such as situational, contingency, cultural, transactional, transformational, charismatic, ethical, and values-based, and other, less developed theories may appear, prima facie, scattered and disparate, and thus could introduce an element of chaos into research and practice. Yet uni-dimensional theory does little to help solve complex and multidimensional organizational, societal, and environmental problems. "Single, unifying theory, while allowing for tidy definitions and visible boundaries, stifles interpretation where it happens in the complex and chaotic world" (Hatcher, 1998, p. 35). The broad spectrum of theories provides leaders with the opportunity to view and understand leadership from a variety of useful and descriptive perspectives.

This chapter presented theory and research within the three primary constructs introduced in this text, namely business ethics, corporate social responsibility, and leadership. Establishing a conceptual framework is an important first step in understanding a phenomenon or field of study. Another important step is to examine related theory and research.

Research and theory that support the notion that HRD has a role in building ethical and socially responsible organizations was reviewed. Business ethics research focused on theoretical and methodological issues; ethical activities, behaviors, and sensitivities; institutionalizing ethics in business and professions; and corporate social responsibility. Ethics theories discussed included stakeholder theory and legitimacy theory. Ethics theories that supported leadership included contingency theory, transactional and transformational theories, and charismatic and ethical leadership. Also discussed were LMX and Vedic theories. CSR theories included stakeholder theory, legitimacy theory, contingency theory, and transcendental theory. Research in CSR focused on links between business and society.

Examining related theory and research grants insights into how ethics, leadership, and corporate social responsibility are related and are in many ways interdependent. This understanding also highlights weaknesses in theory and gaps in research. Such weaknesses and gaps become evident when ethics, leadership, and social responsibility shift from the theoretical to the applied, when we try to behave and lead in ethical and responsible ways. The next chapter illustrates how ethics, leadership, and social responsibility are applied in work-related settings.

The Practice of Ethical Leadership and Corporate Social Responsibility

According to a 2000 study of workers' attitudes toward workplace ethics conducted by the Ethics Resource Center (Ethics Resource Center, 2000), 90 percent of American workers say they "expect their employers to do what is right, not just what is profitable." The survey also found that organizations that pay little attention to ethics put their reputations at risk and impact their ability to attract and keep good people. The study also found that a greater number of U.S. companies are promoting ethics through formal programs that are related to positive outcomes (Ethics Resource Center, 2000). Sadly, results also indicated that of the workers who feel pressure to compromise ethics, almost 10 percent attribute the pressure to corporate leadership.

The fact that some employees are being pressured to compromise ethics and morality to boost business outcomes comes as no surprise to most HRD professionals. Corporate leaders are feeling more and more pressure to increase shareholder value at the expense of stakeholders, even stakeholders with direct and reciprocal relations with the company like employees, consumers, and communities. And even though within the past few years the general public has begun to be more aware of and criticize bad corporate behavior, and regulations like the 1991 Federal Sentencing Commission have increased fines for corporate ethics violations, the sad fact is, it still continues.

No matter how much we might want it to be otherwise, not all of our corporate leaders are ethical. Influenced by culture, circumstances, values, personal background, religion, stress, or a combination of these, leaders struggle with ethics. As a result, not all organizations are moral. To reverse this trend we need to examine how three primary workplace variables, leadership, ethics, and HRD, interact and consequently affect ethical and responsible behaviors in organizations.

Leadership and HRD

The practice of HRD has shown increasing interest in leadership over the past few years. However, it remains a relatively minor concern when compared to other mainstream research and practice themes such as learning and performance. Although not a primary thrust in research and practice, leadership and HRD are related in two distinct ways. First, they are related through leadership development and training programs that build leader skills and knowledge. Second, HRD and leadership are related though HRD's critical role in the shift in many companies from transactional to transformational, and finally, to ethical and values-based leadership.

Because of its close relationship to training, leadership development (LD) as a process to train leadership skills and knowledge is a component of HRD practice and study and is currently the strongest link between leadership and HRD. However, leadership development is a fairly thin slice of the entire training budget pie, only 15 percent of $60 billion total spent on training in the United States, or approximately $9 billion. That's about 12–25 percent of total training dollars spent in big companies. With an expected shortfall of managers and executives in the coming years, this figure is likely to grow. According to *Training* magazine, about 20 percent of top management and 25 percent of middle management positions could be vacant by 2005, and in one U.S. government agency 60 to 70 percent of executives will be eligible for retirement by 2010 (Wellins and Byham, 2001).

The way leaders are developed is also changing. Although classroom training is still the most prevalent delivery method, new methods such as computer-based learning tools are growing rapidly. How successful (the return on that $9 billion spent each year) leadership development training really is remains in question and may be one of the reasons for its lackluster performance. Not surprisingly, then, recent research suggests an increased interest by HRD professionals in evaluating leadership development programs (Moller and Mallin, 1996).

A scan of the Academy of Human Resource Development's (AHRD) international research conference proceedings, and journals such as the *Human Resource Development Quarterly* (HRDQ) from 1995 to 2001, reveals that at least twenty research topics are related to leadership and management development. Given the overall diversity of topics in HRD research, this is a fair amount of research on a specific topic.

Besides leadership development, HRD professionals and scholars have been interested in research and practice of myriad other leadership issues: developing leadership through emotion management, measurement of leadership outcomes such as organizational outcomes like innovation, LD as an educative and developmental endeavor, leader traits and styles such as transformational and ethical leadership, and differences in leaders' styles across cultures, to name but a few. Because HRD needs a stronger connection with business, it is important that continuing and new research and practice address and provide solutions to some of the emerging weaknesses and opportunities in the leadership field.

The second link between HRD and leadership is HRD's responsibility in the shift from transactional to ethical and values-based leadership. Instructional designers, trainers, and other HRD professionals developing, implementing, and evaluating leadership development programs and organization development, performance improvement, and management consultants providing guidance to corporate leaders are in favorable and influential positions to encourage and help build transformational and ethical leadership.

Research on transformational and ethical leadership in the HRD-related literature shows a relationship between success and transformational leadership competencies such as setting a vision, managing change, and displaying professional ethics (Russ-Eft, 1998). Kuchinke (1999) found that the acceptance of transformational leadership might be dependent on culture. And for those who mistrust research, examples of the recent Firestone tire scandal and the Enron debacle are not-so-subtle reminders of the practical relationship between ethical leadership and corporate success.

Transformational leadership competencies are related to competencies that HRD is noted for developing, that is, visioning, change management, process management, technical, and interpersonal and credibility competencies. In addition, many of the competencies suggested for HRD and performance improvement professionals mirror the skills and knowledge required for transformational and ethical leaders. For example, the American Society for Training and Development (ASTD) in its *Models for Human Performance Improvement* included leadership skills and competencies similar to those required by transformational and ethical leaders. The recognized weaknesses in leadership development mentioned earlier offer HRD an opportunity to create and implement leadership development processes that develop the kinds of skills and competencies displayed by leaders who know themselves and who empower and encourage followers' self-growth and shifts in attitudes, beliefs, and values, and thus transform an organization to higher levels, not simply manage tasks or people. The implication is that HRD can and should be in the business of developing transformational and ethical leaders in today's organizations.

Although business ethics have always been important from a moral point of view—to build a good reputation or avoid a scandal—they are now becoming a requirement. The dilemmas and pressures that arise from economics and globalization place an even greater value on ethics and the role of HRD in developing values-based leaders and ethical workplaces. An obvious question is: What is HRD doing to meet these challenges?

Ethics and the Practice of HRD

Looking first at what has been written, a nonscientific review of HRD-related publications from 1996 to 2001 revealed a paucity of research and articles with ethics as a general focus. Publications reviewed included *Training, Training and Development, Human Resource Development Quarterly, Human Resource Development International, Performance Improvement Quarterly, Performance Improvement,* and proceedings from the Academy of Human Resource Development and the International Society for Performance Improvement's annual conferences. Out of over 2,000 articles, columns, critiques, commentaries, and forums, fewer than 100 were found on ethics and HRD, with the large majority occurring after 1998. Sweeping generalizations based on such a nonscientific review are a research faux pas, yet it seems reasonable to assume ethics has not been until very recently a central part of HRD, at least for the people whom these publications represent. This review also assumes that publications reflect the reality of practice.

There are three reasons for this lack of focus. First, the field is relatively new. As Karen Watkins (1990), a well-respected professor of HRD, is fond of saying, "HRD is a field in search of itself," and so is still trying out its "ethical wings." Second, professor Gary McLean, 2001 president of the Academy of Human Resource Development, says: "There is a lack of ethical behavior in the field of HRD" (McLean, 2001a, p. 220). Third, the field may have a vision of itself as free of unethical behavior (McLean, 2001a). Whatever the reasons for this lackluster image of ethics in HRD, there is no doubt that unethical behaviors need to be curtailed and ethical and socially responsible ones should be encouraged by both scholars and practitioners.

Ethics and HRD Professional Organizations

For the past few years, ethics has been a topic of interest in a few of the professional organizations and within the academy in particular. For example, ASTD's *T+D* (professional journal) published several articles on ethics and ethics training. One notable publication by Jennifer Salopek (2001), "Do the

Right Thing," addressed ethics as behaviors that create a return-on-culture, similar to the idea of return-on-investment. She also stressed the importance of values statements and codes of conduct as the infrastructure of good corporate ethics programs. In February 2002 *T+D* started a monthly column that analyzes different ethical dilemmas, thus providing a continuing venue for practitioners in HRD to learn about and discuss ethics.

Arguably, organizations like ASTD and the Academy of Human Resource Development reflect practice. Although dedicated more to research than practice, the academy does seek to bridge the gap between theory and practice by encouraging applied research and conceptual approaches to solving practice-based problems. One could even make the case that since HRD is an applied field, all research is necessarily field-based and practice-oriented (assuming it is quality research on a significant topic and comprehensible). Applied and conceptual research has the potential to lead application. It can set the stage and create a framework for practice. To the extent this is true, it is important to review the work being done within the academy concerning ethics.

The keynote address and theme of the 1996 AHRD international research conference was human resource development with integrity. This was the impetus for subsequent activities leading to the formation of an ethics committee charged with developing a standard on ethics and integrity. The *AHRD Standards on Ethics and Integrity* was first published in 1999 (see Appendix A). Since 1996 several conference presentations have been made on ethics, spirituality, and social responsibility. More notably, the 2000 conference keynote presentation was on the social responsibility of HRD. In addition, the first *Advances in Developing Human Resources* (a quarterly topical monograph published by AHRD), published in 2001, was a book of case studies on ethics and integrity in HRD, and that year both the *Human Resource Development Quarterly* and *Human Resource Development International* published articles on the application of ethics in HRD research and practice. But what does this flurry of activity mean to practice?

An assumption is that the energy expended on ethics in research "transfers" to everyday practice. To illustrate this hypothesis, several activities are ongoing. First, the *AHRD Standards on Ethics and Integrity* are being used as ethical guidelines for HRD practitioners and the *Advances* cases are being discussed in several university HRD programs. Next, the scholar-practitioners involved in the academy's recent focus on ethics continue to publish ethics-related articles in practitioner-based journals, speak to local professional organizations, teach ethics in university courses and workplace training programs, and consult with major organizations on ethics as related to HRD.

Ethics Applied to the Practice of HRD

Human resource development professionals are more involved than ever in establishing ethics programs, designing and evaluating ethics training, and including ethics in orientation and skills-based training programs. In addition, they are developing leadership training programs and mentoring activities that include ethics and values-based components, writing ethics codes, standards, guidelines, and credos, and generally assuming a more involved and visible role in the application of ethics in the workplace.

To accomplish this, HRD professionals and instructional designers are creating ethics-specific training and including ethics as integral parts of orientation, management development, and even skills-based training programs. Several hundred companies in the *Fortune* 500 currently offer ethics training. Ethics training consists of myriad topics that are dependant on organizational context. Generally speaking, ethics training can cover topics such as conflicts of interest, misuse of company resources, procurement integrity, harassment, whistle blowing, social and environmental responsibility, and privacy and confidentiality.

The growth of ethics training is due, in part, to the U.S.-based Defense Industry Initiative on Business Ethics and Conduct (DII), which was formed in 1986 in response to the findings of the Packard Commission (a Reagan-appointed commission that investigated defense contractors' procurement, budget, and management practices), and the more recent U.S. Federal Sentencing Commission guidelines that reduced the penalty for companies with effective ethics programs. Over fifty signatories of the DII have adopted a code of ethics and ethics training, including Raytheon, where over 100,000 employees have received ethics training.

Ethics training programs are becoming a part of most large companies and are growing in popularity in medium and even small organizations because ethical dilemmas know no boundaries of shape or size. And because small companies have small training budgets, ethics training in small organizations is being taught as part of orientation and other ongoing training.

People learn a great deal about ethics through social contacts. One of the reasons orientation programs are still popular is that learning about how work gets done in an organization and the "ins and outs" of a company's culture are just as, if not more, important than learning about benefits. This socialized learning allows a newcomer to quickly figure out what is important, who has power and authority, what groups exist and what their roles are in the organization, what specific tasks to learn first, second, and so on. It is critical for new employees to get a sense of what is considered right and acceptable and what is not. Fitting into a corporate culture may dictate a new employee's success or failure more readily than anything else. And it is not just orientation programs enhancing ethical behaviors, skills-based and other production-oriented training can also be vehicles to build an ethical culture.

Instructional designers are embedding cases and scenarios in training that help build skills and competencies required on the job, and encourage and develop ethical behaviors. For example, in training for a production equipment upgrade, a large manufacturing company designed simulations and role plays enhancing operator skills but also included ethical issues with "simulated" supervisors playing favorites when making work assignments. Skills training coupled with realistic ethical components provides opportunities for people to realize the impact that unethical behaviors can have on productivity and production outcomes. It also gives people opportunities to discuss and work out possible responses to ethical issues in a nonthreatening learning environment.

Leadership development programs provide a real opportunity for HRD professionals to have a lasting influence on ethics. This is true within organizations as well as professions. Leadership training that encourages the kinds of ethical behaviors an organization or a profession expects helps leaders to better understand their own personal values and identifies gaps between individual and organizational and professional ethics. University degree programs are one example of how leaders learn about professional ethics.

Degree programs that offer courses on professional ethics, use professional codes of ethics in courses, or include discussions and role plays on ethical dilemmas likely to occur within a professional setting as instructional methods are preparing future leaders with awareness level knowledge of acceptable behaviors in a given professional field. Engineers, for example, have a code of ethics that is tied to professional certification and licensure. The behaviors that this code advocates are built into engineering school curricula. To ensure compliance, engineering schools are monitored by external professional certifying agencies. This way, the profession of engineering has assurances that graduate engineers not only know how to build a bridge but understand the social and ethical consequences if they do not build it well.

Besides training, another good way for managers to learn about ethics is through a mentor. Formal and informal mentoring programs, if designed and implemented well, have the potential to teach a novice leader about a company's culture and ethics by mentoring with a senior, established leader. However, one ingredient can doom mentoring's ability to build ethical behaviors. That ingredient is an ethical mentor. It is impossible to shape ethical and values-based leaders by placing them with an executive who views ethics as unimportant compared with "getting the job done," or is more transactional than transformational. HRD professionals can assuage this problem by assessing potential mentors' behaviors and values prior to their assignment. Mentors and mentees sometimes face ethical dilemmas together that neither has experienced. Having a code of ethics can provide guidance during times of uncertainty.

Codes of ethics and standards of conduct provide guidance for employees facing ethical dilemmas. Although such codes and standards are not a panacea for all problems of ethics and morality that people face in the messy world of work (Enron had a fifty-page code of conduct), they offer a framework, a model that people can refer to as they wrangle through complex problems. More companies today have such codes and standards than ever before. HRD professionals are being asked by their companies for assistance in the creation and implementation of such documents. In some cases, HRD professionals provide leadership in development of codes of ethics; in others, they offer advice or assistance. Whatever the extent of the role, HRD professionals should be involved in the creation of codes and standards because they are typically responsible for handling ethical dilemmas.

Research suggests that companies with written codes or standards of ethics are more successful than those who do not have them (Pava and Krausz, 1995; Estes, 1996). Companies that encourage ethical behaviors are healthy, quality-oriented, and conduct business honestly. There is a positive relationship between being moral and being successful. However, HRD has been criticized for its inability to add value to organizational success. Thus, if HRD seeks out more responsibility for development and maintenance of codes of ethics, it would in turn benefit from resulting positive outcomes. Of course, it would also be seen as culpable if there were an inverse relationship. Regardless of its practical benefits, a strong relationship with ethics results in HRD becoming more moral and values-based and being "more aware of our professional responsibilities to the community, the society, in which they [we] work and live, and the planet" (Russ-Eft, Burns, Dean, Hatcher, Otte, and Preskill, 1999, p. 3). This accountability beyond our selves, this social responsibility is paramount to our future and to the creation of sustainable organizations and environments.

Corporate Social Responsibility and Ethical and Responsible HRD

For over five decades leaders, practitioners, and scholars have advanced the idea that corporations have not just legal and financial responsibilities but societal and environmental responsibilities as well. Now, as business and industry gain more power in society, it has become clear that they must assume more responsibility.

Joseph Campbell, the famous mythologist, said that the dominant institutions in any society tend to build the tallest buildings; the church's spires towered over all other medieval structures. After the days of Copernicus, the government became the dominant institution and its buildings rose above others. Today, especially in the West, it is obvious who has the tallest and most impressive buildings. Finances and financial companies now define the skyline worldwide. Business's power is ubiquitous and in some sense beyond the reach even of the State.

But does the fact that business has so much power mean that it is automatically responsible for society at large? According to many business leaders, "The business of business is business." Milton Friedman is often cited as saying that business has no other responsibility than to make money, that business is not responsible for societies' nor the environment's ills. Friedman made the case that business is socially responsible by increasing profits, not by addressing issues it was never designed to address. Others have criticized the idea that business has responsibility beyond what the law requires, that by its nature, business is supposed to be unscrupulous and driven by the need for success, so there is no room for ethics or social accountability (Fieser, 1996). The problem with this business is business argument is that it presumes business is separated from and not a part of society or the ecosystem and that only financial or legal ties exist between business and society or the environment.

If the hundreds of people who lost their lives after Union Carbide's deadly chemical release in Bhopal, India, in 1984 and the thousands of animals who died excruciatingly painful deaths at the hands of Exxon at Valdez, Alaska, in 1989 could communicate with us today, they would certainly give us a different view of corporate social responsibility (CSR). So too would the residents of Love Canal in New York, who in the late 1970s suffered serious illnesses and were uprooted from their homes as a result of Hooker Chemical Company's dumping of toxic wastes, and so too would the Ogoni tribe in Nigeria, who have recently fought so hard to reclaim their sacred lands from intrusions by giant oil companies. Those afflicted would no doubt vehemently argue that companies have a responsibility beyond making money. Of course, one could argue that these examples are extremes, which were either accidents or single-case exercises in bad judgment and so are outside the mainstream of typical corporate behaviors. But are they really extremes? Couldn't they merely be newsworthy examples of corporate greed and power run amok?

According to Peter Senge, "The more stress we put on our organizations the more their tendency will be to revert to their most primitive behaviors" (1997, p. 138). The fact is, a company with a myopic goal of making as much money as possible, responding solely to the capriciousness of Wall Street, or both is capable of harming more than itself.

Corporate irresponsibility can be addressed with new and more stringent regulations on monopolies, international business practices, and financial activities. But more government-regulated and -imposed constraints do not make corporations better citizens; in fact, they have proven to cause as many corporate misdeeds as they were designed to alleviate. In a *Business and Society Review* symposium, Lydenburg (1996) interviewed business leaders and politicians concerning government's role in legislating CSR. One respondent said, "I see the prescription for the cure more life threatening than the disease itself . . . incentives are likely to be exploited and penalties are more likely to drive marginal businesses out of business than cause them to behave more responsibly" (p. 40). Government has increasingly less power and influence over business. Of the world's top 100 economies, over half are corporations; less than half are countries (based on a comparison of corporate sales and country GDP), IBM is bigger than Singapore; General Motors is bigger than Denmark; Royal Dutch/Shell is bigger than Venezuela; and the top 200 corporations' combined sales are bigger than the combined annual income of the 1.2 billion people (25 percent of the total world population) living in "severe" poverty (Anderson and Cavanagh, 2000). And a September 11, 2000, issue of *Business Week,* not exactly a venue for antibusiness rhetoric, was dedicated to the subject of corporate power. In the introduction it was reported that nearly 75 percent of Americans think business is too powerful and has gained too much influence over their lives.

The business of business, then, is not solely economic, nor is it solely psychological, social, political, technical, or moral. It is all these things and more. We must fully recognize the mosaic of business, that the full spectrum of human values and behaviors is reflected in it and by it. When our eyes catch the glimmer of a slick corporate logo and we see a reflection in its shiny façade, that reflection is us—you and I. And so, like the powerful yet benevolent church of medieval times, business should take more responsibility for society, take care of and nurture people and community, and sustain the ecosystem. It should not take responsibility for economic, technical, social, psychological, or political reasons but because it is the right thing to do.

Organizations may not possess the same moral status as a person, but they are moral agents with much the same ethical responsibilities and obligations as people. The differences lie in the fact that unlike individuals, organizations have an obligation to address the concerns and desires of their stakeholders and to abide by their charters (corporation, partnerships, or other legal agreements) as applicable. Violating such obligations breaches the social contract that organizations have with society. Because a contract implies an agreement among parties, both the organization and society have interests. These interests may be in the form of production, quality, finances, or social responsiveness and ethical behaviors. A company might expect a community to supply an educated workforce from whom it can attract potential employees while the community expects the company to comply with all employment regulations and laws. In this example, both sides satisfy their interests. However, if the company disobeys employment laws, not only is a legal contract violated but so too is the social contract. The community could respond with legal actions or through loss of reputation potential employees may choose other employers or both. Thus, the notion that organizations have moral status and that a contract exists between them and society further strengthens the corporate social responsibility concept.

A better understanding of corporate social responsibility enables us to develop HRD theory, research, and practice that have the potential to not only accomplish the goals of HRD, that is, create learning and improve performance, but also address societal and environmental ills. This appreciation is complicated by myriad definitions and various terminologies associated with CSR. For example, in addition to corporate social responsibility there is corporate social performance and responsiveness, and with each of these terms comes a range of definitions. Thus, defining CSR is a necessary step in its understanding and application.

Defining Corporate Social Responsibility

Definitions of corporate social responsibility have evolved since 1946 when *Fortune* magazine first polled executives on their social responsibilities and the 1953 publication of Howard Bowen's book, *Social Responsibilities of the Businessman.* In his well-researched article on the evolution of the concept and definition of CSR, Carroll (1999) offered several definitions that have been published over the years as well as some guidance in defining corporate social responsibility.

Differentiating corporate social responsibility, performance, and responsiveness requires viewing responsibility as obligation in response to market forces or legal constraints (Sethi, 1975), performance as the actual outcomes of corporate behavior (Wood, 1991a), and responsiveness as an adaptation of corporate behaviors to societal needs (Sethi, 1975).

Although the idea of companies having social responsibility is not limited to Western business, the idea of CSR as a business construct is primarily a product of twentieth-century America (there is also a strong CSR movement in the UK) and has evolved in tandem with U.S. social, environmental, and economic movements. For example, in the 1960s, Frederick (1960) defined CSR as "a public posture toward society's economic and human resources and a willingness to see that those resources are used for broad social ends and not simply for the narrowly circumscribed interests of private persons and firms" (p. 60). It is interesting to note that Frederick used the term human resources a decade before it was "officially" recognized in the early 1970s as the discipline of HRD.

Reflective of the social and environmental movements of the decade of the 1970s, and the growing concern for performance in business and industry, Carroll (1979) offered a four-part definition of CSR that was embedded in a conceptual model of corporate social performance. This definition implied that first and foremost business has an economic responsibility to produce goods and services that society wants and to sell them at a profit. Second is legal responsibility, that business must obey the law and abide by the rules of the game. Third are the ethical responsibilities business has to society, that extend to behaviors and outcomes that are beyond what are required by laws and regulations. Fourth and finally, there are discretionary responsibilities. These are expectations of society beyond those of ethics and that if not addressed by business would not be considered unethical. Discretionary responsibilities are purely voluntary roles such as philanthropy, providing day care for employees, and employee release time for charitable work.

Alternative concepts and themes and definitions of CSR emerged in the 1980s and 1990s as more research was conducted and published. This research caused scholars and practitioners to begin to see CSR as a construct and field of study that had some validity and sought to better define and operationalize the concept. Researchers such as Cochran and Wood (1984) attempted to further operationalize CSR by trying to find out if it had any relationship to a firm's financial performance. The rationale was that CSR could be bolstered if they could show that socially responsible firms were also profitable. A similar line of reasoning currently exists in HRD in the attempt to show how training and other interventions add value to the organization's bottom line.

Throughout the 1990s tangential themes of CSR were expanded, related research was conducted, and alternative models were developed. By and large, by the 1990s CSR had been established as a concept and as a bona fide area of research, so researchers and scholars placed their efforts into revisiting, further defining, and reframing CSR as a concept and research construct.

Contemporary ethics research is expanding the boundaries of CSR by addressing issues such as environmental degradation, spirituality, financial impact, and its relationship with HRD. Application of CSR and social performance in business and especially international business is a continuous and multifaceted activity that requires observation and assessment by the scholar and practitioner communities. Thus, research and practice continue to shape and reshape definitions of CSR. But even the turbulence of international business and the tedious and often conservative nature of business ethics research have not impacted the development of CSR. As a concept it remains on solid theoretical footing. As Carroll said, even though definitions of CSR may be revised and adapted in the future, "it is hard to imagine that these new concepts could develop apart and distinct from the groundwork that has been established over the past half century" (1999, p. 294).

Examples of Corporate Social Responsibility in the Workplace

The relationship between the definition of corporate social responsibility and its application in a business environment is an important one to recognize. CSR is a concept that is theoretical and basically meaningless to practice unless it is applied in some organizational or work-related context. The same could be and often is said of human resource development. Examining how organizations are interpreting and applying CSR helps us to see how it is implemented and to what extent its application is producing desirable outcomes. It also helps us to see and better understand the relationship between CSR and HRD.

CSR is a process that requires true commitment, diligence, and constant monitoring to ensure success. Of course, just wearing the CSR badge does not necessarily mean that an organization is responsible. Some organizations use being responsible simply as a marketing ploy. But saying a company is "green" and actually being "green" are worlds apart. Putting a recycle symbol on a plastic package that's twice the size of the product inside is as irresponsible as boasting a company moniker that says, "Our people are our only asset" while moving factories offshore.

Jumping on the responsibility bandwagon without a real commitment and without clear strategic initiatives to do so is reminiscent of the thousands of companies in the 1970s and 1980s that too quickly brandished the "total quality" banner without really understanding that what it meant was a new philosophy and a new way of doing business. Many companies did not comprehend that achieving total quality was a process, not an event. The outcome was elusive and the goal was a moving target. What was really important was the doing—the striving for quality, the never-ending quest to improve. CSR is like that, a process, not a position, the doing, not the achieving, the constant passion to be socially responsible and financially successful. However, it is not unattainable as some would have us believe. What organizations that are considered socially responsible strive for can be identified and defined.

Generally speaking, social responsibility can be categorized into four major areas of impact or performance: human resources—development and protection of people; community, cultural, and societal involvement and philanthropy; environmental protection, waste reduction, and sustainability; and product, consumer, and service contributions and protections. Although not prescriptive, the ethical policies and practices listed in Table 5.1, "Determinates of Corporate Social Responsibility," taken in toto help to create a socially responsible culture.

TABLE 5.1 Determinates of Corporate Social Responsibility

Social Responsibility Area of Impact	Policies and Practices
1. Human resources: Development and protection of people	• Providing employees a safe, clean, healthy, and pleasant work environment.
	• Protecting employees from harassing and oppressive work environments based on gender, ethnicity, or sexual preference.
	• Provide policies to cover grievance and employee representation.
	• Helping employees with family responsibilities.
	• Fairly compensating employees through wages and benefits for their labors and not undermining their right to organize under the law. Provide for incentives and rewards and other means for employees to share in an organization's success.
	• Encouraging employee participation and creativity and providing opportunities for teamwork and team development in support of achieving the organization's goals. Create an atmosphere that encourages risk taking, lifelong learning, and creativity of employees. Educate employees on environmental principles and challenges to sustainability.
	• Reward people for humanitarian, environmental protections, human rights, and sustainability efforts.
	• Provide employees with adequate training and educational opportunities in a timely manner that enhances organizational and personal career goals.
	• The organization shall not engage in nor support organizations that engage in child labor or slavery in any form.
	• Providing equal opportunities in hiring and promotion.
	• Disclose credible and rigorous annual financial reports and accounts.
2. Community, cultural, and societal involvement and philanthropy	• Being sensitive to the cultural and human rights of indigenous people.
	• Reducing corporate pressures on lobbying, campaign financing, and other political efforts in support of narrow corporate financial ends.
	• Obeying all applicable laws and regulations.
	• Avoiding doing business in repressive and/or tyrannical regimes that are oppressive to basic human rights.
	• Supporting world peace through resistance of the transfer and sale of military goods, weaponry, and technology to unstable and repressive regimes and developing peacetime industries to the degree possible.
	• Conducting international business in a professional and nonexploitive manner consistent with acceptable ethical conduct in organizations' home culture.
	• Giving back to the community in which the organization resides, does business or impacts on stakeholders in terms of philanthropy, donations, foundations, volunteerism, or other contributions.
	• Supporting educational, humanitarian, and/or environmental causes with financial donations or volunteer assistance or other socially responsible investments.
	• Participate in community environmental programs and forums that seek to protect the environment, support human rights, restore biodiversity, and enhance sustainability.

(continues)

TABLE 5.1 *(continued)*

3. Environmental protection, waste reduction, and sustainability	• Adoption of recognized environmental guidelines such as the CERES (Coalition for Environmentally Responsible Economies) Principles, ISO 14000, or BS 7750. • Seek to introduce environmentally friendly processes and practices though continuous improvement policies. • Identifying and reducing in every way possible the overall damage the organization does to the environment. • Appreciate, maintain, promote, and seek to restore biodiversity. • Adoption of clear policies relating to the elimination or minimization of negative welfare impacts on animals and nonhuman species, the conservation and protection of endangered species, and avoidance of negative impacts on genetic manipulation or bioengineering. • Humanely treating animals by avoiding animal testing and seeking alternatives to animal testing when obvious alternatives do not exist. • Applying environmental and sustainability standards to purchasing and vendor relationships. • Reduce energy demands in production and service, adopt alternative energy sources, maximize energy efficiency in all manufacturing and production, and use efficient equipment and materials. • Identify and reduce wastes in all wastes streams. • Recycle everything that can be recycled. • Reduce use of water and all consumables. • Purchase only energy saving and recyclable equipment and materials. • Reduce employee travel and use of travel-related consumables and energy by providing alternative means of travel and communications such as teleconferencing, cell phones, and web-compatible computers, flexible hours, work at home options, and public transportation passes.
4. Product, consumer, and service contributions and protections	• Provide guidelines and means for consumer protection in accordance with applicable laws and regulations. • Design products and services for the environment that use fewer raw materials and less energy in production or implementation. • Replace nonrenewable materials with more sustainable materials in products and services. This includes using organic materials, locally produced and recycled. • Design products to minimize consumption of energy and production of wastes, including reduction in packaging requirements. • Consider the entire life cycle of the product, including recyclability potential uses by consumers and recoverability. Use a "cradle to grave" approach to design. • Provide truthful information on the known environmental impacts of the organization and its products and services. • Embrace socially responsible purchasing, including contracting with minority, indigenous peoples, and women-owned businesses, and establishing relations with other socially responsible vendors.

Seeking to meet each of the initiatives listed in Table 5.1 requires constant vigilance, continuous evaluation, and a passion for ethics and social responsibility. But the striving, the seeking to be responsible and ethical can also place an organization in a position to be criticized.

Organizations that wear their responsiveness to societal, ethical, and environmental issues on their sleeves are targets for criticism. When they falter or fail, because they are held to higher standards they have farther to fall than organizations that are either aversive to or ambivalent about CSR. Ben and Jerry's Homemade, Inc. is a good example of a company that has from meager beginnings tried hard to do the right thing, to be responsible to people and the environment and remain socially active. It endured continuous attacks from the media and a fickle public whenever it stumbled in its attempts to be socially responsible. But despite its trepidations it managed to remain financially successful for over twenty years before being recently sold to Unilever for the tidy sum of $326 million.

In 1978 Ben Cohen and Jerry Greenfield, a couple of guys who were more at home at a Grateful Dead concert than in the executive suite, renovated a gas station in Vermont and took to making really good ice cream with local, natural ingredients. They built a multimillion-dollar international company that has continued to support projects for social change and in 1997 had $174 million in sales.

Although the company received criticism, it thrived on doing well by doing good. For example, a shop was opened in partnership with an alliance of several local community action groups in Minneapolis. Ben and Jerry's donated the franchise to the groups that own and operate the store. Proceeds go to community action agencies and programs that serve low-income families.

One reason for the doing well part of the socially responsible equation is the relationship between social responsibility and employees. By serving as a home for people seeking work outside mainstream corporate environs (the corporate culture at Ben and Jerry's is described as comfortable and informal—with dogs and kids roaming the halls) and as a sanctuary for those who seek more than financial meaning in their work, companies like Ben and Jerry's offered employees more than a place to be for eight hours a day. The store manager of the donated shop in Minneapolis took a pay cut of $5,000 to work at Ben and Jerry's. She said the social mission aspect of the job encouraged her to make the change.

Socially responsible companies offer a way to relate work to something outside us, something bigger than we are or the company is; a way to feel good about the way we make a living and to actually witness that organizations are part of society, the environment, and us. Of course, not all that glitters is actually gold.

In the late 1980s Ben Cohen gambled on a truly unique corporate venture called Community Products, Inc. CPI was designed to save the rain forest and benefit other worthy social causes by donating a whopping 60 percent of profits to progressive causes. Its goal was to import nuts harvested from the rain forest by native cooperatives. This would theoretically aid the cause of low-impact agriculture, help local economies, and in the long run help save the rain forest (Welles, 1998). In addition, its manufacturing facilities would create jobs in areas of chronic underemployment. What happened is a case study in bad timing, bad management, bad judgment, and bad luck.

Almost as soon as CPI got started, the market for Brazil nuts collapsed, driving prices sky-high. Next, the quality of nuts began to suffer; there were even complaints of coliform bacteria. As a result of the quality problems, only 5 percent of the nuts CPI used from 1989 to 1994 came from native Amazonian cooperatives (Welles, 1998). This nixed the cause of saving the rain forest and forced CPI to start saving itself. Over the next few years, problems with carpal tunnel syndrome injuries to workers in its plant, a series of new company presidents, and tax troubles plagued the company and as a result CPI began to fall apart at the seams. Although it gave away half a million dollars and was for a brief time a true cause marketer and shining success, it imploded and in 1997 filed for Chapter 11 bankruptcy. Cohen tried to build a new enterprise by melding the corporate charter with social causes, only to discover that sometimes even the best of intentions are not enough to succeed in business. More than anything else, his distancing of his personal involvement with CPI and inability to reconcile corporate realities and social responsibility goals may have been its death knell. What successes Ben and Jerry's Homemade had as a socially responsible enterprise was a result of the passions of its founders to create a responsible organization.

This is true of the leaders of many well-known ethical and socially responsive companies such as Dave and Tami Longaberger of the Longaberger Company, Ray Anderson of Interface, Inc., and Anita Roddick of The Body Shop. Roddick is an example of a top executive who has not lost sight of the relationship between the corporation and the community. Her company has continued to make a difference with social causes such as helping out the environmental activism group Greenpeace in lobbying against dumping of hazardous wastes in the North Sea and providing logistical support for human rights organizations like Amnesty International.

The Body Shop International is not only striving to be socially responsible, it is also successful, one of the most successful companies in the UK. Founded in 1976 in Brighton, on England's south coast, The Body Shop sells environmentally friendly beauty products in some 1,700 stores all over the world. In 2000 it posted retail sales of over $800 million although recently it has decided to "soften" its campaigning image due to "mixed results" from its strategy of fighting for social and environmental causes (Curtis, 2001).

To these ends The Body Shop has carried out many short-term and longer-term programs designed to help communities and people in need both in the UK and internationally. For example, the company financed the *Big Issue,* a UK newspaper for the homeless and other socially excluded people that helps find jobs and shelter and provides training and education opportunities as well as hundreds of jobs. Internationally, The Body Shop developed a program called Community Trade, which provides a fair price for raw materials from communities in need in areas such as the Philippines, Zambia, Nepal, and India (Quarter, 2000). Children on the Edge is a longer-term program that provides funding and volunteer services to renovate orphanages for the thousands of children abandoned after the 1990 fall of the Ceaucescu regime in Romania.

In conjunction with its social activism, The Body Shop has been a leader in innovative and caring human resource issues, such as offering paternity leave to all male employees. In 1998–1999, faced with layoffs (called *redundancy* in the UK), The Body Shop conferred with local community caregivers such as religious leaders and charity groups and offered redundant employees outplacement support, retraining, and a program geared to set people up in small businesses of their own. Services were offered to partners and households of employees as well (Woodall, 1999).

Not all organizations that seek to be ethical and socially responsive do so simply because their executives "got the faith" or are possessed by a burning desire to drive their favorite social issues. Some organizations are more socially responsible as the result of cooperative grassroots movements between corporate leaders and the workforce and many more are starting to view CSR as a strategic initiative. A good example of a passionate and insightful leader who recognized that his company could change only through tapping into the same passions in his people is Ray Anderson, chairman and recently retired president of Interface, Inc.

Atlanta-based Interface is the largest commercial carpet manufacturer in the world with facilities on four continents and sales in 110 countries. Founded by Anderson in 1973, Interface was not always the model of sustainable manufacturing it is today. For over twenty years, Ray described himself as a "plunderer of the Earth" and his company settled for compliance. But in 1994 he was transformed by Paul Hawkens's (1993) book, *The Ecology of*

Commerce. Thus began Anderson's journey to become an environmental crusader and to create the world's first sustainable manufacturer. He began his crusade by developing a vision beyond environmentalism toward sustainability by managing human and natural resources with the same vigor applied to the management of financial resources.

By combining a kind of ecoextremism with good business practices, innovative engineering, continuous learning, and systems thinking, Anderson and Interface have succeeded where others have failed at doing well by doing good. In 1996, their first year of being ecoefficient, Interface decreased its use of raw materials by 20 percent and saw its sales soar by the same percentage. Since then, Interface has undertaken several hundred sustainability initiatives that include designing carpet fabrics that are 100 percent recyclable and offering customers a carpet or floor covering leasing arrangement instead of buying.

But more than a focus on product alone, Interface approaches sustainability from concept to raw material to production to product life cycle to client use to the impact it has on the global community, and back again. With a firm commitment to the CERES Principles (see Table 5.2), Interface produces its own annual CERES report and development of its own unique sustainability. The tangible results have been nothing less than dramatic. "On sales of 1 billion in 1996, our second year into this journey, the total extracted material was, by our very best calculation, very nearly the same at 1.23 billion pounds, or about 19 percent more efficient usage of the same amount of extracted material as in 1995" (R. Anderson, 1998, p. 128).

The 2001 recipient of the prestigious George and Cynthia Mitchell International Prize for Sustainable Development chosen by a National Academy of Science (NAS) selection committee, Ray Anderson is a veteran corporate mogul whose blood happens to run eco-green. NAS president Bruce Albans said, "No corporate leader in the United States has done more to set an example that moves us into the world of the future, where new models of operating sustainably must become the standard." This leadership is also responsible for Interface using its knowledge of sustainability to create a strong corporate culture that is engaged in a continuous dialogue about the company and its employees' personal values and concerns.

Discussions about Interface's approaches to sustainability, its changing values, and employees' concerns about these approaches, started by Anderson, were cascaded down to every employee in the company. According to Anderson, at the end of the first year "we had 2,800 different English language words to express people's values . . . we boiled them down to a list of ten common values and also distilled down the mainstream concerns, the next year

TABLE 5.2   CERES Principles

Coalition for Environmentally Responsible Economies—CERES Principles

Protection of the Biosphere
Reduce and make continual progress toward eliminating the release of any substances that may cause environmental damage to the air, water, or the earth or its inhabitants. Safeguard all habitats affected by operations and protect open spaces and wilderness, while preserving biodiversity.

Sustainable Use of Natural Resources
Make sustainable use of renewable natural resources, such as water, soils, and forests. Conserve non-renewable natural resources through efficient use and careful planning.

Reduction and Disposal of Wastes
Reduce and where possible eliminate waste through source reduction and recycling. All waste will be handled and disposed of through safe and responsible methods.

Energy Conservation
Conserve energy and improve the energy efficiency of our internal operations and of the goods and services we sell. Make every effort to use environmentally safe and sustainable energy sources.

Risk Reduction
Strive to minimize the environmental, health, and safety risks to employees and the communities in which we operate through safe technologies, facilities, and operating procedures, and by being prepared for emergencies.

Safe Products and Services
Reduce and where possible eliminate the use, manufacture, or sale of products and services that cause environmental damage or health and safety hazards. Inform customers of the environmental impacts of our products or services and try to correct unsafe use.

Environmental Restoration
Promptly and responsibly correct conditions we have caused that endanger health, safety, or the environment. To the extent feasible, we will redress injuries we have caused to persons or damage to the environment and will restore the environment.

Informing the Public
Inform in a timely manner everyone who may be affected by conditions caused by our company that might endanger health, safety, or the environment. Regularly seek advice and counsel through dialogue with persons in communities near our facilities. We will not take any action against employees for reporting dangerous incidents or conditions to management or to appropriate authorities.

Management Commitment
Implement these principles and sustain a process that ensures that the board of directors and chief executive officer are fully informed about pertinent environmental issues and are fully responsible for environmental policy. In selecting our board of directors, we will consider demonstrated environmental commitment as a factor.

Audits and Reports
Conduct an annual self-evaluation of our progress in implementing these principles. We will support the timely creation of generally accepted environmental audit procedures. We will annually complete the CERES Report, which will be made available to the public.

SOURCE: Coalition for Environmentally Responsible Economies (CERES), *www.ceres.org*

we started the process again to address with our people these values and concerns, and next year we'll do it all over again." Learning to engage the workforce in its entirety is one of the reasons for Interface's success. It helped to create and reinforce a culture that has, according to Anderson, "Enormous pride and feeling of worth in being associated with our higher purpose . . . a transcendent reason to go to work."

Today, Interface, with Ray Anderson as its chairman and head cheerleader, is poised to continue to lead the world toward sustainable development and to embrace learning as a means toward social responsibility and ethics on a global level. For many companies like Interface, becoming global might mean a startup in a foreign country or hiring an overseas sales force, but for others it challenges the very core culture, what makes the company unique.

One such company is the Longaberger Company of rural Newark, Ohio. Founded in 1973 by Dave Longaberger, the Longaberger Company is the world's largest manufacturer of high-quality, handmade baskets with annual sales of $1 billion. Longaberger employs more than 8,000 people in three production facilities; in addition, it has a unique, nationwide network of almost 70,000 independent sales associates, making it one of the nation's largest and most successful direct-sales, entrepreneurial organizations. It is also family-held and family-run, with Tami Longaberger as CEO and sister Rachel as chair of the Longaberger Foundation, its charitable arm.

Two things make Longaberger unique, intensely ethical, and responsible: The "family" culture and its handmade, high-quality product. Being family-owned and -operated pervades the entire organization from the first time you see the company's Newark, Ohio, headquarters, which is shaped exactly like one of their baskets, only 160 times bigger at seven stories and 180,000 square feet. Family is also what sets the workforce apart, especially the sales associates. This army of autonomous and fiercely loyal employees is passionate about the company's products and about being a part of the Longaberger family.

Family and community is something Longaberger knows about. Its roots run deep in central Ohio, the heartland of America. Already an entrepreneurial spirit working in the family's small restaurant and grocery store, Dave, the company founder, sensed the public's desire for things handmade, and in the early 1970s decided to start hawking his dad's handmade baskets to local shopkeepers. He also discovered that the only way the public could justify the high price of his baskets over the cheap competition was to explain to customers how they were made—to get them involved by telling a story (Longaberger, 2001). The rest, as they say, is history. Today, some three decades and thousands of baskets later, the pride in creating and selling an American handmade quality product is still the soul of the business.

Not relying on retail outlets, but using person-to-person sales at home showings, committed and enthusiastic sales associates tell the story behind each basket, their design, and how they are made, so customers are an intimate part of the process, not just a faceless consumer. They become a part of the community, a part of the family. The company's CEO, Tami Longaberger, echoed this sentiment by saying, "We don't sell a product, we sell a lifestyle . . . our mission is to stimulate a better quality of life for our employees, their families, and the community." This commitment helps to create a relationship with the community that few organizations this size and this successful can claim. "It's a bond that runs deep . . . a pride in a community," said Longaberger.

Through the Longaberger Foundation the company has given away nearly $6.5 million to charitable causes, much of which stays in local communities. Its Charitable Champs program awards $500 to local community organizations for each employee who clocks twenty-five hours of volunteer work in a six-month period. In 2000, employees raised more than $500,000 for local organizations. Also adding to local coffers, the company donated half a million dollars for the construction of a local wellness center and $2 million to help with the construction of a new high school, located only a few miles from "The Basket" (what locals call the corporate headquarters).

Being charitable means writing a check, which is certainly admirable, but being socially responsible means helping to change a community depending on its needs, and this is what Longaberger does well. It also recognizes that "community" can mean more than the local high school or health center; it also means the environmental community.

Made from all raw materials, basket making at Longaberger is an environmental process without compromise. The existence of the company is dependent on the forest.

> We appreciate the environment at a front-line level, with us being in the forests so much—we are extremely concerned with the environment. Our environmental philosophy is . . . we are committed to preserving the environment by practicing sustainable forestry and environmental initiatives that insure that those forests, wildlife habitat, conservation of soil, air, and water, are maintained not only for us today but for future generations. (T. Longaberger, personal communication, May 15, 2001)

Recycling nearly all production scrap and even using the wood from downed trees from the construction of a golf course as the finish wood in their corporate headquarters, Longaberger's environmental passions come not only from the top but also from employees. An employee involvement team won the 2001 Rochester Institute/*USA Today* Quality Cup Competition for developing a new material delivery method that reduced material waste and returns, thus saving precious natural resources. Employee learning and training is at the heart of Longaberger's obsession for ethics and social responsibility in everything they do. Promoting from within is part of the culture, so Longaberger maintains career development programs that allow people to explore job opportunities and develop the strengths necessary to qualify for advancement—the kind of old-style career development that most companies ignore today.

Since the baskets are made by hand, one at a time by tradespeople—craftspeople—a sense of ownership and pride reminiscent of the days of apprenticeships and revolutionary Americana permeates the Longaberger workshops (what most everybody else outside their community calls a factory). Craftspeople are trained in much the same way Dave the founder was, on the job and one on one. Not exactly the model of cost-efficient training that Corporate America is pleading for. Yet for Longaberger, this is how the skills and dedication required to create lasting quality and pride in workmanship are passed down.

Longaberger is another example of a company that builds its ethical framework not only on the vision of its leaders but also on the shoulders of its employees, and it understands the crucial role that training and education play. Unlike many companies that might "teach" ethics, Longaberger sees ethics as part of the day-to-day environment, in how people are treated. "I cannot imagine having to have an ethical seminar here. I would feel like we would have failed as an organization. It's that important to us!" remarked CEO Tami Longaberger. So, Longaberger is an ethical place to work and is successful to boot, but how does a company with such strong ties to a local community and a dependence on a homegrown workforce grow? How does it go global?

When asked how Longaberger might respond to pressures to reach international markets, Tami Longaberger replied, "Globalization will be an interesting challenge for us—what we do well is make quality crafted, handmade baskets in America—our brand is really home and lifestyle in the United States . . . what we have as much as we have a basket business is a relationship business, and that's the business we are in." Whether a product that represents a culture as much as Longaberger's baskets do can be transferred to a global market remains a challenge.

Whatever the plans are for Longaberger's future, it will most assuredly include a continuous determination to maintain high quality, nurture a highly skilled and dedicated workforce, preserve the environment, and, as the company purpose says, "To stimulate a better quality of life with all those we touch." Finally, it is important to this study of HRD, ethics, and corporate social responsibility to add that embedded in Longaberger's mission statement and in most everything they do is the resolve to do the right thing. "There's no reason why we cannot continue to grow as an organization and continue to do things the right way. If we have to do things the wrong way to grow—we won't grow! The next step is to continue and strengthen our commitment to create a work environment that gives people the opportunity to live up to their potential—it's the American dream, it's what my father and in turn our family has had the good fortune to live," said Tami Longaberger. And in a suddenly more global world where environmental and human-made disasters and ethical misconduct are increasingly the norm, maybe that's enough.

These examples of how organizations go about the business of being ethical and responsible illustrate the depth and breadth of CSR and its various interpretations. Even though each of these companies portrayed a slightly different reason for and approach to corporate social responsibility, some common themes emerged.

Socially responsible organizations typically draw direction and inspiration from a passionate leader and care about their stakeholders, the people who influence and are influenced by the organization. This is especially true of their employees, who typically are engaged in training and continuous learning. Training and learning are common and frequent activities among socially responsible and ethical companies. A positive relationship seems to exist between the time and resources invested on training and education and organizations' ethical and socially responsive activities. There also seems to be a strong bond between being ethical and responsible and a fierce attention to product and service quality, or both. Organizations that are dedicated to producing high quality in whatever they do are more likely to be responsible to their employees, constituents, and other stakeholders. To be a quality organization requires a fanatical dedication to taking care of the social and technical needs of employees and building close and respectful relationships with customers. Companies that know how to create quality also know how to create value for stakeholders. For a quality-oriented company to treat its employees badly, disregard its impact on the communities it serves, or foul the environment would jeopardize its ability to deliver a quality product or service. It just would not be logical for a company that is dedicated to product or service quality to disregard its ethical and social responsibilities. Socially responsible organizations not only see their employees and customers in a different light, they also have a different view of their relationship with the environment.

For many ethical organizations the environment is a comparable stakeholder, with all the rights and responsibilities afforded employees, the community, clients, suppliers, and the law. Seeing the environment in this way enables a company to build the same kinds of strategic initiatives for the ecosystem as it does for its customer. Thus, the environment gets at least the same respect as a company's best customer. But the stakeholder approach, although a worthwhile and creative way for an organization to enhance its social responsiveness, is not perfect. It assumes that a company treats each of its stakeholders with equal admiration, respect, attention, and intensity. It assumes no variability in the way an organization interacts with its stakeholders and that environmental factors such as the economy or changing regulations have relatively equal influence on each stakeholder. Taking a systems view, changing government regulations on the limits of particulate emissions from a plant's smokestack would most likely impact each stakeholder in some way. However, in reality it would require an organization to address stakeholders differently. In other words, although it is true that changing regulations will impact each stakeholder in some way at some time, a company typically reacts to such a change by first addressing the stakeholders that are immediately and obviously impacted. This seems prudent and efficient, at the same time illustrating the difficulties in applying stakeholder theory. Although it is an imperfect way to ensure ethical and socially responsible corporate behaviors, stakeholder theory can provide a systematic way for a company to acknowledge, address, and satisfy all its stakeholders; typical of organizations like Ben and Jerry's Homemade, The Body Shop, Interface, and Longaberger.

The conclusion to this discussion of the practice of CSR focuses on an omission, an oversight in socially responsible companies, a possession that many organizations today seek in a nearly blind and fanatical way: technology. None of the exemplary companies discussed seemed to be as overtly intent on technology as companies that might be considered less socially responsible. That is not to say socially responsive companies are not technically savvy or that they do not work very hard at achieving technological superiority. It is just that they seem to understand much better than most that technology is only one in a number of issues they must address to sustain long-term success. Being obsessive about any one issue is unhealthy. Lacking constant attention to research and development of new products and testing and enhancement of existing ones would quickly reduce a company's international dominance. Even companies that are not as technically oriented seem intent on achieving the right mix of technology and technical positioning. For example, the Longaberger Company has moved almost all its contractor management and customer service to a web-based environment and plans to increase its Internet technologies in the near future. Socially responsible organizations recognize and appreciate technology as a tool, as a means to an end, not the end itself; a tool like many others that help them better address their economic, environmental, and social performance.

Summary and Conclusions

The most significant issues shaping organizations must be better understood for us to be able to know how they impact the way we learn, how we improve performance, and might enlighten people as a part of our organizations. The more we know about these issues, the better are our abilities to handle the uncertainties about the consequences they bring. This chapter focused on how people and organizations are moving toward ethical and socially responsible outcomes and the difficulties they face along the way. The next several chapters delve into the reasons why this road is so bumpy and so infrequently traveled.

Part **3**

Contemporary Issues Influencing Societies, Organizations, and HRD

Globalization

Globalization is one of the most significant and pervasive issues shaping organizations, influencing leaders, and transforming cultures, societies, and the environment. It is an expression, a metaphor, an idea, and a word that is used, misused, abused, and tossed about by business and HRD professionals, generally with little or no understanding of its true nature or consequences. Globalization is in many respects a conundrum, a paradox. To date we have a real love-hate relationship with it. On the one hand we seek to enlarge our global markets and pad our portfolios but at the same time we are sickened by its propensity to quicken environmental and cultural degradation.

But globalization is not something that might happen or that we are busy planning for, we *are* global. We are global as consumers, producers, leaders, and as citizens. We drive autos with parts made in Germany and Hong Kong and assembled in Indiana. We use computer software designed in India, manufactured in Malaysia, and marketed in the United States. We visit villages in the Third World and see flickering images of Coke commercials emanating from color TVs inside thatched-roof huts. We read about riots all over the world protesting Western ways of life. And we recoil in horror as we watch thousands of innocent people die at the hands of terrorists determined to destroy the burgeoning and predominately Western-led global village; but why? Why isn't everyone proglobalization? Why aren't more cultures, especially those in the Third World, on the global bandwagon? To begin to answer these questions, we need to explore the relationship between businesses and governments and between globalization and the values of individuals and societies.

With globalization comes a new way to do business. Organizations are beginning to call the shots, not governments, and certainly not cultures. Our corporations are capable of influencing authority, cultures, society, and the ecosystem without hindrances or even much interruption from government. "Silicon Valley and Bangalore have generally played more important roles than Washington, D.C., and New Delhi, and they will probably continue to do so" (Micklethwait and Wooldridge, 2000, xxii). This power is not only economic, but also social and political. Not knowing or having a say in who controls what or who is calling the shots creates fear and anxiety for many individuals, especially those who have little or no power to begin with. And sometimes simply not having enough of the right kinds of information can cause anxiety, and that can turn into fear leading to hate.

As a mature businessperson and scholar it has been my observation that many people who profess to understand globalization have until recently viewed it primarily in a positive light and tended to respond to managements' demands to "globalize" their respective organizations without any real assessment of its impact on people and the environment and its potential for good and evil. I have often heard HRD professionals discuss globalization with limited understanding of how it affects or has the potential to affect what they do. With the exception of a few publications by a handful of scholars and practitioners, little has been published about HRD in a global economy and even less has been published about the true and bipartisan impact that globalization can and is having. Even writers and scholars whom we might consider proponents of globalization are somewhat skeptical about globalization's ability to create sustainable environments. The reality is that we need to better understand globalization and its relationship with HRD.

Many of our organizations and many of us are already global or are quickly getting there. Yet even with all the influence and power that supposedly comes with globalization, we struggle daily with how to prepare workers for international assignments and how to deal with inevitable ethical dilemmas when cultures interact. We struggle with what globalization really means. We struggle with how globalization influences us and the way we do business, the way we treat people and the environment, our worldviews and the way we live. To better understand globalization's ubiquitous nature it is instructive to address how people are affected by it and are reacting to it. It is also smart for us to recognize that it is becoming a touchstone, a real powder keg for people and groups who see it in a less than favorable light.

Defining Globalization

Globalization is the most fundamental redesign of Earth's political and economic arrangements since at least the Industrial Revolution (Mander and Goldsmith, 1996). It is not a fad. It will not go away. It is "not just a passing trend. It is an international system—the dominant international system that replaced the Cold War system after the fall of the Berlin Wall" (Friedman, 2000, p. 7). Burbules and Torres (2000) wondered whether or not ". . . we are facing a new historical epoch, the configuration of a new world system, or whether these changes are significant but not unprecedented, paralleled for example by similar changes in the Middle Ages" (p. 12). Whether it is unprecedented may be in question but there is no doubt that it is one of the primary driving forces behind current organizational change and is having a tremendous impact on all organizational stakeholders. It is without a doubt one of, if not *the,* leading change effort that HRD professionals are being asked to address.

Like many abstract economic and social ideas globalization is hard to pin down, hard to define with much certainty. Some view it as corporate globalization where companies are involved in open market international competition, expanding resources and trading goods and services throughout the world with little or no interference from government; others see it as the driving force behind damage to the environment and destruction of culture. But globalization is more than simply business being conducted globally, which has been going on for nearly half a century.

From a systems perspective, globalization is the dominant international economic and social system that replaced the old Cold War system and "influences the politics, environment, geopolitics, and economics of virtually every country in the world" (Friedman, 2000, p. ix). Almost everyone is feeling the influence, constraints, and opportunities to adjust to the system of globalization. The World Bank defines globalization simply as the ability of individuals and firms to transact business across national boundaries. Others have characterized globalization in economic terms such as the amount of international flow of capital or numbers of international transactions, whereas others such as Nader and Wallach (1996) describe it as an economic model that "establishes supranational limitations on any nation's legal and practical ability to subordinate commercial activity to the nation's goals" (p. 94). Velasquez (2000) described it as the "process by which a company places its operating units in more than one nation, thereby becoming what is sometimes called a 'multinational enterprise' . . . referred to as foreign direct investment" (p. 343). According to Friedman (2000):

> Globalization is everything and its opposite. It can be incredibly empowering and incredibly coercive. It can democratize opportunity and democratize panic. It makes the whales bigger and the minnows stronger. It leaves you behind faster and faster, and it catches up to you faster and faster. While it is homogenizing

cultures, it is also enabling people to share their unique individuality farther and wider . . . it enables us to reach into the world as never before and it enables the world to reach into each of us as never before. (p. 406)

Globalization is a fundamental transformation of many diverse economies into a single integrated "free" market and subsequent organizational and social responses to this transformation. Wartick and Wood (1998) added, ". . . it is not just the economy that is globalizing. Globalization of social and political issues is becoming the rule rather than the exception" (p. 8). Then again, social and political globalization may simply be a response to or outgrowth of economic globalization.

Free market implies autonomy, lack of restrictions, and the ability of businesses to exchange goods and services unfettered from what many view as oppressive governmental and trade restrictions. But such freedom may also be examined, according to Paul Hawken, "in an entirely different way, because its freedom is partially immune to community accountability" (1993, p. 78). Other well-known economists like E. F. Schumacher and David Korten believe that global markets have autonomy and effects beyond mere partial immunity to community accountability and believe that global markets have near absolute freedom and power. Schumacher, one of the first economists to recognize problems with the interaction of big business and the natural environment, including culture, believed that large organizations inhibit freedom, creativity, humanity, and are unfriendly to the ecosystem (Schumacher, 1973, 1979).

The disequilibria caused by globalization leaves people in organizations wondering to whom they are responsible and wresting with a decreasing sense of commitment. This minimizing of accountability uproots people and "renders us isolated and anonymous. It heightens our longing for community and personal context but also allows us an invisibility from which it is easy, and often self-advancing, to avoid obligations and cut corners" (Dalla Costa, 1998, p. 20). To the extent that it is easier to avoid responsibility and with little or no conscience or concern do things like externalizing the costs of environmental compliance to an unsuspecting public, then we must turn our attention and energy to the ethics and social responsibility of our global decisionmakers.

The Global Manager and Public Accountability in Globalization

Managers, executives, and other decisionmakers assume the role of moral manager, a manager who "conforms to a high standard of ethical, or right, behavior . . . and redefines their companies role in society" (Carroll, 2000, p. 39). Personal ethics and the role of the leader in social and environmental responsibility of global organizations are discussed in more detail elsewhere. However, what is important to underscore here is that we are now able to cloak our personal morality and ethics under the banner of globalization, to isolate our responsibility and assume an anonymous posture when making decisions about public accountability. An example is the continuing practice of externalizing costs such as waste disposal from the private to the public sector without the public's consent. Instead of assuming total costs, consider lifetime costs of a product like a refrigerator. A company relinquishes its responsibility for the product as soon as it is sold to an unsuspecting public and an overburdened waste management system. The public, typically through increased taxes, is then responsible for the refrigerator for as long as it exists in the environment.

Progressive business leaders such as Ray Anderson of Interface, Inc., an international flooring company, believe that global organizations should be accountable for products for their lifetime and are thus making waste reduction not only a part of being ecoefficient but as a profit-enhancing process. This lack of accountability can cause a decrease in responsibility, an attitude of looking the other way, and finally downright deviousness.

Two of the more notorious outcomes of a lack of public accountability are destruction of the environment and human rights violations. An example is the many maquiladoras—factories along the U.S.-Mexican border that assemble goods for export, mainly to the United States. With endless supplies of cheap labor and little or no enforcement of lax environmental regulations, these plants represent free trade as a "race to the bottom" by the world's workers and in many cases a dumping ground for toxic wastes and industrial refuse. Fueled by the 1994 North American Free Trade Agreement (NAFTA), many mainly U.S. firms dumped their high wages and highly regulated factories and headed south for the cheap labor and almost nonexistent pollution laws provided by a lax Mexican government. Over 1 million workers in 3,800 factories toil typically six-day workweeks with grueling ten-hour shifts.

Even the few environmental regulations that do exist are not enforced. Many maquiladoras do not comply with minimum regulations for the safe disposal of hazardous wastes, which in the case of a U.S. firm is supposed to be returned to the United States for disposal. However, evidence suggests that this law is too often overlooked. One of the worst examples is Metales y sus Derivados, a U.S.-owned battery recycling and lead smelting facility. According to reports by the Environmental Health Coalition, although it was shut down by the Mexican government, the factory continues to leak more than 5,000 tons of toxic waste, including lead, sulphuric acid, and arsenic, into the ground. These toxic chemicals are carried downstream into the water supply of Colonia Chilpancingo, a village of about 10,000 people close to Tijuana. There are reports of villagers suffering from high rates of health problems including birth defects like hydranencephaly—babies born with almost no brain. This is only one example of U.S—owned companies along the U.S.-Mexican border with abysmal environmental and human rights abuse records.

Most of the factors that expose the dark side of globalization have to do with exploitation of some kind—environmental, worker and human rights, child labor, and loss of cultures (McLean, 2001b). The Dalcon shield, Exxon's Valdez, Union Carbide's Bhopol, asbestosis caused by products made by companies like Johns-Manville, tobacco lobby efforts to convince the public that tobacco is harmless, Texaco's recent racial problems, and Enron's problems in Nigeria and with "innovative" accounting are all nasty examples of companies and corporate leaders that have been caught. The worst case of unethical behavior, that is, corporate crime, costs an estimated $400 billion a year in health care fraud alone. There is little doubt that corporate illegal and immoral shenanigans costs us money and makes good fodder for the evening news. However, these examples are only the ones that were exposed. If this is the tip of the iceberg, then, like the ill-fated *Titanic*, are we necessarily on our way to the bottom?

But the good news is that most companies are not evil entities; they are not all bad. There is no doubt that there are ethical and moral people working or who did work for bad companies and in most cases the organizations cleaned up or at least apparently attempted to clean up their moral and legal messes. The fact is that most companies and even industries, like people, are neither all good nor all bad; they fall somewhere in between. They can and do shift either way on a kind of good-bad continuum from time to time. An obvious target for any discussion of corporate bad behavior spurred on by globalization is the U.S. tobacco industry.

Organizations such as the World Health Organization estimate that every year, 4 million people around the world die from tobacco-related illness. In the United States alone, smoking is the leading preventable cause of some 400,000 deaths annually. The tobacco companies are now target marketing cigarettes to youths and women in Third World countries, thus reversing public health progress, which has traditionally been minimal or nonexistent. In many developing countries, the tobacco companies target market "lights" and "low smoke" cigarettes, which are the preferred brand of women who are led to believe that they are healthier products. A report from the World Health Organization stated, "Transnational tobacco companies have increasingly turned their focus to the developing world, with aggressive marketing campaigns aimed at women and girls." Finally, a recent exposé by the watchdog organization the Center for Public Integrity accused major tobacco companies of smuggling tobacco products from one country to another in a global effort to secure market share and lure generations of new smokers.

The tobacco industry is capitalizing on the naïveté and economic neediness of the Third World. Globalization, with its lack of regulations addressing shady marketing, also makes smuggling and dumping of harmful products easier and more lucrative for ethically challenged companies and industries. But to address our questions, could ethical leadership impact such an obvious violation of basic humanity? And would a focus on being socially responsible alter the outcomes in any way? The initial response is: Probably not much would have changed. If a company's leadership chose not to play in this global shell game I wonder how long the stockholders would play opossum as stock prices plummeted, as they no doubt would? The second question concerning social responsibility is a bit more complex to answer. To begin with we must ponder the dilemma of whether a company producing a harmful product can be socially responsible. If we are interested in developing human resources, if we ascribe to a set of basic human rights, and even if companies are ethical in their dealings with workers and their stockholders, the results of production, that is, the unmistakable devastation of disease and suffering in the case of long-term tobacco use, simply cannot be ignored.

So where does this leave the HRD professional seeking to enhance his or her company's social responsibility? How does one reconcile the apparent ethical and moral implications? Geary Rummler, a well-known performance improvement expert, said, "Pit an outstanding performer against a bad system and the system will win almost every time" (Rummler and Brache, 1995). To an extent this is true. The ethical and moral performer must make a decision to either challenge the bad system or, as Rummler may be implying, self-select out of a system unwilling or unable to change. We are then left with the bad system and the subsequent pain it causes. Could it be that society has not accepted or acknowledged the pain? Or could it be that through psychological avoidance, we simply ignore that which is painful? Whatever the reasons for our ennui, the fact remains that we are often unable or unwilling to act in the face of an overwhelming system. Luckily, globalization also has a positive side.

The Benefits of Globalization

Globalization has the potential to eradicate a great deal of global human suffering and fiscal strife by providing economic support in the form of infrastructure, medical, agri- and food technologies, and communications that provide vast amounts of information sharing, education, and knowledge to people who previously had little or none. With globalization "the potential for wealth creation becomes geographically dispersed, giving all kinds of previously disconnected people the chance to access and apply knowledge" (Friedman, 2000, p. 51). Just as there are plenty of examples of environmental and cultural damage as a result of globalization, examples of its positive impact are equally impressive. There are few cases of a poor nation working itself up to a decent standard of living without embracing globalization and without addressing the training and education of its workforce.

Before trade and free markets can translate into sustainable growth, governments must first establish political stability, viable commerce, and an educated and trained workforce. Governments that understand the requirements for skilled workers create educational and skills development opportunities for their citizens and thus realize a return on their investments in education and training. A world-class example of this is the Penang Skills Development Center (PSDC) in Penang, Malaysia.

The PSDC is an industry-led training center for the manufacturing industry in northern Malaysia. The center offered its first sixteen courses to some 300 participants in 1989 in response to rapid globalization and skilled labor shortages in the region. Today, it graduates over 10,000 students annually. Led by the chief minister of Penang and the American Business Council, the PSDC's unique mission is to establish a mechanism to coordinate and use resources from industry and institutions through the support of some twenty-four member companies. Many of Penang's 700 or so factories participate, operated by a veritable *Who's Who* of high-tech firms. Multinational corporations such as Intel, Advanced Micro Devices, Hewlett Packard, Motorola, National Semiconductor, and Robert Bosch provide the center with donations, loans of state-of-the-art equipment, and expertise to design industry-specific curriculum. These firms have greatly benefited from Penang's dedication to creating a global workforce by focusing on skills and knowledge of incumbent and potential workers.

Skills and knowledge development, especially in Third World and developing countries, is an example of one way that globalization can have a positive impact on people, organizations, and the community and is certainly a point of influence and interest for HRD professionals. Globalization benefits countries and regions like Penang that have something to offer the world's market. But how do the poorer and less educated get on the globalization bandwagon and join those who have benefited?

Although the above examples tend to serve as rejoinders to the negative influences of globalization, the question remains: To whom does globalization currently bring most of its benefit? Today, forty-seven of the top 100 economies in the world are actually transnational corporations (TNCs); 70 percent of global trade is controlled by just 500 corporations; and a mere 1 percent of the TNCs on this planet own half the total stock of foreign direct investment (Korten, 1996; Anderson and Cavanaugh, 2000). But even if only a few multinational organizations (MNOs) or transnational corporations are in control, it does not necessarily mean that cultures, communities, countries, and other organizations are not somehow benefiting from globalization.

There is no doubt that globalization has brought with it a certain amount of organizational control and manipulation of finances and economies. Yet this wide dispersion of resources also provides funds for many people who had no previous access or ability to receive money for new business startups or development of infrastructure. The Grameen Bank of Bangladesh is a good example of how globalization has positively influenced people on a one-to-one basis as well as globally.

Grameen Bank and its founder and director, Professor Muhammad Yunus, has turned conventional banking practice upside down by completely eliminating collateral. He created a banking system based on mutual trust, accountability, participation, and creativity. (When was the last time you got a mortgage on mutual trust and creativity?) To the poorest people in rural Bangladesh, Grameen provides miniscule credit as compared with most credit lines. With a loan of only a few dollars (the average loan is between $20 and $160 U.S. dollars), borrowers who make bamboo stools by hand and previously cleared only pennies a day can pull themselves out of grinding poverty a few dollars at a time. Grameen is an example of a catalyst in the overall development of socioeconomic conditions of the poor and an example of how globalization works first on a small scale, then globally.

Dr. Yunus, a former Fulbright Scholar, reasoned that if financial resources could be made available to poor people on terms and conditions that are appropriate and reasonable, millions of small people with their millions of small pursuits can add up to create a development wonder. Currently, Grameen Bank is the largest rural finance institution in Bangladesh. It has more than 2 million borrowers, over 90 percent of who are women. With some 1,000 branches, it provides services in almost 40,000 villages, covering more than half of the total villages in Bangladesh. The repayment of its loans is over 95 percent. But microlending in one Third World country is a local issue, not global. What is globalizing about this example is the fact that the ideas behind microlending have now taken off at a startling pace. For example, a Microcredit summit that was held in 1997 in Washington, D.C., drew over 2,900 people, representing 1,500 organizations from 137 countries. Bankers, financiers, multinational organizations, nongovernmental agencies, and community self-help groups interested in learning more about and replicating microlending and the Grameen concept attended the summit.

More than 4,000 people from some 100 countries have completed Grameen's training and exposure programs over the last ten years. Some of those visitors have returned to their countries and replicated the Grameen Bank financial system to help poor people in their own country to overcome poverty. Further, the success of the Grameen concept has been extended beyond banking. As a result, a new global model for development theory and practice is emerging. This is globalization at its best: positively changing people's lives without overtly destroying anything in the process.

Globalization is influencing human resource development beyond the obvious economic impact. It is a transforming force for organizational learning and is encouraging many HRD professionals to rethink their notions about technology, diversity, leadership, the environment, ethics, and social responsibility. Mike Marquardt, a recognized expert in the role of HRD in a global market, said that globalization ". . . takes power and corruption away from governments to wage war, aggrandize themselves, select those who will be favored and creates competition and training that ultimately raises wages, opportunities and resources for workers."

When organizations become global, we cannot assume that everyone is along for the ride. Dalla Costa (1998) added that "the economy may be global, but people are not—or at least not yet. So whereas the shape and priorities of the global economy may be clear, the form and substance of the larger global community is still an open issue, with largely unasked questions" (p. 15). Globalization also impacts political and social attributes of organizations. Some HRD scholars and practitioners go so far as to suggest that HRD faces a real ethical dilemma in helping organizations go global. One of the Academy of Human Resource Development's 2001 International Conference keynote sessions was on HRD's ethical responses to and responsibility for globalization of organizations. One issue that surfaced during this discussion was that globalization is multifaceted, with many more possibilities and contradictions than those of simple economics; that the impact on culture and the sovereignty of indigenous peoples and their relationship with nature must be considered and addressed as a strategic issue, not as a hindrance to triumph over or disregard. The extent to which HRD responds to globalization in a culturally and environmentally friendly manner and how we react to changes in our personal and societies' values as a result becomes the standard by which our organizations base their own approaches to and attitudes toward globalizing.

Changing Values and Shifting Societies

People's values change. Society and cultures change. Global restructuring of capitalism (and subsequent shifts in politics) and the technological revolution just discussed are responsible for many changes in the way we think and act, our values and beliefs, and the way we develop and run our organizations. Values are not always easy to understand; they are sometimes hard to conceptualize and to quantify.

Values are an exclusively human characteristic. They may be communal, universal, or end-state, what Rokeach (1973) called instrumental values, or they may be illustrative of a particular mode of conduct such as responsibility, integrity, or honesty. Values allow us to grow as individuals and as a part of society, protect us against real or perceived threats, and help us to meet needs. They are important because they tend to be structured and somewhat stable over time. That is, values are acquired and hierarchically organized to become part of a relatively enduring system of values that when broadly applied to a specific context, organization, or profession, are collectively known as ethics.

Once we develop a value it becomes a criterion of significance for us (Rokeach, 1973; Hultman and Gellerman, 2002). A thing has value if we appreciate it, approve of it, or prefer it. Values are related to interests, pleasures, likes, desires, obligations, wants, needs, and attractions, and are a primary determinant in action. Generally speaking, we act on what we value within the constraints of mores, laws, and moral standards such as codes of ethics. Actions in conflict with values usually result in ethical dilemmas.

Values are linked to practice. Theoretically, value structures provide individuals with an ordered framework for resolving conflicts and making decisions and solving problems. It is through their influence on decisionmaking and problem solving that variations in value structures motivate individual behavior and affect specific actions. In addition, it is during times of decision and choice that differences in culturally based value structures may arise. For example, an HRD professional who personally and culturally values the positive impact the company makes on the community may view community-based learning as more important than individual learning. The structure of values may therefore be used to understand how potential behaviors are ordered in a given situation or within a specific organization or industry.

When goals or outcomes are achieved as a result of actions, they contribute directly to the satisfaction of certain values, values that can and do vary from individual to individual and from culture to culture. Thus, certain behaviors tend to support or oppose values and are assigned importance based on this relationship. The result is that we prefer certain behaviors to others because they support our values. When applied across a profession, values provide standards of conduct and behavior that may not be dependent on context. In other words, a value remains a value regardless of the situation.

Values can provide potentially powerful explanations of individual and societal behaviors. For example, values have been applied to account for the performance of teams (Maznevski and Peterson, 1997), the behavior of organizations, and the productivity of nations and societies (Hofstede, 1980).

Society and individuals are bombarded by a wide spectrum of technology and global influences that are restructuring every aspect of present and future experience, both on and off the job. But economic, organizational, and political changes do not happen without sociocultural change. This triad is the foundation of modernization theory espoused by Marx, Weber, Deutsch, Bell, Toffler, and others. Modernization implies that societal and political changes are a result of changes in the workforce, changes in communications and formal education, and changes in the economy. Cultural patterns and cultural shifts are closely linked to human values. The current postmodern shift is linked with different beliefs from those that characterized modernization.

In many of today's postmodern societies, the West in particular, the long-standing focus on economics is slowly being overridden by an increasing emphasis on quality of life issues. Individual self-expression, diversity of lifestyles, construction of reality, changing gender roles, differing nonsecular (religious) beliefs, and the importance of tolerance, creativity, emotions, and intuition characterize this shift in values.

Changing business values, some of which we are already experiencing, include less maintenance of order and control and more employee empowerment, democracy, freedom of expression, and workforce diversity. Post-modernism unfortunately also includes conflicts between differing ideologies, ethnic groups, and genders. We are witnessing an increase in violent conflicts of ideologies on a global basis. And there is more concern about the state of the environment than the nationalization of our industries.

But postmodernism brings with it no standardization of values, no consistency of values across cultures. On the contrary, it tends to reveal differences in value structures. At first view, it appears there are some common values, universal values everyone could agree on, but there are in fact few values that cut across all cultures and religions. Some values like peace, compassion, justice, and the like, listed in documents such as the United Nations' Declaration of Human Rights, are espoused as universal but are constantly challenged by alternative meanings any time they are used by divergent groups or cultures. In other words, they are always viewed through the lenses of a culture and therefore are interpreted by and subservient to various cultural mores and norms.

Understanding values gives us a wealth of knowledge about what people, groups, and societies consider important. It also helps us to identify value differences across cultures, groups, communities, societies, and individuals. This knowledge helps to create workplaces that have the potential to nurture values by providing opportunities for people and cultural groups to express their values and value structures and to better understand what motivates people to action. Values that are reflected in the goals, missions, and visions of organizations help us to recognize real and potential conflicts between individual and organizational values. Conversely, not understanding or being unsympathetic to values or values-based differences limit our abilities to develop positive corporate cultures, fulfill organizational needs, or to create effective interventions.

To understand values we must be able to somehow assess them and then evaluate them. This can be a daunting task, not only because of the skills required but because it places the people or groups being assessed in self-protective positions. People can and do become defensive when questions about their values arise. One reason for this defensive behavior is that values are not neutral. Most values have either a positive or negative impact on actions. Decisionmaking, problem solving, implementing a change process, designing a strategic plan, or teaching a class are improved or impaired by the values of the people involved. Values justify everything from downsizing and plant closings to developing employees and environmental stewardship. When leaders care more about profitability than people or value organizational efficiency over a company's environmental impact, such instrumental values must first be acknowledged, and then evaluated for their long-term impact. Similarly, HRD professionals who value performance over learning or disregard the transcendent nature of human beings because they do not value spirituality impact their own work-related behaviors and accomplishment of tasks. The ability of front-end analyses, instructional development and design, training, and evaluations to enhance an organization and the people within it can be just as adversely affected by the values of HRD personnel as by their competence or incompetence. So, understanding the values and value structures of individuals, groups, and societies is critical to our ability to effect positive change.

Research on values, especially in the field of HRD, has not received the attention that research on competence or performance has received (Bates,

Hatcher, Holton, and Chalofsky, 2001). This dearth of research is particularly obvious when we attempt to identify and apply changing societal values. Measuring societal values, research organizations such as Gallup and Harris provide access to changing attitudes and values of adults from all over the world.

Gallup and Harris polls are public opinion surveys that take the pulse of citizens on a wide variety of current issues and topics including crime, the death penalty, workplace gender equity, religion, race relations, employment, the economy, morals, families, smoking of tobacco, school violence, and honesty and ethics in business and industry. These and other concerns are periodically assessed and reported so that shifts in societal values and attitudes can be monitored.

Gallup frequently queries the public about values toward work and employment. For example, a September 2001 poll asked a sample of almost 600 adults about job satisfaction. A majority of respondents indicated satisfaction with workplace safety conditions, relations with coworkers, flexibility of work hours, the opportunity to use skills, job security, vacation time, the overall contribution employers make to society, and the immediate supervisor (J. M. Jones, 2001). In a similar study, a 2000 Harris poll of over 650 U.S. adults suggested that people are satisfied with their jobs and that giving people control over their work influenced job satisfaction (Taylor, 2000).

Because they use randomly selected respondents from the public, these surveys are a good general indicator of values and changes in value structures for American society. Similar polls taken in Europe, Asia, the Middle East, and the Orient provide information on values of representative cultures. The strength of opinion surveys is their ability to capture prevailing values and help business and HRD leaders to make better decisions about predicting shifts in values and attitudes that might impact commerce and the workforce. Their weaknesses lie in their generic versus specific nature and in difficulties addressing cross-cultural values that would be important to international and multinational organizations.

To better understand values of different societies requires assessing a cross-section of people from different countries and representing diverse cultures. An important and well-documented cross-national study is the *1990–1993 World Values Survey,* an analysis of the values and attitudes of people from more than forty societies around the world, representing 70 percent of the world's population and covering the full range of variation.

It surveyed societies with per capita incomes as low as $300 per year to societies with per capita incomes of more than $30,000 per year; from long-established democracies to authoritarian states; from societies with market economies to societies that still had state-run economies at the time of the survey; and from societies that were historically shaped by a wide variety of religious and cultural traditions, from Christian to Islamic to Confucian (Ingelhart, Basaòez, and Moreno, 2001, p. 1).

Questions in the *1990–1993 World Values Survey* ranged from examinations of generational differences to whether or not respondents associated more with materialist or postmaterialistic values. Of particular importance were inquiries that sought answers to questions about work, jobs, leisure, family, the environment, social welfare, social change, personal responsibility, technology, education, communities, gender issues, and religion. This report facilitates cross-cultural comparisons. For example, responses to the question "How important is work in your life?" one finds that in India, 86 percent of the respondents rated work as "very important," while in the United States, Austria, and Italy a little over 60 percent of the public rated work as "very important." And when you consider other national data such as relative economic levels based on per-capita gross national product (GNP), information is revealed about how and why poor versus richer cultures view work. In this example, an emphasis on the importance of work in poorer countries may be related to survival (Ingelhart, Basaòez, and Moreno, 2001).

Although research such as this cross-cultural study help us make generic decisions about value structures of cultures, other, more focused studies help us make sense of what people want and expect of the future within a single group or national boundary. Studies such as those by Paul Ray and Sherry Anderson (2000) illustrate shifting values.

Ray and Anderson's (2000) research is based on values and lifestyles survey studies conducted over a decade with over 100,000 people in the United States, with surprisingly nonhomogenous demographics. That is, they vary in terms of age, income, geography, politics, occupation, and education. Their research revealed an emerging cultural phenomenon that they coined the "cultural creatives." This is a shift from modernistic beliefs in materialism, consumerism, and technology, and more traditionalists' beliefs in male dominance, conservatism in politics and religion, and nationalism toward a culture that integrates and values idealism, activism, globalism, communitarianism, xenophilism (love of travel to foreign places), environmentalism and sustainability, feminism, altruism, spiritualism, self-actualization, optimism, relationships, social responsibility, and alternatives to purely scientific approaches to health. Ray and Anderson estimate that there are 50 million cultural creatives in the United States and millions more in Europe. These creative, optimistic millions are at the leading edge of several kinds of cultural change, deeply affecting not only their own lives but the larger society as well (Ray and Anderson, 2000).

These national and cross-cultural studies are of special importance to HRD professionals because of the lack of values-related research in HRD. Although there has been a general interest in ethics in HRD recently, little empirical research on values has been conducted and published. This is especially egregious in an emerging field such as human resource development, a field in urgent need of identifying its professional values and beliefs.

The foundations of any field of study include what the people doing research and practicing in the field believe in and value. This is especially true for a relatively new field such as HRD, which has been characterized as an interdisciplinary field in search of itself. Thus, a better understanding of people's values helps us to develop foundations and philosophies of what the field of study considers valuable and important, acceptable and unacceptable, and good or bad.

We are just beginning to understand the values of HRD professionals. Results of preliminary conceptual and empirical studies suggested that HRD professionals operate from a set of normative values. For example, in a preliminary study, Bates, Chen, and Hatcher (2002) found that people who value creating empowering work and building caring organizations tended to give high priority to the normative, problem-solving value of HRD. Much work is needed to better understand the values of scholars and practitioners in HRD. This is especially pertinent today as cultures and value structures are changing and impacting organizations, companies, and professionals in obscure, hard to understand, and complex ways. And as societies become more dependent on the knowledge of experts and their professions, it is vital that values, the underlying predictor of behaviors, be acknowledged. Studying values also helps to illuminate worldviews and the core values from which people operate and the standards that frame research and practice; values that help us deal with ambiguity and uncertainty in a changing and oft-times tumultuous and increasingly international work environment.

Coping with uncertainty means finding one's way in the midst of change. Values and ethics provide a roadmap for this journey. However, values can be subservient to and usurped by the oppressiveness of the marketplace. Studies such as Allen and Davis (1993) in particular have illustrated a disturbing trend in personal values being overcome by the pressures and demands of global work environments, wildly fluctuating economies, or simply making a living. But some individuals and even cultures seem to be less susceptible to external economic or social pressures. Their values are solid, unwavering, less fluctuating, and less fungible; some values may be better at weathering the storm of change than others.

A strong case has been made recently for development of core competencies in business and industry. Because values and beliefs are an integral part of organizational culture, it is critical for us to acknowledge and present the idea of core values as equally important as core competencies in current business practice. Core or terminal values like peace, equality, freedom, respect, and sustainability are desired outcomes or ends that do not change dramatically over time since they represent an end state or outcome (Gilley, Quatro, Hoekstra, Whittle, and Maycunich, 2001; Hatcher, 1993). Organizations that exhibit core values such as stakeholder service, social responsibility, ethics, and sustainability are able to transcend the conflicts that arise between human fulfillment, environmental protection, and economic success. "As a core value, sustainability can provide the understanding that economic success and ecosystem survival are both worthy and necessary goals for individuals, organizations, societies, and Nature" (Stead and Stead, 1996, p. 130).

As our values change, ecologies are transformed and cultural diversity is decreased. Therefore, the level of our vigilance in ensuring that all people, including employees, are treated humanely and with respect should increase. Beyond the recognized worker's rights to whistle blowing without recrimination, collective bargaining rights, and freedom from discrimination, recent human rights violations around the globe have shed light on the inequities and oppression that occur, in many cases with the complicity of corporate leadership. Although much has been accomplished over the past two decades to minimize human suffering, people in every part of the world are experiencing human rights violations that impact our ability to develop people and create humane workplaces. Just as an engineer would not or could not design a pump that defied the laws of thermodynamics, we cannot and should not create workplaces that defy the rights of workers, and/or all stakeholders, or both. But not all abuses are obvious. We must be aware of human rights violations beyond the factory walls, violations and mistreatment that may not be apparent or directly under our control but may only be addressed through corporate or individual political and economic influence.

Human Rights

HRD has a primary responsibility to ensure the basic rights not only of employees but also citizens of the communities in which our corporations operate and have economic and political influence. "In fact, the growing power of multinationals, the relaxing of international trade barriers, and the increasing flight of manufacturing from industrialized nations to third world countries all make human rights the key corporate responsibility topic"

(Reder, 1994, p. 215). This means that, like executives with Levis Strauss and Co., we become involved in decisions such as whether or not to do business or locate in a country known for human rights violations, and help our organizations define the true implications of such a move when it is inevitable. This responsibility requires that we appreciate the complexity of and ethics underlying global human rights as well as how to recognize and address their violations.

Even with the creation in 1948 of the United Nation's Universal Declaration of Human Rights (UDHR), the recent fall of the Soviet Union, the activism of groups such as the National Association for the Advancement of Colored People (NAACP) and the National Organization for Women (NOW) in the United States and global organizations like Human Rights Watch, Greenpeace, and Amnesty International, human rights violations remain persistent and unpredictable, especially in developing nations. See Appendix B for a summary of the UDHR.

Corporations continue to be at the core of some of the world's worst human rights violations, from Bangladeshi children working in sweatshops to make clothes for Wal-Mart, to the implication of Royal Dutch Shell in the deaths of Nigerian environmentalists and activists, to the alleged abuses of local villagers in India by Houston-based Enron Corporation, to corporate abuse of domestic workers with special visas and Hispanic child farm workers in the United States.

Even when corporations profess political neutrality, argue that they have no responsibility for human rights in the places where they trade, invest, or locate facilities, or argue that they enhance the local community by providing employment, medical care, and other benefits, it is almost impossible for companies to do business in some countries without support of military and paramilitary regimes and their pervasive violations of human rights. This has been especially troublesome in the oil and gas industry, where companies must go where the reserves are and thus do not have the luxury of deciding not to move into unstable, corrupt, and politically volatile areas. Companies such as Royal Dutch Shell and Chevron have been accused of ill treatment of civilians and the environment in the Niger Delta region of Nigeria, charges they have denied. In response to continued admonishment by groups such as Greenpeace, Friends of the Earth, and Human Rights Watch, and challenges by the investment community, Royal Dutch Shell has done more than most other oil companies, especially American oil companies, to respond to human rights violations and respect of the environment. In the six years since the death of Ken Saro-Wiwa, the Nigerian activist, Shell has revised its policies and corporate objectives on human rights and the environment into its general business principles and has tied these objectives to performance. Of course, it remains to be seen how these principles will impact performance over the long term, yet companies like Shell and others are beginning to address the changing expectations of the global community for them to be intimately involved with protecting human rights. In addition to meeting human rights guidelines such as the UDHR and Amnesty Internationals' Human Rights Principles for Companies (see Appendix C), organizations are beginning to recognize that the distinction between business and society is artificial, that businesses are social entities, interdependent and interrelated with cultural, political, sociological, and environmental systems; that human rights issues can and do arise. Human rights violations occur through daily HR activities such as employment, recruiting, training, promotion, and laying off employees. Therefore, by ensuring the security of employees and facilities, identifying and managing environmental issues, and attempting to make a positive contribution to the societies and cultures within which companies operate, HRD is intimately involved in human rights in many organizations.

The capacity of individual HRD professionals to mitigate these and other human rights abuses is in most cases limited. However, collectively, as a profession and field of study, we can and should make a significant contribution to upholding human rights. Practical ideas and ways to accomplish this are discussed in Chapter 10.

Summary and Conclusions

This chapter reviewed the growing influence of globalization on society, the environment, and the field of HRD. Its definition, the role of management and accountability, disadvantages and benefits, and the role of values and changes in society were discussed with an emphasis on how these are and might be changing HRD.

The future is unknown. No one knows for sure what it might bring. But even though we cannot predict the future, we can make sure that we do everything in our power in the present to lay the foundations for a future that is positive and sustainable. We have the intellect to design and develop global systems and international organizations that enhance life. But the question remains, will we?

We are at a crossroads. With almost ubiquitous and ever-growing power our businesses are now capable of dictating to, even bullying all but the most powerful governments, and even the most powerful acquiesce to corporate edicts when faced with anemic markets and tumbling stock values. This power can enable companies to pull people from abject poverty or to obliterate an ecosystem. The extent that organizations either build or destroy as they attempt to go global rests with the people who are given the responsibility to create vision and to the people asked to turn those visions into reality. The human resource development profession is in a precarious position. HRD can help corporate leaders to create and execute a positive and nurturing vision for global commerce within societal and environmental boundaries, or it can become a tool for businesses to disregard everything in favor of profits.

Globalization could have two possible outcomes. One is a global environment where people have equal opportunities to grow economically and socially. The other outcome leaves us with a globalized world where suffering is standard fare for most citizens and organizations are oppressive and abusive to cultures.

We need to evaluate these scenarios, to debrief where we are now against where we want to be in the future. And we need to better grasp how we get to where we want to be, to know the means by which we will progress, the tools, like technology that will hopefully enable a positive global environment. Senge, Carstedt, and Porter (2001) said, "Global markets, capital flows and e-commerce open up new opportunities for emerging economies, but they also create new generations of technological haves and have-nots" (p. 25). The next chapter discusses technology, its definition and role in society, economics, and globalization and its use in learning.

Technology

Technology. We read about it, hear about it on TV and in the news, work with it, play with it, and are surrounded by it. We manipulate it and it manipulates us, we are part of it and it is part of us. There are few places left on the planet where technology has not reached and every day there are fewer people that have not been touched by it in some way.

Technology makes communication easier, transportation faster, entertainment more entertaining, and it makes us healthier, smarter, and more mobile and global. But it also shuts down, misinforms, makes us crazy when it quits even for a second or two, frustrates and mystifies us, and stresses us out faster than almost anything. And we are just now beginning to contemplate its role in our lives and to recognize limits to its ability to help or hurt us.

To know technology's true nature and capacity for humanity and business requires that we know about its relationship with us and society, and that it can do harm as well as good; to move beyond its inert tool-like character and to come to terms with the control it has over our lives. To see technology for what it really is.

The Nature of Technology

The instant dissemination of information on a worldwide basis through computer-based technology is one of the primary catalysts for globalization. It is hard to imagine a magazine article, a TV show, or generally any discussion about business without an immediate reference to e-commerce, e-learning, or e-something related to how technology is changing our organizational lives.

Technology is more than capable of helping us to create a world free of disease and poverty, a world where people communicate for and nurture humanity. Medical technology sees into our brains and hearts, laser-beams our nearsightedness back to 20/20 vision, rebuilds shattered bones and heals burned skin, and makes diagnoses almost flawless. It literally saves our lives and gives us a better quality of life than ever before. Communication technologies allow us to be closer, faster than ever before, and open a veritable Pandora's box of too much information, and the wrong kinds of information and images from too many unknown and unreliable sources. We can now get hundreds of TV channels and access to web sites on everything from buying a vintage automobile to research on the African dung beetle—all instantly and with little effort. A single computer sitting on a desk in almost any American household has more computing power than existed on the planet less than sixty years ago. Computers have given us instant access to more information than we could ever absorb, and gives us the capacity to learn what we want when we want it. And this is all now, right now! What of technologies of the near future?

Consider nanotechnology, where miniaturization is taken to the point where things are built one atom at a time, sort of manufacturing at the molecular level. Advances in genetics may soon enable us to factor out life-threatening conditions and grant us a glimpse into immortality. These advances and opportunities have almost limitless possibilities. But they are not universal—yet. The current reality is that they apply almost exclusively to people lucky enough to be living in industrialized nations.

Developing countries and less advanced cultures are not reaping the full benefits of technology. And oftentimes they end up being the dumping ground for technologies' dregs, the "toxic and radioactive wastes" of technology. Examples of technology being a contributor for technological dumping are the maquiladoras along the U.S.-Mexican border discussed in the previous chapter on globalization, and the recent surprise move by the Russians seeking to become the world's radioactive waste repository. Of course, one could argue that these examples are more socioeconomic than concerned with technology. But they certainly would not be happening without the fall-out, the refuse created by it.

In our businesses technology has given us on-line conferencing, intranets that help to build corporate culture, and ubiquitous e-commerce. Yet tough questions are arising about employee and consumer privacy, surveillance, and issues about the way some technologies depersonalize communication and can provide a cloak of anonymity for those seeking to hide or prey on the innocent. Although technologies' waste is being dumped in a few Third World countries, others are benefiting. Through industrial technology, Thailand went from being a poor Third World rice producer to the world's second largest producer of pickup trucks and one of the world's top producers of motorcycles (Friedman, 2000).

There is little doubt that technology has the potential to positively change humanity and provide a way for less advanced nations to progress. But the question remains, will it? What we must begin to seriously consider is not a specific technology or tool or even specific processes within a technology—although those are important. We must consider the overall impact of technology in toto and its place in society. We must also consider the fact that we in HRD typically do not give much thought to this aspect of technology because we are usually too busy trying to work with and control it (or keep it from controlling us) and need to better understand the relationship between technology and human values if we are to come to terms with ethics, social responsibility, and the role of HRD in shaping sustainable organizations.

The Foundations of the Technological Society

It is beyond the scope of this chapter or this book to provide a comprehensive treatise on the philosophies and theories underlying a technical society. The social, political, and philosophical theories of Jacques Ellul, Henri Marcuse, Neil Postman, Langdon Winner, and others concerning technological society are complex, but they cannot nor should not be overlooked, especially by HRD professionals struggling with implementation of learning technologies. Some insights into the philosophical ideas of these great thinkers are important in any discussion of technology and its role in society.

Over the years since the Industrial Revolution the ties between science, technology, economics, and modern society have grown stronger. What appears to have become a belief, and even a religion for some, is that the goals of our Homo sapiens culture, namely health, prosperity, security, and knowledge, can be achieved only through the effective use of technology. We have become more and more dependant on and in many ways subservient to technology. An obvious illustration is the chaos that ensues when the computer server "goes down" in any modern office. We have no alternative process by which to get information even to the person in the next cubicle. Physically talking with them over the partition wall seems to be the last thing we think of. This control, although it has caused covert fear of dependency and for some even addiction, has been repressed or simply ignored by a general public eager to purchase the latest Windows application and glitzy computer. Certainly, most business leaders and HRD professionals view technology, especially computer-based technologies, with a certain awe and trepidation veiled in reverence. This is particularly true of HRD professionals who might be technophobes.

We have become conditioned by technological civilization (Ellul, 1964). Western culture is oriented to technology. Those who control particular technologies preside over us and possess a certain amount of tyranny over those who have no access to technology or the specialized knowledge required to control it. French philosophers Ellul and Marcuse believed that the dominance of a technological society can be continued only through saturation of ideas—propaganda in the form of advertising, marketing, and public discourse that creates a contented population that values propaganda and is thus blindly happy with technology. Jeremy Rifkin (2000), a contemporary, supports this idea of a market-driven populace in his book *The Age of Access.* In it he says that we as humans are being commodified. "We are making the transition into an 'experience' economy, a world in which each person's own life becomes, in effect, a commercial market" (Rifkin, 2000, p. 7).

Defining Technology and the Technological Society

Technology is not a twentieth-century invention. It has existed throughout human history as the ways and means that humans have attempted to shape their environment: a shard of flint honed for an arrowhead or a wheel to move goods. Technology can also be a method applied to solving a problem. Although it certainly includes tools and machines, technology also includes processes, knowledge, and preference. Technology has shifted its meaning from a limited and relatively precise description of things like machines, tools, factories, and engineering to a more "vague and expansive, and highly significant and haphazard collection of phenomena" (Winner, 1977, p. 10). This is Ellul's *la technique,* a "vast, diverse, ubiquitous totality that represents modern culture." So we have always lived in a technological society and have seen development and adoption of new technologies throughout history. What is different now is its omnipotence.

Technology causes us to respond in a certain way, to shape our decisions in a particularly mechanistic and technical way. Thus, technology is not neutral (Winner, 1977). We are "modified by technology; by consumption, by technical work, by news, by television, by leisure techniques . . . all of which are techniques . . . we are no longer dealing with an ethics of choice with regard to possible futures" (Ellul, 1964, p. 24). And technology goes far beyond the idea of a device like a computer, used to get a task done. Ellul argues that the technical dominates our thinking and thus our actions.

But is technology autonomous? Is technology the force that shapes society or does society shape technology? Autonomous technology, according to Ellul (1964), "has fashioned an omnivorous world which obeys its own laws and which has renounced all tradition" (p. 15), and where the quest for efficiency drives out all other human values. This technological determinism holds that technology is autonomous and causes social change; that technological change is the single most important source of change in society. However, many different forces such as politics, religious practices, corporate development, climate, geography, the economic market, and a host of other variables also cause social change.

Other scholars believe that any activity, including technology, initiated by humans must be inside of, a part of society; that society shapes technology. This social determinism holds that society sculpts technology and thus technology can never be autonomous. Of course, if technology is not governed by society then it is autonomous and there can be no human autonomy in the face of technical autonomy (Ellul, 1964).

Whether technology is autonomous or is governed by society, it is a fact that its development and implementation almost always causes unintended results. Some of these results are good, others not so good. An example is the unanticipated growth of the World Wide Web as a result of computer and communications experimentation and our growing feeling of isolation and loss of privacy. So technology does more than it was intended to do; "we know this so well that it has actually become part of our intentions" (Winner, 1977, p. 98). Both positive and negative side effects are accepted and expected aspects of technology. We have learned to live with such consequences as loss of privacy that is not of our making but shapes what we do. An acceptance of a certain amount of ambiguity, of not knowing exactly what the end view will be, is not, however, a relinquishment of control.

Postman (1993) said, "Those who have control over the workings of a particular technology accumulate power and inevitably form a kind of conspiracy against those who have no access to the specialized knowledge made available by the technology" (p. 9). The question that HRD and other business leaders must ask is to whom will technology give power and whose power will be reduced by technology or limits to access to technology?

In many ways technology changes the way we perceive reality. "New technologies alter the structure of our interests: the things we think about. They alter the character of our symbols: the things we think with. And they alter the nature of community: the area in which thoughts develop" (Postman, 1993, p. 20). Virtual learning is redefining our religion, art, family, politics, history, truth, and what we call privacy. Because information technology is so ubiquitous, "other forms of traditional communications that take place in the shared culture through direct face-to-face communications—rituals, ceremonies, festivals, the arts, religion, civic discourse—become less relevant and have less impact on human relations" (Rifkin, 2000, p. 170).

One of the most important activities that HRD addresses in today's organizations is culture development and change, thus this reduction in relevance of the very heart of organizational culture may have a profound and far-reaching impact. At a minimum we are struggling to understand what impact technology, and the Internet in particular, will have on our abilities to develop corporate culture. It may cause the concept of corporate culture to collapse or it may enhance the creation of an entirely new "virtual" networked culture. There is growing evidence that virtual organizations do have a specific culture, that networks of people and organizations develop rituals, ceremonies, and civic discourse as would any culture. But not everyone is a proponent of or believes in the sanctity of technology.

Those who scorn or criticize technology or seek other worldviews that do not include ubiquitous technology are either seen as despots or are marginalized. It does not make them illegal or immoral, but Postman said it makes them irrelevant. Those who presume to question technology run the risk of being branded as antitechnology: a Luddite. Luddite is a moniker given to people who naively oppose technology. It is based on the 1812 Luddite revolt in England when textile workers revolted against new weaving machines that displaced them. Ned Ludd was reported to be the leader of the revolt.

But if not a full-blown Luddite, then why not at least be a critic? Seriously questioning the intent, the sponsorship, and outcomes of technology helps us to demystify and better analyze the best uses of it in our society and in our organizations.

Technology poses specific challenges to business and to HRD; it affects individual privacy; it has potential for ubiquitous social control within industries and organizations; and technology plays a role in workplace democracy. Inferred from documents such as the U.S. Bill of Rights, the right to privacy and controls over the abuse of confidential information call for personal anonymity within public venues such as the Internet. There are more regulations and rules being developed around data privacy now than at any time in history. In 2000 alone there were over 200 bills on privacy introduced in the 106th Congress of the United States. Companies such as Microsoft have recently signed a U.S.-Europe "safe harbor" agreement on data privacy and most U.S. companies struggle to comply. These rules seek to protect the sovereignty of individuals by ensuring varying amounts of control over one's personal data. HRD professionals are caught in the middle between the need for effective learning technologies and ensuring individual privacy.

Technology is not the sole source of a reduction in privacy, however; it is also the people who control the technology. Technology is simply the tool they use. However, it does make the monitoring, surveillance, storage, processing, and dissemination of personal information much easier and therefore more likely. And all this is without our permission and usually without our knowledge. Through ID smart card technology the restaurant industry monitors the bathroom hygiene of employees, and VDT strokes per minute are counted, e-mail and voice mail are monitored, and closed-circuit TVs capture our workplace behaviors. Workplace monitoring is ubiquitous and surprisingly more accepted than one might think, and HRD professionals are in some ways responsible. Almost three-quarters of respondents to a survey of HR professionals said their companies monitor Internet use. The same group said they believe their employers have the right to know what web sites employees visit, how much time they spend on line, and what they send or receive through company e-mail ("Internet Use Surveillance Rising," 2001). Even off-duty behavior that comes under employer scrutiny and control is condoned. A recent survey of Society for Human Resource Management (SHRM) members found that almost a quarter believed monitoring of off-duty behaviors, including political activities and smoking regulations, to be appropriate. Combined with policies that through required cholesterol testing control what employees eat, and whom they date and wed (policies against supervisors and competitors dating and marrying), a pattern is emerging of *Brave New World* technological control (W. S. Brown, 2000).

Are our organizations becoming total institutions with panoptic power? A panopticon, based on the early work of philosopher Jeremy Bentham [1748–1832], and updated by Zuboff (1988), is a polygon-shaped structure sheathed in glass that makes it possible to monitor and controll people's behavior. It was designed to control social deviants such as criminals and paupers. The metaphor of the panoptic organization is certainly not lost on modern companies that hide video cameras in workers' break rooms. "Such systems can become information panopticons that, freed from the constraints of space and time, do not depend upon the physical arrangement of buildings. They do not require the mutual presence of objects of industrial administration. They do not require the presence of an observer" (Zuboff, 1988, p. 322). The effects of such constant controlling and intrusive devices diminish our personhood. We become a means to an end. Lack of privacy may even have psychological affects. W. S. Brown (2000) found that loss of privacy creates feelings of vulnerability, violation, and shame at the exposure.

Privacy is also important for societal growth. In a "society that esteems personal growth, creativity and progress . . . allows great thinkers to experiment with unorthodox ideas . . . scientists to produce revolutionary breakthroughs, and everyone to adapt to life in an ever-changing society," privacy is important (Williams, 1997, p. 15). On the other hand, in a free society such as the United States, where televised surveillance in department stores, continuing mining and sharing of electronic personal information, and daily exposés of the sex lives of public figures is commonplace, citizens are becoming more accepting of intrusions into their private lives. This explains in part our ambivalence toward information technologies, and our malaise toward societal-level hegemony over our private lives. But does this ambivalence spill over into our work lives? Will we accept the same level of control from our employers that we do from society? And if so, how do we maintain corporate loyalty, enhance employee empowerment, and strive toward learning organizations while our privacy, independence, and inner selves are threatened? How can HRD professionals create corporate cultures and build autonomous work teams while technology thwarts any semblance of workplace democracy?

Making the workplace more democratic may be a way to address the challenges of learning, performance, and e-commerce, but it may also be a moral right. In a democracy, the workplace should mirror democratic national governance (Haque, 2000). The threat to democratic values that technology makes possible encourages decisions that impact people and the environment to be made with little or no employee discourse or accountability. Coercive and controlling technology makes possible the substitution of digitized responses for active participatory exchange (Nelkin, 1997, p. 25), and reduces workers' capacity for reflective engagement in the workplace.

Democracy seems more plausible in learning organizations where the expansion of learning among all participants is the goal, not division of labor or command and control. Democracy arises in response to coercion. It is flight from oppressive ideology, not a response to life in an organization where learning is culture, and open and honest communication is the modus operandi. Whether technology is a catalyst for a democratic workplace or the tool of organizational tyrants is an ethical dilemma. Because HRD is involved in learning, information, and productive technologies, and plays a role in encouraging workplace democratic values, it is a facilitator of the choice and use of technology that enhances ethical and socially responsive workplaces.

Technology as Information

Technology is not only creating issues around autonomy and control, it is creating an information glut that Postman calls "information chaos." This chaos, this confusion of too much information, destabilizes our ability to apply technology to anything but instrumental and economic needs and values. Our inability to cope with information detracts from our ability to address our social problems. The irony is that in the face of technology capable of solutions to medical traumas and other scientific difficulties ". . . our most serious problems are not technical, nor do they arise from inadequate information" (Postman, 1993, p. 119).

Are the problems in the Middle East or anywhere there is conflict due to a lack of information? Is it lack of information about how to grow food that keeps millions at starvation levels? Is it a lack of technology that racism is again on the rise? "If families break up, children are mistreated, crime terrorizes a city, education is impotent, it does not happen because of inadequate information" (Postman, 1993, p. 119). Technology and the information it creates appear inept in helping us solve many of our most pressing social problems.

Computers give us reams of information, store our words and numbers, compute our statistics and empirical problems, and allow us access to the World Wide Web, but what has computer technology really brought to humanities' table? Postman says that it "has not yet come close to the printing press in its power to generate radical and substantive social, political, and religious thought . . . and in its capacity to smooth over unsatisfactory institutions and ideas, is the talcum powder of the mind" (1993, p. 116).

Technology is enabling new work environments by making instantaneous communications between workers a way of life. Stories of bad behaviors and lousy attitudes are trumpeted over e-mail and on web sites. There is literally nowhere left for people in technical work environments to hide. The challenge for HRD professionals will be to establish and nurture communication technologies wisely by addressing individual rights to privacy and keeping in mind acceptable norms and ethics.

The nearly schizophrenic quality of technology is that it entertains us, helps us to learn, keeps us healthy, and lets us know who's doing what to whom, all while holding a gun to our heads in terms of its ability to enhance humanity and society and transcend beyond the instrumental and the materialistic. In an article published a few years ago I asked: "Have we become so infatuated with technology, so blinded by its promise, that we have neglected pursuing a *deeper* understanding of humanity and preparing for a more humane future?" (Hatcher, 1998, p. 44). Yet in retrospect technology's true abilities and potential to fundamentally change the way we live and learn is inimitable and in many cases enhances our ability to create sustainable organizations. The web gives us access to the majesty of art and the degradation of pornography at the click of a button and also provides instant information on unethical and socially irresponsive people and corporations. This instant shift in how we perceive an organization wields a great deal of power and challenges us to be conscientious consumers of information.

Technology as Cultural Change Agent

We need to know how technology is altering our conceptions, and of most importance to HRD professionals we need to know how it is altering our learning and cognition and the way in which we perceive reality. As Postman reminds us, new technologies alter our interests, our symbols, and the nature of community: the arena in which thoughts develop" (Postman, 1993, p. 20). If, in fact, technology has the power to alter the essence of community, what are the implications for control of technologies that have the power to impact international social stability, global sustainability, or both?

Individual technologies such as television, computers, telecommunications, and genetics, taken separately, have specific and defined roles to play. We tend to analyze their virtues on an individual basis and thus conclude that all technology is useful or entertaining or we simply would not use it. "But to base our ultimate conclusions about technology mainly on our personal experience leaves out the social, political, and ecological dimensions; in other words, it overlooks the effects outside ourselves" (Mander, 1996, p. 346). Together, these and other technologies combine to form a megatechnology that overwhelms diversity and works to reshape culture. For example, solar power technologies have very different social and intrinsic characteristics than fossil fuel or nuclear-based power technologies. And what are the implications of each kind of technology? Mander asked, "What kind of technology relates to what kind of society?" (1996, p. 348). Television has Americanized almost every culture on the planet with the technical infrastructure to support it and the World Wide Web is slowly infiltrating even the poorest and most isolated Third World cultures. As this process of monoculture, this homogenizing of the worlds' diverse cultures and customs increases, more and more indigenous peoples and their way of life may fall victim.

Where is technology's moral underpinning and where are the social institutions that typically spring up to mediate and resolve social conflicts? With few exceptions such as the United Nations, social institutions established to reconcile or at least attempt to monitor the results of technology and its impact on humanity are rare. "Technological society, after all, has never shown any great commitment to self-reflection, self-criticism, or the study of its own history" (Winner, 1977, p. 128). This leaves organizations to try and mediate technology-based conflict and attempt to divvy out technology in an equitable manner. HRD may be asked to assume more of this responsibility within organizations. HRD professionals should respond by addressing the ethics of accessibility to and use of technology and work toward workplace democracy.

Technology and Expertise

Expertise means skills, knowledge, and proficiency in an explicit field of study and application. Expertise can and typically does result in a limited technological viewpoint that implies: "I am not responsible for the human consequences of my decision. I am only responsible for the efficiency of my part of the system." An expert is an important technical means by which technology strives furiously to control information (Postman, 1993).

Experts are generally badly informed about any matter not directly related to their area of expertise. However, technical experts claim "dominion not only over technical matters but also over social, psychological, and moral affairs" (Postman, 1993, p. 87). Experts concentrate on one field of study, filter out all that is not pertinent, eliminate that which is irrelevant, and use what is left to solve a problem. "This process works in situations where only a technical solution is required or where there is no conflict with human purposes. . . . And it is disastrous when applied where efficiency is usually irrelevant, such as education, law, family life" (Postman, 1993, p. 88). Technology applied in the social sciences creates the belief that a survey or a test can tell us things they cannot. "We come to believe that our score is our intelligence, or our capacity for creativity or love or pain. We come to believe that the results of opinion polls are what people believe, as if our beliefs can be encapsulated in such sentences as 'I approve' and 'I disapprove' (Postman, 1993, p. 89).

As HRD professionals work with subject matter experts this technological elitism should be acknowledged as a barrier to the development of interventions that are equitable and able to reach diverse audiences. For example, basing an intervention solely on the input of one or two experts should be suspect. Not only because it is an unacceptable design method but also because a lack of breadth resulting from the expert's limited data could result in training that limits understanding by diverse groups in the workplace.

Technology may be a panacea for some modern ills but it may also reinforce traditional barriers to advancement and potential for some and may create hindrances for others. We must constantly ask and be willing to answer the questions, To whom will technology give power and who will be denied? Who will be our experts and to what extent is technology exclusionary? HRD professionals must be cognizant of technological elitism in our profession and in our organizations and be diligent in providing equal access to training and other technology-based, career-enhancing activities.

There is growing concern about the differences between male and female use of technology, especially web-based technologies and the lack of women in technology-based careers. Shade (1998) reported that the statistics for women in the computer science field are dismal, revealing that only a small percentage of computer scientists and computer professionals are female, with over 90 percent being male. Usage of computers and computer networking is also disproportionately male. Shade added, "Women are still underrepresented in almost every aspect of computer culture, from programming, to product design, to everyday use" (1998, p. 5). However, there is progress in helping to overcome the general underrepresentation of women in almost all fields of public interest. The Declaration of Quito of 1994 and the GK'97 Gender Declaration, treatises that recognized general equality for women in socioeconomic environments established basic principles to ensure equal opportunities for men and women involved in information and communication technologies. Technologies such as the Internet enable communication and learning across time and space. Yet technology-based learning has seen limited use in teaching diversity or developing societies based on equality.

Technology and Learning

Technology's dependence on business for support has created education limited primarily to job orientation. This has led to the rapid dominance of scientific and technical education and "has helped turn philosophy into linguistics, linguistics into mathematics, psychology into rodentology, sociology into methodology, and music into computer cacophony" (Douglas, 1970, p. 10). We seek to improve learning through the metaphor of "instructional technologies." But why should we involve technology in learning? Postman (1993) says the answer is to make learning more efficient and more interesting. This is an adequate answer since in a technological society efficiency needs no justification. It is usually unnoticed, then, that this answer does not address the question: What is learning for? Efficiency is a technical response, an answer about means, not ends; "and it offers no pathway to a consideration of education philosophy" (Postman, 1993, p. 171).

When we never query what learning is for or why we are building certain skills and knowledge and not others; when we use education solely as an instrument for efficiency and productivity or to develop humans as corporate resources, we block whatever transcendent, political, spiritual, or social ideas that might be advanced. Informal learning or noninstrumental learning not directly related to production and economics that might further our understanding and add meaning should be encouraged and enhanced. In addition, systems thinking and divergent viewpoints should be encouraged, especially in young children, to enable us to see the relationships and interdependencies between technology, globalization, and humanity. And what and how we teach, our curriculums and methods, should also reflect this need for more interdependence and holistic thinking. For example, application of adult learning principles (andragogy) to design and delivery of web-based learning enhances the learning experience for the adult learner by encouraging him or her to seek connections with and application of the learning to everyday life. University-level HRD curricula should include lessons on systems thinking separated from its instrumental value to business by being more focused on its ability to enhance our understanding of the interrelatedness of business, society, the environment, humanity, and the role of HRD. Skill acquisition, although important, should be subservient to understanding. We should keep in mind that technology "encourages an insensitivity to what skills may be lost in the acquisition of new ones. It is important to remember what can be done without computers, and it is also important to remind ourselves of what may be lost when we do use them" (Postman, 1993, p. 120).

A study at Carnegie Mellon University reported in the September 25, 2000, *US News and World Report* found that teenage computer users showed signs of more loneliness and isolation and that they tried to replace people with the computer. Do we need a person who is educated or one who possesses skills? Do we really need more isolated and lonely people with no commitment and no point of view but with plenty of marketable skills? Is our education system addressing only technical skill needs? Shouldn't that be the business of business? And is business really prepared to take up the understanding-level learning slack, to provide knowledge that is incapable of being attached to a return on investment figure? Even if we could wrestle through who gets taught where and what, the question "Is technology really a good teacher?" although a common topic at HRD and e-learning conferences, remains unanswered.

The rise in technical knowledge and the resulting loss of mastery in more visionary and transcendent pursuits manifests itself in a decline in our abilities to judge and control technology and see the bigger picture of the problems facing society and our organizations. More and more powerful technology hampers our ability to move into what Wilber called the second tier of consciousness, where humanity moves from individualism to transpersonalism, from "relatavism to holism . . . from pluralism to integralism" (2000, p. 12).

The steady increase in application of the technological worldview has created a knowledge-based economy—that is, an economy in which scientific-technical information is the "legitimate basis of action and, at least for a growing part of the population, a goal in itself" (Douglas, 1970, p. 15). Thurow (1996) called it the third industrial revolution—steam being the first, and electrification the second. To participate in this knowledge-based economy, nations and people must be seen as attractive production bases for multinational companies; thus, nations must provide well-educated workforces with the technical skills required to compete. The result has been a continuing increase in knowledge-based occupations and jobs, which creates more need and a continual commitment to the technological worldview. The prevailing economy is based not so much on knowledge, which implies understanding, as it is on information. "What makes the market superior is precisely that it organizes economic activity around *information*" (Drucker, 1993, p. 181). Knowledge as a commodity moves it out of the purview of education or learning and into economics. Knowledge then becomes a marketable product or service with no more economic, and thus in a consumer-driven society, social value than an electronic device or a bushel of apples.

There are obvious dangers to this shift. For instance, public education has been steadily moving toward an instrumental activity valuing the practical over fundamental knowledge and wisdom, where a test is more important than social skills and a degree or certification is more important than understanding or meaning making. The other dilemma this shift to a knowledge-based economy is causing is class conflict between knowledge workers and the majority who are not. The former U.S. secretary of labor, Robert Reich, coined knowledge workers symbolic-analysts; these systems thinkers, consultants, scientists, lawyers, engineers, bankers, and university professors who live and work in walled, secure postmodern structures, are more highly valued because they can trade their services, their knowledge, and skills on a global basis. All other workers who cannot trade their skills globally are and will be left behind (Reich, 1991).

Have we come this far in our evolution to believe that technology and science is the only system within which people can be successful or the only system of thought capable of producing truth? Or that technology is the highest form of human achievement? Shouldn't we be allowed the freedom to interpret science and technology on our own human terms, to question science's view of the universe as the random act of quarks and superstrings with no direction and even less meaning? Have we lost something, in our quest for faster modems and artificial intelligence?

In a time when we need to assume more responsibility for our actions, technology, computer technology in particular, allows us, even cajoles us, to relinquish this responsibility. "The computers are down" is another way of saying that no one is responsible. Winner added that much of technology "amounts to a triumph of instrumentation—virtuosity in measuring and comparing quantifiable variables—rather than an earnest effort to advance our understanding" (1977, p. 7). Science allows us to rationalize, to step outside ourselves to relinquish, even shirk, our responsibility. We want others to tell us how to behave, what to do, and how to feel. And we listen to the experts not because like ancient shamans or tribal leaders or the wise elderly they speak to us "as fellow humans who have lived longer, or experienced more of human suffering, or thought more deeply and reasoned more carefully about some set of problems, but because they consent to maintain the illusion that it is their *data,* their procedures, their science, and not themselves, that speak" (Winner, 1977, p. 161). Experts are the predominant directors of current research dominated by and dedicated to technology. Nowhere is this more evident than in academe and research.

Technology, Academic Freedom, and Research

Not so long ago, it was common for researchers to sacrifice their financial and reputational self-interests in the "name of science and humankind" and adding to the truth about reality. Today, however, scientific development is dependent on corporate support and the industrial-technological society. This interdependence creates a conditional and unhealthy needy relationship between the creators of science and the owners of power. Thus, scientists, and this includes HRD scholars and professionals as social scientists, become the servants of power.

Today's technology gurus and experts are "invested with the charisma of priestliness." Some of our priest-experts are called psychiatrists, some sociologists, some statisticians, and some HRD scholars. Their god speaks of efficiency, precision, and objectivity. They come from a moral universe that is irrelevant to the theology of expertise. And so the priests of [technology] call sin "social deviance," which is a statistical concept, they call evil "psychopathology," which is a medical term, and the economic idea of the development of humans as "resources." "Sin and evil disappear because they cannot be measured and objectified, and therefore cannot be dealt with by experts" (Douglas, 1970, p. 90).

Many uninformed people in the public see science and social science as a subset, which HRD is a part of, as value-free and unbiased. Yet even when we think we are doing value- and bias-free research in HRD, we are under the covert trusteeship and influence of technology-based business and the watchful eye of many scientific-military focused governments. And whether we realize it or not, with few exceptions the federal dollars and grants we use to fund our programs and research with originate from technology and science-based funding agencies. Some of the most monetarily attractive grants come from government-related agencies such as the National Institutes of Health and philanthropic foundations like the Ford and Kellogg Foundations. But where do these organizations get *their* dollars? Primarily from individuals and corporations seeking answers to economic more than social questions.

The corporatization of higher education in the United States is a concern for many scholars and researchers. Recent articles in the *Chronicle of Higher Education* have focused on the assertion that universities are trying to serve two masters and that "conflict-of-interest policies and standards of disclosure that universities rely upon don't do much to protect academic freedom or the integrity of research in an environment where corporate interests are playing a growing role" (Blumenstyk, 1998, p. A42). Universities are our repositories of information and expertise disseminating to the public results and recommendations from research supposedly unfettered by corporate financial influence. But when autonomy is compromised, when academic freedom is replaced with corporate coercion, then we lose our primary source for independent and trustworthy research and our most important source of experts willing and able to pursue pure research and study unfettered by a corporate mission.

This control over research has grown substantially over the past three decades. As a result, we generate products and processes in the practitioner arena that have been developed and in many ways controlled by technology-based business, science, and government. I am not saying that this is all bad, just that we need to be more aware of this domination and possible manipulation over our ideas and subsequent outcomes that were not really created in an open forum. On the other hand, where would we be without the financial support of some of these same entities? Would we still have rampant epidemics like polio or smallpox or would we still be flying people all over the globe just to have meetings or to take a few hours of training? Probably.

But shouldn't we as informed and relatively free global citizens have more control over our destinies or at the very least be more informed about the impact that certain technologies may or may not have on society and people before they are implemented? Hamelink (2000) asks, How realistic is it to expect that society would conduct an ethical dialogue about technology choices?

As much as we would like to think there is a dialogue between technology, ethics, and HRD, the fact is that technology just goes on. Questions of ethics are relegated to after-the-fact scenarios. The prevailing sentiment is that problems such as learning are technical, not social and thus can be solved by technological means that require little or no ethical reflection. The inability to ask questions of right and wrong about technology and to adapt it to social needs is corroborated by the fact that "in most countries technology choice is a highly undemocratic process, not involving even minimal accountability to the public" (Hamelink, 2000, p. 8).

Democratization of technology is no small feat. It requires adherence to basic human rights to participation in the governance process and that everyone's voice be heard. In capitalist economies, however, the market, not the public, assumes responsibility for decisionmaking about technologies that enhance competitive positioning. Thus, decisions about technology are based more on return on investment decisions than on considerations of societal needs. Only the voices of business and industry are heard. And the gap between those who can afford technology and those who cannot widens.

The daunting task of initiating an open debate about technology's role in society may be in our future—and it may not. Given the formidable power of technology in a global and increasingly consumer-oriented world, and the supporting worldviews of those in power, the prospect of a public dialogue seems remote. It seems unlikely that we, as Hamelink points out, "could mobilize counterforces against a world order which provides an uneven access to the world's communication resources" (2000, p. 175).

But even if we cannot think globally, we can act locally. Providing initiatives to ensure that everyone's voice is heard, people have equal access to technology, and a healthy dialogue exists between ethics and technology at the level of the HRD profession and in our organizations is not unattainable. Asking questions about the long-term impact of new technologies based on the needs of people and the environment, in addition to basic economic and technical needs, does not limit competitiveness of our organizations. In fact, it enhances an organization's ability to seek a balance between economic, technical, and social needs. Winner suggested that we need programs to "study the various impacts of new technologies and to provide citizens and policy makers with advance information 'intelligence' concerning possible alternative futures" (1977, p. 90).

HRD has a professional and ethical responsibility to respect the fundamental rights, dignity, and worth of all people and to be sensitive to issues around differences in power between people and groups. "HRD professionals are aware of their professional responsibilities to the community, the society in which they work and live, and the planet . . . and seek to contribute to the welfare of people" (Russ-Eft, Burns, Dean, Hatcher, Otte, and Preskill, 1999, pp. 2–3). Thus, HRD is responsible for equitable uses of technology. Much can also be done at the organizational level. HRD professionals are encouraged to revise needs analyses to identify not only what technology is needed, but also assess the overall potential of technology for the organization and individuals and for both good and bad. During the development, implementation, and evaluation of performance improvement interventions such as training, questions should be raised about the ethics of technology and its equitable use. Finally, HRD can be a mediator when issues of privacy, employee surveillance, and other technology-based ethical issues arise.

Summary and Conclusions

Technology's nature and its impact on humanity and business and its relationship with society and HRD were examined in this chapter. That technology is capable of great good as well as harm was explored. The philosophical foundations of the Technological Society were summarized in light of the ubitiquousness of technology in modern business and industry. How technology creates dependence and its relationship to learning and education were also considered.

Technology has much potential to heal our broken bodies and minds or destroy our ecosystems. But it does not have to be a tool for destruction or a tyrant over us. Because controlling ideas is more powerful than controlling space and physical capital technology can be a "kind of global nervous system enveloping the world" (Rifkin, 2000, p. 16). How we choose to delineate technology's place in our society and in our lives remains in question. We have a responsibility to wisely choose and use technology.

As a tool, technology has been used to develop communities and for the growth of societies. But not all growth and development has produced positive results. The next chapter introduces a different definition of development and growth and examines alternatives to development based on traditional economics.

Development and Economics

Our concepts of development in the Western world are based on classical economic theory. The ideas of development and economics are intertwined. It is important for business leaders and HRD professionals to better understand how to interpret economics and development and how we use this knowledge to lead people in organizations. It is instructive for us to begin by understanding pertinent concepts of development and their relationship with economic theories.

Concepts and Definitions of Development

Modern international development began with a speech—the State of the Union address delivered to Congress in early 1949 by President Harry S. Truman. The speech introduced a proposal called Point IV, which was about a new policy of helping "poor" countries, the "under-developed" nations with foreign aid from richer countries. This patronizing point of view of development, or more rightly underdevelopment, ushered in a new perspective that all nations progress, just some more slowly than others, and it is the duty of the faster, more developed to assist the underdeveloped. It also suggested that the worth of a nation is based on its production, its ability to produce something, not whether its people are spiritually fit, its families resilient, or its environment pristine. Sachs added, "Truman conceived of the world as an economic arena where nations compete for a better position on the GNP scale" (1995, p. 429). Coming on the coattails of the Marshall Plan, which preserved Western Europe's social and business structures after the devastation of World War II, there was and still is some disagreement over the rationale for the mechanism of this proposal.

Although Truman ushered in the modern era of development, it is still a term viewed through multiple lens. When we think of development we typically think about progress, growth, and expansion, and assume that it provides a better life for those affected by it. Applied in a corporate setting, we typically see development as labor productivity, physical growth, and profit. Of course these viewpoints of development are not absolute and many believe that they are outdated to the point of being detrimental. Negative accounts of development come primarily from reports that it is synonymous with destruction of natural and cultural resources.

As human and physical resources are developed, entire areas of the planet are destroyed or drastically altered and cultures are disrupted and often emasculated. This one-dimensional account of development causes bias, especially in light of new technologies and the modification of land. A multidimensional approach to development provides us with an opportunity to view it within a taxonomy that includes politics, society, technology, environment, and culture. But even if we acknowledge this multidimensional approach, our sphere of influence shapes our interpretation of its meaning and value.

The notion of development is synonymous with economic and technological growth, where bigger is better and more is desirable. Development as it has been applied in Western society means that Wal-Mart wins out almost every time over little "ma and pa" operations that positively contribute more than just money to a community.

One of the key problems with development is the way it is defined and how it is institutionalized by organizations and professions. Peet said, "Development is a founding belief of the modern world. Progress has long since replaced God as the icon of our age" (1999, p. 1). There is no more misused word in the English language than "development," whether we refer to development of land, humans, or a particular economy.

Defining Development

For most people in modern cultures and certainly within modern organizations, development is synonymous with economic growth.

> We speak of land development, and typically mean stripping the land of vegetation and paving it over with asphalt. We speak of human development, typically meaning destroying traditional community and conditioning people to survive

in an urban environment. We speak of economic development, implying that it is equivalent with improvement of well-being, but typically we mean increase of economic production and consumption. (Harman and Porter, 1997, p. 256)

Peter Senge added that for "business people the best rate of growth is fast, faster, fastest. Yet virtually all natural systems have intrinsically optimal rates of growth. The optimal rate is far less than the fastest possible growth" (1990, p. 62).

Many economists make a distinction between growth and development and on occasion their definitions appear to contradict one another. Growth is a quantitative measure that implies an increase in size by the assimilation and processing of materials or resources. Development means to come into being, to realize potentialities and bring into a fuller, more stable state. Hawken added that development "means the qualitative improvement in the structure, design and composition of the physical stocks of wealth that results from greater knowledge, both of techniques and of purpose . . . a growing economy is getting bigger; a developing economy is getting better" (1993, p. 140). Peet said, "Development differs from economic growth in that it pays attention to the conditions of production, for example, the environments affected by economic activity, and to the social consequences, for example, income distribution and human welfare . . . human emancipation . . . and finer ethical ideals and higher moral values" (1999, p. 1). According to him these self-congratulatory views of development have been and continue to be challenged, and increasingly becoming the subject of intense skepticism.

These diverse definitions of development and growth are illustrative of their complexity and the uncertainty with which they have been used. Although the definitions appear disjointed, it is clear that in most cases the idea of development is one of economics fueled by corporate growth, productivity, efficiency, and profit.

Outcomes of Development

The advocates of development and growth maintain that economic growth is key to ending human suffering, wars, and poverty and for achieving society's goals. The number of people living in abject poverty has actually kept pace with the population growth: both have doubled. And the ratio of the share of the world's income that went to the richest 20 percent and that which went to the bottom 20 percent has also doubled (Korten, 1995, p. 39). Development creates its own breed of victims:

. . . peasants relegated to peripheries drained of their youth, "nimble-fingered" women assigned the most boring tasks in computer chip mills, colonized societies raided for resources, their people moved at random to satisfy the whims of corporate leaders, or manipulated for mass market as goods, such as cigarettes, now deemed too dangerous for Western lungs. (Peet, 1999, p. 2)

Over the past several decades, business has taken a much harder view of its role in economic development and growth. One of the primary reasons for this shift to a strictly bottom-line focus is the advent of the unprecedented growth in the stock market, especially in the United States. Ironically, during the "bull market," many companies that traditionally were socially responsible actually decreased their philanthropic activities. Reports show that philanthropy, as a percent of gross corporate income, had not increased even in a time of substantially increased profits. Even the estimated $60 billion spent annually on corporate training, and identified as a variable in organizations considered socially responsible, has shifted more toward instrumental and technical training and skill building, versus a more education, learning-oriented or human development focus. It is rare indeed that we see training as training *and development*.

The preponderance of corporations and the viewing of development solely in terms of economic growth in particular characterize industrial and Western societies, and there is growing concern that non-Western societies are following suit. This economic rationality forces organizations and the people within them to focus almost exclusively on economic production and consumption. "No other society has attempted to guide a society with decisions shaped primarily by economic considerations. No other society has taken as its highest value acquisitive materialism . . . there is no reason to assume that economic rationality will lead to decisions that are wise from human, ecological, compassionate, and spiritual standpoints" (Harman and Horman, 1990, p. 57). Passionate words for sure, but even the most supportive advocate of pure economic development should be able to see that a way of life devoted to development for profit alone is bringing us as humans more and more into the commercial arena, that our very existence is becoming commodified. We are moving from development that is "metamorphosing from commodifying goods and services to commodifying cultural experiences" (Rifkin, 2000, p. 29). But what of the results of development? What outcomes should we expect?

Development and HRD

As business has grown, so too has the need for structures and functions to develop employees and improve processes to add instrumental and economic value. Human resources, training, and performance improvement have always been willing yet basically uninformed partners in economic development. Willing, because management has viewed them and they have reacted as a subservient function, as a "resource" to be consumed, and uninformed, because the true consequences, the long-term impact of their actions, are seldom acknowledged outside the organization's walls, much less analyzed with an unbiased eye. As organizations become more global HRD's role becomes more important in how we approach development.

Theoretically and historically, HRD enhances the learning and performance of individuals and organizations—to do good, not put neighbors out of business or foul the environment or support any number of other socially irresponsible or unethical behaviors. But the reality is that HRD is helping to create and make successful "big box" organizations like Wal-Mart that gobble up entrepreneurs and small local businesses, and adding value to organizations who are destroying the environment and consulting with companies with a history of exploiting foreign workers. Of course we are also adding value to many socially responsive and ethical organizations like Interface, Inc., organizations trying to do the right thing for society, the environment, and themselves.

As we interpret organizational goals to increase profit, expand a company's customer base, or improve learning and performance, we are automatically adding to development and growth responsible not only for enhanced quality of life for many people, but also for environmental and social and cultural dilemmas. Unfortunately, as a rule we are not in a position to decline managements' requests to help. But what would a strategic plan or organizational development or training program look like if people and their cultures really mattered or if corporations and their leaders truly cared about the ecosystem? Would these activities and outcomes look substantially different? Would we revise the way we do needs analyses to methods that force us to address environmental and social issues? Possibly. But before we attempt to answer these questions, it is crucial to take a closer look at how we are defining and interpreting the ideas of development within HRD and better understand the economic theories that support these definitions and concepts.

Corporations are the most powerful players in development. Therefore, it is inevitable that the profession of HRD is an integral part of the development process, whether or not it is consciously acknowledged. Inherent even in the name human resource development, the word development is a clear signal that HRD adds not only to individual but also to economic growth. In their review of cross-cultural research on HRD, Hansen and Brooks (1994) found that the term HRD was offensive to some cultures (the Dutch in particular) because it implies human exploitation and the view that people are commodities; an economic concept. Value based solely on economics, on money, improperly equates nonsentient assets of a company, such as equipment, with human assets and land. This exposes people and Earth to potential for exploitation and capricious decisions based solely on finances.

As we sense the need to redefine development and growth, it becomes increasingly clear that human resource development in particular needs a new metaphor to address the negative connotation many associate with the current definition of development. One possible solution to this problematic metaphor is to change human resource development to a name that is less economic, a more inclusive term, one that supports sustainable growth and development. One such designation might be *sustainable human resources.* This name maintains the business-oriented idea of humans as resources but also suggests that HR may lead to a sustainable future in the positive light of sustainability. Thus, we as people in organizations enhance the long-term viability of the ecosystem and society and add long-term value to our organizations as a part of, not separate from society and the ecosystem. Here we must balance human needs with those of the environment. We must begin to intimately understand that we are not separate from but are a part of our environment and that there is a limit to the amount of consumption that can be sustained indefinitely without degrading capital stocks—including natural and human capital. Natural capital is the physical soil, water, air, atmosphere, plant, and animal biomass; human capital is intellectual and social resources.

HRD can do much to ensure that basic human needs are taken care of when our organizations make decisions concerning allocation of available ecosystem resources—often called development. We can also increase the accountability and sustainability of our economic organizations by encouraging and educating our leaders to be more aware that resources allocated to global enterprises might be reallocated to local communities or entities, thus increasing localized markets and developing more sustainable growth.

The idea of a morality-free market is being applied to society wholesale (Dalla Costa, 1998). "When the government is focused on competitiveness, and society is fixated on budgets, growth [development] assumes greater importance than quality of life" (Dalla Costa, 1998, p. 59). We must reverse this trend. We must define development differently from economic growth in order to address the environments affected by production; the social and human consequences of productive activity. Because development and growth are seen as economic, it is important to get a better feel for the theories and concepts that underlie development, how we measure economics, and the extent we base corporate activities like HRD on such measurements.

Economic Theories and Economic Measurements

To rethink, reexamine, and readjust our ideas about ethics and social responsibility in HRD and other organizational pursuits, we need to take a look at the role that economics plays in constructing our ideas. Economic theories are the guiding dogma behind business and govern the assumptions, beliefs, values, and structures that underlie the way we do business and many of our organizational behaviors. If we consider economics as one of the theoretical foundations of HRD, and if, as one researcher has reported, we really believe that economics is having the most influence on our practice (Hatcher, 2000b), then we should improve our understanding of economic thought and its power to shape our consciousness, profession, activities, and behaviors. I will provide a discussion of the classic school of thought, neoclassical economics. I will also discuss capitalism as an outcome of neoclassical economics and will introduce contemporary environmental economic theory that better serves not only the field of HRD but society as a whole.

Neoclassical Economic Theory and Capitalism

Theory helps to explain things; it provides principles and tests models. Theory cajoles us to try and understand, to better comprehend a phenomenon by shedding light on its values and ethics. In economics, theories help us to understand how we allocate and manage limited resources. It is not my intent to try to fully explain or critique economic theory; there are just too many theories and hundreds of well-written and detailed books and articles on the subject. But what many of these publications fail to address and what HRD and other business leaders need to understand are the limitations that conventional economic theory places on us and how these theories compel us to make decisions that are questionable and often unethical and irresponsible. Just knowing that contemporary economic theory is flawed is an important first step to understanding. We also need to be aware of alternative economic theories that could help us in our quest for more humane, ethical, and socially responsible workplaces.

Neoclassical economics has its foundations in agricultural society, where supply creates increasing demands, and is founded on rationalism. Proponents of this theory believe that all knowledge is derived from reason. According to them, only rational structures of analysis are valid and human qualities such as values and feelings should be excluded. As Korten notes, "This commitment to rationalism has given standing to the claim that economics is the only objective, value-free science" (1995, p. 72). Burk added,

"Rationality is probably the last and most improbable basis on which to erect a theory of human behavior" (1994, p. 319). Since HRD deals with human behavior, it stands to reason that neoclassical economics is just not a very good fit.

In its truest sense neoclassical economic theory implies that starting from zero consumption, people as self-interested individuals will seek to maximize consumption of goods and services. It also supports organizational and HRD leaders acting only in the interests of the owners of capital, and not acting as moral agents for themselves, the profession, society, or the ecosystem. Economic logic posits that this autonomy leads to stockholder wealth maximization that in turn purportedly causes positive social outcomes. Examples abound of the application of this cause-and-effect relationship that proves its fallacy. The fact is, the hypothesis that neoclassical economics improves society has not only been soundly questioned but has been charged with causing much suffering within organizations, societies, and the environment. For example, if we apply neoclassical economics to real world problems such as discrimination, environmental degradation, or crime, then we are forced to conclude that they must be efficient practices or they would not exist. Because of its focus on wealth maximization and individualism it should come as no surprise that neoclassical economics is considered to be an explanation of capitalism.

Capitalism is the most powerful, ubiquitous, meritorious yet potentially harmful economic system the modern world has thus far devised. Capitalism is a system in which people compete to accumulate wealth by buying the rights to use land, labor, and capital to produce goods or services with the intention of selling them in a market at a profit (Saunders, 1995). As an instrument of growth it has "collapsed distance, overcome space, and pulled the world together into an integrated (yet somewhat precarious and often dangerous) global system" (Saunders, 1995, p. 10).

Hawken, Lovins, and Lovins identified the "mind-set" of the capitalist system:

- Progress occurring best in a free-market system where reinvestment makes labor and capital productive.
- Competitive advantage is gained when producers are more efficient and produce more product and services to expanding markets; more Gross Domestic Product (GDP) maximizes human well-being.
- Environmental concerns must be balanced against economic growth to maintain a high standard of living.
- Market forces will allocate people and resources to their highest and best uses (1999, p. 6).

Again, free market capitalism is typically viewed as moral dogma, unquestioned, and morally correct. The ideal of free market capitalism should not be encumbered with governmental interference or regulation and thus results in the most efficient and socially optimal allocation of resources (Korten, 1996). It also means that there is perfect competition, perfect and assessable information, and that no barriers, no taxes, no monopolies or price controls or transaction costs to trade exist. Obviously, free market capitalism described above is not the market in which most business happens today. Does a manufacturer in the West have the same competitive advantages as one in the Southern Hemisphere, where labor rates are a fraction of those in the West? These economic assumptions simply do not apply in the real world.

The imperfections in market-based economics are causing problems for individuals and organizations, but of most pressing concern is the allegation that free market economics is debilitating our environment. Although free market capitalism has been associated with improvements in legal systems and enhancing democracy on a global scale, it is also frequently accused of cultural and environmental degradation. Because of environmental problems such as the destruction of the ozone layer, global warming, and increases in carbon monoxide and environmentally related diseases, there is an urgent need to develop and employ economic theories that address the greater environment in which economic and all other systems on the planet are embedded. We simply can no longer afford to separate economics from the environment.

I will continue to explore economic theory, but before I address environmental economics allow me to reiterate our purpose. Globalization, technology, and economics are the causes, the raison d'être why we are the way we are, why HRD looks the way it does today and what it may become tomorrow. It is important to understand the role of globalization, technology, and economics in shaping the values, ethics, and social responsibility of HRD as a field of research and practice.

Environmental Economics

Calls for new economic theories are not new. For many years economists, sociologists, scientists, philosophers, management scholars, and even CEOs have proposed alternative theories based on society and the ecosystem. Notable are Ray Anderson, Wendell Berry, Kenneth Boulding, Fritjof Capra, Anthony Carnevale, Robert Costanza, Herman Daly, Amitai Etzioni, Edward Goldsmith, Willis Harman, Paul Hawken, David Korten, Aldo Leopold, Arne Naess, E. F. Schumacher, George Sessions, Edward and Jean Stead, and Margaret Wheatley. Although each of these scholars and practitioners has painted a slightly different picture of what they see as a healthier economic system, each of their divergent views is based on the assumption that unlimited economic growth and development is not possible within a finite ecosystem and that current economic systems are unsustainable.

Economic development and growth has always involved transformation of the natural environment, but in the last 200 years the pace and magnitude of development has reached a fever pitch, ". . . and the relationship between human beings and the natural environment has changed fundamentally as a result" (Saunders, 1995, p. 53). Hawken added, "Economics separated production processes from the land, the land from people, and, ultimately, economic values from personal values" (1993, p. 11).

The problems associated with unlimited economic growth have stimulated economists and others to develop economic theories based on the assumption that neither consumption nor money are the dominant variables and that business is not solely an economic institution with only economic responsibilities to a few stockholders. Economic theories such as ecological or environmental economics are based on the proposition that growth has reached an unsustainable trajectory. Unsustainable means that the amount of consumption exceeds natural and social capital's ability to be sustained indefinitely. Traditional economics implies that capital is wealth only in terms of investment in tangible resources such as a factory or equipment; yet an economy requires human, financial, manufactured, and natural capital to be sustainable. The problem is that capitalism as we know it "neglects to assign any value to the largest stocks it employs—the natural resources and living systems, as well as the social and cultural systems that are the basis of human capital" (Hawken, Lovins, and Lovins, 1999, p. 5).

If we are to wipe out the endless conflict between economic and ecologic and cultural interests we must embrace economic theory that places economics as a subsystem under the larger ecosystem, which includes culture and society as well as the physical environment. Environmental economic theory and natural capitalism are related concepts that HRD and other business leaders should immediately recognize as providing for human, social, and environmental wealth and point out just how inadequate neoclassical economics is in addressing human and environmental needs and dilemmas.

A. C. Pigou, an English economist, in the 1920s first introduced the idea that the costs associated with environmental and cultural damage should be borne by producers. As Paul Hawken (1993) points out in his book *The Ecology of Commerce,* Pigou pioneered the economic strategy where immediate and future damage caused by production systems is internalized, thus actually increasing efficiency by forcing more ecoefficient designs and production processes on producers—corporations and organizations. And with publication of *Small Is Beautiful* in 1973, the economist E. F. Schumacher introduced the modern concept of environmental economics, so it is not a new concept. By not externalizing as neoclassical economic models encourage, but internalizing the environmental costs of doing business, environmental economics assigns value to resources, pollution, and wastes so that optimum levels of resource depletion, pollution, and waste generation that the ecosystem can tolerate can be determined (Costanza, 1991; Stead and Stead, 1996).

Unfettered economic growth based on consumption and the rationality that people will consume without limits results in the environment being viewed simply as a product to be consumed. But it is not enough to know economic theory. We must know how theory is applied. We need to know how economics are measured and to understand how these measures impact us. We also need to understand why current measures need to be changed and discuss alternatives.

Economic Measures: Gross Domestic Product and Beyond

There is a saying in business that "we measure what we value." The problem, however, is not so much the measures themselves but what we end up doing with the resultant numbers. Through measurements abstract concepts such as economics are justified, presented, and accepted as if they are the gospel truth. The economist Kenneth Boulding said, "The danger of measures is that they become ideals." Whether this is true at a public or national level is debatable, but most certainly measurements such as the Gross Domestic Product (GDP) and the Gross National Product (GNP) (the U.S. government switched from the old GNP to the GDP in 1991), the prime interest rate and stock prices capture not only corporate attention but also our mutual consideration. The United States and most of the rest of the world holds its collective breath when Alan Greenspan, currently chairman of the U.S. Federal Reserve Board, talks about changes in the prime interest rate. The truth of the matter is that measurements such as these are not set in stone, and in many cases are not even all that valid or reliable. Yet we bank a lot of important decisions on them.

The primary way that production is measured in industrialized nations like the United States is through measurements that consider all economic activity, whether positive or negative, as "gain." Such a measure is the Gross Domestic Product. The key word being "gross," the GDP offers little more than an aggregate, a total output in terms of dollar values of finished goods and services while making no distinction between costs and benefits, productive and destructive activities, or economic and social and environmental outcomes. The GDP treats every action in the market the same, as adding to the benefit of humanity. This includes crime, divorce, the *Exxon-Valdez* oil spill, and almost all other kinds of social and environmental erosion.

Since everything produced is considered "goods," this flawed measure is blind to what kind of activity is measured or whether the activity adds anything of real value to our well-being or to human welfare. Almost all social and environmental degradation adds to GDP. "The GDP not only masks the breakdown of the social structure and the natural habitat upon which the economy—and life itself—ultimately depend; worse, it actually portrays such breakdown as economic gain" (Cobb, Halstead, and Rowe, 1995, p. 3).

Problems with the GDP are not new or unclear. It is just that between history and power plays in government and industry to maintain the status quo, any real calculation of human or environmental progress poses a genuine threat. Stemming from economic challenges of the Great Depression and World War II, the GNP (Gross National Product, as it was called then) served a very different set of economic priorities. In the 1930s and 1940s, the environment seemed an infinite source of resources, and few people questioned its ability to absorb the limited amount of wastes that industries of the time produced. The days of the Hoover administration, the New Dealers, and John Maynard Keynes witnessed inadequate infrastructures to bolster a national economy reeling from a depression and preparing for a world war. Keynes, who also helped to develop economic systems for the UK, and Robert Solow created the foundations of GDP, which helped to win a world war and thus set the stage for a consumer-based postwar economy. The Employment Act of 1946 institutionalized the GNP into official policy (Cobb, Halstead, and Rowe, 1995). The economic model of efficiency and production that made recovery from a deep depression possible and the defeat of the Nazis and Japan a reality became the same model that set economic policy for the next sixty years.

Economic measures such as the GDP do not have the conceptual apparatus to deal with existing social and environmental problems. The market in Keynes's day was minuscule and the environment was pristine; neither occupied much space in people's collective consciousness as compared to today. Our myopic focus on economic measures ignores social and environmental erosion. As a result, they have increased tenfold over the past few decades. As long as crime and environmental disasters actually add to what we consider progress and prosperity, our corporations will continue to find themselves caught in a time warp of ancient economic theories and flawed measurements. Without changes in the way we measure true progress, sustainability will remain a pipe dream and organizations that want to do the right thing will be forced to develop new and different economic measures and strategic models or remain in constant conflict.

Measurements that more closely approximate social and environmental concerns and deduct for such things as pollution that do not add to a sustainable future while currently seeing limited application, have a rich history and are well developed. Accounting for nature, or internalizing instead of externalizing environmental costs of doing business, environmental economics is a recognized field of research and practice that considers how to calculate the value of resources that are not privately owned such as air, the oceans, or biodiversity. Incentives such as taxes and regulations can be used to assign values to these resources. Other models of ecological economics include Herman Daly's (1977, 1991) steady-state economy theory, Hicksian Income, proposed by Sir John Hicks (Stead and Stead, 1996), and the Genuine Progress Indicator (GPI). The GPI, developed by Halstead and Cobb (1996), broadens the focus of economic life and offers a more accurate measure of sustainable progress. The GPI takes into consideration five factors that never show up in traditional economic models:

1. *Resource depletion, pollution, and environmental damage.*
   Consumption and depletion of natural resources, wetlands, farmland, soil, as a current cost, is weighted against short-term economic gain from this depletion (Halstead and Cobb, 1996). The GPI subtracts the costs of air and water pollution as measured by actual damage to human health and the environment. The actual costs of nonrenewable energy consumption, the use of ozone-depleting chemicals, loss of forests, radioactive and toxic wastes, and similar costs are calculated along with costs of replacements.
2. *Community-based and voluntary work.* Rates for the health, welfare, and education of citizens done in the home and community are calculated at rates equivalent to what it would cost to hire out or contract.
3. *Under- and unemployment and loss of leisure time.* Hours of chronic unemployment and underemployment and hours of lost leisure time at market rates are calculated.
4. *Crime and personal safety.* GPI assigns value to intangible medical, lost-opportunity, and psychological costs of crime. It also accounts for the costs of defensive measures such as alarm systems, air and water purification filters, and so forth.

5. *Life span and consumer durables and infrastructure.* The length of time people receive service from a product is considered. Typical measures count only the costs of an appliance, not its life cycle service value. This consideration also includes measures of the life span of a product and deducts for planned obsolescence.

Although traditional measures like the GDP are tracking a slowing economy, measures like the GPI are simultaneously tracking the economy's impact on people and nature. A GPI report on 1999, a "boom" year in America's economy, revealed that Americans were paying a price for their wealth through overwork and rising personal debt. In addition, the data suggested a reduction in savings, a widening income gap, an overall decline in quality of life, and that natural resources were being depleted ("Redefining Progress," 2001).

Traditional economic measures are difficult to apply in an effort to enhance humanity or the ecosystem. New measures that do not reward unhealthy, unsafe, and unethical behaviors are replacing the old. Public and consumer demands for environmental stewardship are leading the charge for business and industry to use new economic measures that ensure we are measuring the right things in the right way.

Summary and Conclusions

Postmodern, neoclassical economics shape our concepts of development in the Western world and increasingly the world. Business leaders and HRD professionals must understand how organizations react to and interpret economics and development and how this knowledge can be used to lead organizations. This chapter also posited new ways of measuring economic development that better reflect the need for sustainable and humane work-related systems.

Society is under the impression that current economic systems support quality of life and are environmentally friendly, but reality suggests the opposite; they encourage waste, overconsumption, and underutilization. These antiquated measures that helped pull a sagging economy out of a depression and a world war five decades ago will most likely not see us through the twenty-first century. Innovative and sustainable economics and new ways of defining growth and development help us create systems that enhance our quality of life, both inside of and external to organizations.

Economics' impact on natural systems is quickly driving us to a point of no return. We must reverse this trend or suffer the consequences in terms of waste, pollution, disease, and overall quality of life. Environmentally and human-friendly economic measures are an obvious first step, but to ensure a sustainable future requires more than changing numbers on an economic trend line.

We need people-centered development, not growth as we have encountered it thus far; development that is the "creation of life-centered societies in which the economy is but one of the instruments of good living—not the purpose of human existence" (Korten, 1995, p. 7). However, "life-centered" development is dependent on a healthy and abundant ecosystem. The next chapter examines current environmental issues and their impact on humanity, business, and HRD.

The Environment

There is little doubt that globalization, technology, development, and economics are influencing commerce and industry in varied and significant ways. Whatever impacts business and industry also impacts our abilities to learn, change, and perform. But these influencers do not happen in isolation, separate from the environment. The importance of the environment in developing sustainable workplaces cannot be overstated. It is critical for HRD and other business leaders to understand environmental issues and how they influence organizational performance so that research and practice can address resulting problems and opportunities. It is also important to understand the relationship between a focus on environmental protection and ethics and social responsibility.

Environmental Issues Impacting HRD

What if we got a thousand or so of the world's most respected and accomplished scientists together and they submitted proof that Earth could not sustain itself on its present course? Wouldn't that be an important step in emphasizing the importance of environmental issues? Surely we'd listen to such noted scholars, wouldn't we? Ironically, and rather sadly, that's already happened.

In 1992, a gathering of over 1,500 respected scientists, 104 of whom were Nobel Prize winners, issued the *World Scientists' Warning to Humanity,* which summarized their trepidation about human population, industry, and the destabilization of Earth's ecosystems. Yet I imagine that the large majority of business and HRD professionals never heard of this meeting or the report, much less acted on it.

Even before this warning, the environmental movement, at least in the United States, took a backseat to economic growth and prosperity and with all too obvious and expected results. "The natural environment is close to reaching a threshold where it will be just too frail to sustain *homo economicus*" (Dalla Costa, 1998, p. 52). Although not all organizations that keep track of how the environment is doing agree on every issue concerning the extent of damages caused by pollution or global warming, they do agree that the environment is not healing itself quickly enough to recover from long-term abuse and in fact is in jeopardy.

As business professionals we have a tendency to ignore things that do not keep our attention and do not give us immediate feedback, either positive or negative. Human resource development professionals and most business leaders are so caught up in the minutiae of daily responsibilities, so myopically focused on the immediate spreadsheet or current training program that we tend to lose sight of and often are quite unaware of what is going on around us, particularly events that are external to our organizations. Again, understanding systems is important. To provide ethical and socially responsive leadership we need to look to what we do in terms of organizational systems and their environmental impact. What do our organizations and us do to or for the environment and how is the environment responding?

Our organizations are part of the environment no matter how much we choose to ignore, overlook, or minimize its importance. We impact the environment and it impacts us. We pollute, it responds with disease.

We are facing multifaceted and decisive problems impacting our environment, our organizations, and thus HRD as a business function and a field of study and practice. To address environmental problems we must acknowledge that they do in fact exist and get a better handle on their complexity, importance, and urgency. We need to understand and acknowledge environmental dilemmas; lay out our facts so that we can make better decisions about the true extent of the environmental crisis; and address those who would minimize the predicament in which we find ourselves.

Before Aristotle and even later during sixteenth-century navigation, most people believed Earth was flat. People have not changed much in several hundred years in their unwillingness to accept what eventually becomes accepted ideas. Not so long ago people believed cigarette smoking was a harmless pastime. In 1977 Ken Olson, the founder and chairman of Digital Equipment Corporation, said, "There is no reason anyone would want a computer in their home." Seems ridiculous today, but at the time these were accepted, and conventional concepts. Recently, I overheard several noted HRD scholars expressing their disdain with environmentalists, those left-wing radicals with skewed data as their ammunition—that there really is no environmental "crisis" to speak of, and the notion that Earth's ecosystem and cultures are in trouble is nothing but a fairy tale. Obviously, not everyone is on the environmental crusade bandwagon.

Regardless of the prestige of the source or specifics of the claim, there is much consternation that "our environment is becoming ever less capable of sustaining the growing impact of our economic activities" (Goldsmith, 1996, p. 78). And it is not just the radical fringe throwing rocks outside a World Trade Organization (WTO) meeting who are calling for some immediate damage control. From business scholars like Peter Drucker, Lester Thurow, and Peter Senge to business leaders like Ray Anderson and Paul Hawken, mainstream economists, scholars, and bottom-line CEOs are sounding the alarm that our environment cannot take much more abuse. Examples of degradation abound. It is hard to go anywhere anymore and not see, hear, or read about some signs of environmental and cultural harm.

Environmental degradation is a complex issue. It is beyond our scope to identify and discuss all of the different kinds of environmental threats and problems and their subsequent health effects, or to fully debate whether or not there is an environmental crisis. However, there are currently several environmentally related issues important to HRD that warrant discussion. Examples of environmental and cultural degradation that help to make the point that our environment is in trouble and are especially pertinent to HRD include population growth, disease, resource depletion and loss of biodiversity, pollution, and global warming and climate changes. A brief discussion of each issue follows.

Population Growth, Disease, Resource Depletion, and Loss of Biodiversity

The world population has doubled in the last forty years and is expected to double from its current just over 6 billion people to over 11 billion sometime in the next three decades. The world's gross national product (GNP) will have to increase from five to thirty times over its current $25 trillion just to provide basic life necessities to this increased population (Shrivastava, 2000, p. 24). This level of economic production to meet population demands is unsustainable. Problems associated with population are not restricted to the streets of New Delhi or to hamlets in the Third World. There is an urgent need for industrialized countries to reduce population because they are the ones responsible for most of the worlds' overconsumption and pollution. In developing countries, even with rampant disease and infant mortality rates five times higher than in more developed countries, the need to reduce population because of food and health protection shortages is dire. Some scientists go so far as to say that today's population of 6 billion is substantially more than Earth's biological capacity (called carrying capacity) to sustain current standards of living.

The National Academy of Science reported that the incidence of infectious disease, which now kills 17 million people a year, particularly young people in the developing world, is increasing. According to a United Nations' 1999 *Earthwatch* report, global warming could create from 50 to 80 million new cases of malaria as disease-bearing mosquitoes move into new areas. There is also growing fear that the heavy use of antibiotics causing antibiotic contamination of the natural environment could result in resistance in communities of nondisease organisms. International travel makes it possible to spread drug-resistant microbes to all parts of the world, so no one is safe. A U.S. Office of Technology Assessment report said that up to 90 percent of all cancers are environmentally induced and theoretically preventable and the smallest doses of toxic and radioactive chemicals cause a significant percentage of cancers.

Many of Earth's natural resources are being mined, cut down, or otherwise altered for profit. This is especially true in the resource-rich but economically poor Third World, where it is easier for a corporation to convince a weak and needy government to allow unsustainable destruction of its natural resources for a few dollars. Of course, as forests and jungles dwindle, so too do the diverse and native populations that live in and rely on them for survival. For example, Ethiopia, one of the poorest countries in the world, lost 30 percent of its forest cover in less than four decades, causing mass relocation of its indigenous people and radical changes in their land-based culture. As the number of species declines, so too does the opportunity for people to sustain their cultures and rituals. As a result of global capitalism, Khor said Third World countries are "losing their indigenous skills, their capacity for self-reliance, and, in many cases, the very resource base on which their survival depends" (1996, p. 48). Systems thinking, one of the foundations of HRD, should allow us as professionals more than others to be acutely aware that loss of one species or one ritual can have devastating effects on an ecosystem or an entire culture.

Declining biodiversity may be the most serious of all our environmental problems. Loss of hundreds of species each year is impacting Earth's total biodiversity. Although many of these species are bugs and weeds, not adorable Pandas or something we would expect to see on a PBS special, many noted scientists believe that loss of diversity is the most important process of environmental evolution because it is the only process that is completely irreversible (Stead and Stead, 1996). Diversity is the wellspring of life and of humankind. It is the "foundation of evolutionary potential" (Korten, 1995, p.

272). Economic success depends on local cultures, for if they are weakened or eliminated, social trust and social capital, the very foundation of commerce and trade will disappear (Rifkin, 2000).

Pollution

One of the by-products of consumption and production is waste, and a universal outcome of waste is pollution. The primary output of today's modern organization, whether it is a manufacturer, a service company, or e-commerce, is waste (Anderson, 1998). Less than 10 percent of everything extracted from the planet by weight becomes usable products or services, and from 90 to 95 percent becomes waste. "So while businesses obsess over labor and financial capital efficiency, we have created possibly the most inefficient system of production in human history" (Senge, Carstedt, and Porter, 2001, p. 28). But solid waste is only one among many different kinds of pollution.

Air, water, and noise, as well as solid and hazardous wastes, are pollutants. Some pollutants are toxic and some are radioactive. Some are biocidic, directly harming tissue or organisms, and some are locucidic, adversely affecting the natural environment or habitats of species (Santos, 1999). The most serious impact that pollution has on people is on our health, and health influences our ability to think, reason, learn, and perform.

Since the publication of Rachel Carson's *Silent Spring,* whom many believe kicked off the environmental movement in the early 1960s, pollution has steadily increased in pockets around the globe with the Third World having the worst record. This is especially true with air pollution. Since the Industrial Revolution the amount of carbon and carbon-related compounds such as CO_2 spewed into the air has increased by 40 percent and according to a 2000 National Academy of Science report on climate change, CO_2 is rising at a rate of 1.5 parts per million per year. Subsequent health problems are exacerbated by these environmental changes. For example, asthma and allergies are on the rise, a direct result of a radical increase in pollen production of some 400 percent (United States Department of Agriculture Release No. 0278.00, 2000). As disease and illness caused by pollution increase, the opportunities for people to grow through education, training, and career development decrease. People who work on the Great Lakes may have less capacity to remember than others who do not. A June 2000 *Environmental Health Perspectives* article reported that people consuming at least twenty-four pounds of fish from Lake Michigan every year were less able to recall a story after hearing it than people who ate less than six pounds of fish. And plenty of studies link cognitive and academic deficits with blood lead concentrations and other toxic chemicals (Needleman, 1979; R. T. Brown, 2000). An obvious and troubling question for HRD professionals is: To what extent are employees experiencing effects of toxic chemicals on their ability to learn and perform on the job?

Global Warming and Climate Changes

Related to increases in carbon dioxide is global warming. Scientists have found that CO_2 levels and global temperatures have closely paralleled one another over the past 160,000 years and both have risen significantly since 1800 (Stead and Stead, 1996). According to the U.S. Environmental Protection Agency, if current predictions prove accurate, by the year 2100 CO_2 will reach concentrations of more than 540 to 970 parts per million, or 30 to 150 percent higher than today's levels. As a result of the burning of fossil fuels, trace gas emissions of dangerous substances such as sulfur dioxide, methane, and nitrogen oxide are more than twice the rates today than they were in the 1950s (Stead and Stead, 1996). According to a 2001 U.S. Environmental Protection Agency global warming report, fossil fuels burned to run our cars, heat our homes and businesses, and power our factories are responsible for 98 percent of emissions, 24 percent of methane emissions, and 18 percent of nitrous oxide emissions. The results of development by way of increased deforestation, landfills, and industrial production also contribute to air pollution.

Another by-product of the increase in CO_2 and other greenhouse gases is the reduction in the effectiveness of the ozone layer to filter damaging ultraviolet rays. Environmental scientists believe that even a slight depletion of less than 10 percent in the ozone layer would lead to a 25 percent increase in skin cancers, or an additional 300,000 cases per year worldwide. These and other climate changes cause changes in temperature that even though they seem slight, are thought to result in massive crop losses, a reduction in arable land, and influence the incidence of infectious disease. Scientists expect the average global surface temperature to rise between 1 and 4.5 degrees Fahreinheit in the next five decades, and between 2.2 and 10 degrees Fahreinheit in the next century.

Global warming and other climate changes could have a devastating impact on our ability to maintain dependable, safe, and secure work and home environments as well as provide adequate food and nutrition necessary for developing and nurturing human intellect and building work-related skills. If people have to focus on safety and security or if they cannot ensure their families' safety, or they are scrounging for food and water or fighting off disease, then they are certainly not ready to learn or build job-related skills. Neither will they be creative or innovative or motivated to do much else besides seek sustenance, security, and health.

Environmental problems affect not only our physical health, but through decreases in security, addictive behaviors related to overconsumption, and the increasing detachment of humans from Earth, it negatively impacts our psyches as well. Some have even implied an ecological unconscious, similar to Jung's collective unconscious, where we are "actors on a planetary stage who shape and are shaped by the biosphere system" (Roszak, 1995, p. 14). Such scholars contend that we should redefine sanity within an ecological context, that understanding human psyche does not stop at our skin or the city limits. Could we be so tied to Gaia (mother Earth) that we cannot restore our own mental health, our sanity, unless we restore or at least cease to destroy the health of the planet?

The way we respond to our environmental problems is similar to the way we respond to most other psychologically based problems: disbelief, denial, fear, despair, anger, rage, retaliation, and sometimes acquiescence. We simply give up in the face of what we see as insurmountable odds. Yet we have no good way to address these problems as we would a recognized mental illness such as depression. Fortunately, HRD professionals have knowledge of psychological issues. Through the HRD theoretical foundation of psychology we have knowledge of a discipline that can help us find ways to begin to address the complex conflict between our psyches and environmental destruction.

Understanding that people may be not only physically affected, but also psychologically impaired by pollution or loss of a rain forest helps us to identify potential causes of changes in individual and organizational performance and learning; disabilities that we would typically not address nor even be aware of. This understanding broadens our conception of psychology to include the relatively new and growing field of ecopsychology (Roszak, Gomes, and Kanner, 1995) and the strong relationship between our psyches, related behaviors, and what is happening in our environment.

Environmentalism as Business Strategy

Many business leaders would consider the acknowledgement of the environment as part of our psyches and part of our professional responsibility and behaviors a contemporary and innovative idea. But it may already be dated, and, as far as implementation and instrumentality is concerned, already playing second fiddle to the environment as a business strategy. Until recently environmentalism was seen as a necessary evil, a compliance issue within the domain of public relations and in many cases simply corporate rhetoric. Today the environment is not a side issue, it is an essential part of doing business that many business leaders are capitalizing on. "Greening" of business objectives and marketing, ecoefficiency, Design for Environment (DFE) and environmental management system (EMS) are now more than rhetoric, more than "buzz words" echoed in CEOs speeches, they are the modus operandi for many successful companies. And more and more international environmental and social responsibility standards like ISO 14000 and SA 8000 are being viewed as vital for business success. Business leaders, consumers, and the public are beginning to expect environmental stewardship.

The reasons for the current growth in environmental management and concern are based on pressures from a few key sources. These sources include competition, the increasing costs and reactive nature of mere compliance to regulations, stakeholder activism, and increasing knowledge and concerns about environmental and social issues.

The creation of bodies and regulations such as the U.S. Environmental Protection Agency (EPA), the Occupational Safety and Health Administration (OSHA), the European Union's EEC-Treaty amended by the Single European Act of 1987 and the 1999 Treaty of Amsterdam, the 1995 United Nations World Summit's Copenhagen Declaration, and myriad international environmental acts and decrees, laws and regulations, governing everything from air and water pollution and commercial wastes to requirements for material safety, environmental labeling, and ergonomics have proliferated and become more and more stringent. See Appendix D for a listing of environmental organizations, programs, laws, declarations, and regulations that HRD professionals should be familiar with.

There are currently over 9,000 local, state, and federal laws and regulations dealing with environmental safety and health on the books in the United States alone. The costs to business and industry to comply with these myriad environmental regulations each year runs into billions of dollars and eats up valuable human and physical resources. Compliance adds almost no real value to corporate objectives or to a company's stock value and in most cases has negligible return on investment. Stamping out fires and placing Band-Aids over festering environmental problems by continually trying to stay one step ahead of relentlessly changing regulations, new permits programs, and drastically increased civil and criminal liabilities is simply not efficient, effective, smart, or an ethical or socially responsible way to conduct business. Comprehensive and strategic approaches to environmental management ensure ongoing compliance, really do provide competitive advantages, and from an ethics point of view are simply the right thing to do. More and more companies are incorporating international environmental management standards such as ISO 14000 and social responsibility standards like SA8000 into their strategic planning and operations. See Appendix E for a description and overview of ISO 14000 and SA8000.

Business and industry has not always been a friend of environmental regulations and in fact in many cases has vehemently fought compliance. Many business leaders, scholars, and HRD professionals are critical of the escalating costs associated with what they see as overbearing, irrational, complex, changeable, and often inconsistent laws and regulations, resulting in battle lines being drawn between "green" environmentalists (liberals) and business capitalists (conservatives). Over the past twenty or so years this conflict has escalated from name calling to large-scale demonstrations to physical destruction of property and even some intermittent physical violence. It is at the heart of the recent brutal demonstrations against the World Trade Organization's summits on globalization and global trade held in Seattle, Washington, and the meetings to ratify the Kyoto Accord held in Italy, which the United States declined to participate in.

It is beyond the scope of this chapter to lay out the complex and emotionally charged arguments on either side of the two camps of environmentalists and capitalists, nor is it my intent to argue for or against either side. However, because I believe that HRD can and should serve as a conduit, an arbitrator if you will between the two sides, it is important for HRD professionals to better understand this conflict. Environmentalism requires systems thinking, which is one of the foundations of HRD, and at least a portion of environmental compliance and implementation of environmental management systems tends to fall on the shoulders of HRD professionals. It stands to reason that we might gravitate toward a better understanding and appreciation of environmental issues within our organizations. Because environmental management, waste reduction, ecoefficiency, environmental training and education, and other related activities are so pervasive and crucial to good business strategy today, it makes sense that HRD leaders would seek such involvement.

Environmentalism is changing the nature of competition in industries that are resource intensive, energy intensive, or pollution intensive and "ecological variables are increasingly being used to establish competitive advantage" (Shrivastava, 2000, p. 25).

Examples of environmental and cultural degradation and transformation should be a wakeup call for us to act in more ethical and responsible and environmentally friendly ways. It should also serve as a catalyst for HRD and other business leaders interested in sustaining the environment, which we now know includes all business for future generations and encouraging cultural and biodiversity that we understand is required for organizational success.

Summary and Conclusions

This chapter highlighted the importance of the environment in developing sustainable work places. It addressed the importance of HRD and other business leaders understanding environmental issues and how they influence organizational performance so that research and practice can address resulting problems and opportunities. The discussions included the relationship between a focus on environmental protection and ethics and social responsibility.

Globalization, technology, development, and economics influence business and industry. Our ability to learn, change, and perform is influenced by external factors such as these. But these influences do not happen in isolation. They happen as a part of the environment. Understanding environmental issues is critical in helping to develop sustainable workplaces. Sustainability has biophysical and socioeconomic dimensions, but it also has moral dimensions. The focus of sustainability is that we are not separate from the natural environment; rather, we are a part of it and have a moral responsibility for its stewardship. The collective *we* includes individuals, cultures, groups, communities, ecosystems, organizations, business, industry, and commerce. The environment and commerce must assume a more symbiotic relationship if we are to ever create organizations that do not support economics at the expense of the environment.

The sooner that we as humans accept that we are not the center of the universe, but a single species that cannot survive without the web of life that is all around us, the better we will be able to develop work-related systems that sustain us and future generations. HRD and business leaders are just beginning to see the interrelationship and interdependency between business and natural systems and that we cannot separate them.

Chapters 6, 7, 8, and 9 introduced several issues that impact business and industry. Because issues such as globalization, technology, development, economics, and the environment influence organizations and work-related systems, they also influence HRD's goals and how it accomplishes them. The better informed HRD professionals are about how these influencers are changing work-related systems the better equipped they are to develop or adapt methods and processes to solve problems and deal with opportunities.

Human resource development as a field of practice and study is an active discipline seeking solutions to performance problems, analyzing organizations for critical learning needs, researching possible causes of skill deficiencies, and evaluating the impact of training on people and organizations. With few exceptions, HRD professionals are inquisitive and analytical by nature. The next chapter describes several activities and imperatives that, if accomplished, could add real value to our organizations, our ecosystems, and to us. These imperatives are not intended to be prescriptive. Rather, they should be used as a jumping-off point for HRD scholars and practitioners. The HRD scholar may view these initiatives as research problems or as research agendas, whereas the practitioner may see them as opportunities to add value to an organization or as problems to solve. In either case, there is a pressing need for HRD as a discipline and field of inquiry to seriously consider these and other related initiatives. A profession values and understands its ethical and social responsibilities. It is time HRD became a true profession.

10

The Imperatives of HRD

This chapter introduces several HRD-related imperatives that if implemented have the potential to greatly enhance an organization's and the profession of HRD's ethical and socially responsible behaviors and outcomes. HRD professionals should recognize that they might not "own" the imperatives. But even if not directly responsible for each imperative, there is an important role for HRD professionals to play. To the extent that we are able to effect sustainable changes in our organizations and thus positively impact society and the environment rests with our ability to not only provide ethical and responsible training and education, but also to become more involved in organizational planning, designing of strategies, and leadership.

The imperatives are divided into two main categories: theory, structure, and philosophy, and strategies, programs, and interventions. Each imperative is described along with illustrations of what HRD professionals can do to realize each one.

Theory, Structure, and Philosophy

The three imperatives that I will discuss under the heading of theory, structure, and philosophy include how to establish a climate of integrity, how to keep the organization change ready, and how to emphasize ethics in HRD.

How to Establish a Climate of Integrity

Having a values statement on the bulletin board is not enough. A climate of integrity requires building an organizational infrastructure that supports and nurtures ethical as well as rebuking unethical behaviors, and builds an ethical culture through training, orientation, and story telling; setting reasonable ethical expectations, and recognizing that punishment of negative behaviors may not result in desired ethical conduct; addressing employee privacy and confidentiality; and using systematic ethical decisionmaking processes.

Build an Ethical Infrastructure. Codes, ethics officers, ombudsmen, ethics "hot lines," EAPs (employee assistance programs), community development, and philanthropy are a few of the activities that underlie an ethical work environment. Although HRD may be restricted in its capacity to implement such activities, HRD professionals must be aware of the ethical infrastructure in order to know their potential role in its development. For example, the decision to hire an ethics officer may be made by upper management, but developing job descriptions and even hosting the position in the human resources department could intimately involve HRD in organizational ethics. Any activity that enhances an organization's ability to act in an ethical and socially responsive manner should be identified and analyzed by HRD to assess its prospective role and potential outcomes. Analysis, systems thinking, intervention design, facilitation, and evaluation skills enhance an organization's ability to create an ethical infrastructure. For example, using systems thinking, HRD professionals could identify ethical disconnects. Or during needs assessments an analyst might look for disagreements and lapses of trust between departments or company functions by seeking out information on how the bottom-line focus and "tough" leadership style in one department impacts the functioning of other departments.

Even if HRD is not directly involved in organizational ethics activities, HRD professionals can indirectly impact ethics and social responsibility by creating training, education, and organization development activities and programs around ethical objectives and outcomes. For example, developing stories about employees who have achieved superior results while modeling integrity can be used in training programs, especially new employee orientation programs that set the tone for workplace culture.

Set Ethical and Socially Responsible Expectations. Most people want to do the right thing and will if they believe such behaviors are attainable and they know what is expected of them. In training, education, and all performance evaluation processes, show how ethics results in positive outcomes for people and that those who act with integrity are recognized and rewarded. Caution should be exercised when dispensing punishment for behaviors that are less than ethical. There is little empirical evidence that punishment results in positive outcomes. Researchers have noted a number of complexities such as the kind and intensity of the punishment and the relationship between parties that affect behavioral-oriented punishment. To establish equity, HRD professionals working with personnel and line managers should compare how others are treated in similar situations before setting targets for punishment of unethical behaviors. Ensuring that the punishment meets the crime, that is, matching the severity of the punishment with the severity and consequences of the misconduct, can alleviate negative reactions.

Consistently Address Confidentiality and Privacy in an Open Environment. People feel violated when private or confidential information about them is made public. Provide required information, at the same time ensuring that personnel and related confidential data remain private. For organizations to develop cultures and work environments built on trust and honesty requires that employees are seen to have broad moral rights to be treated fairly and with respect and to have rights to privacy. This includes the expectation that personal and private data, including training and other performance-related data, will be accessible only on a limited, need-to-know basis. HRD plays an integral role in this important task by training all users on the needs for limited access and security of key company data, how to use and handle electronic databases, proper use of software and hardware, and the use of audit trails that track all transactions. Integrating codes of ethics from information and computer technology professional organizations such as the Code of Ethics of the Information Systems Security Association (ISSA), with applicable HRD or organizational codes, may help to establish a climate of integrity around employee privacy and confidentiality of data. Although employers and many HR personnel have a right to access certain employee records, the bigger issue of employee surveillance is impacting organizational integrity and ethics.

With employee surveillance on the rise, a climate of integrity is becoming harder to accomplish. Technology, e-mail, PC-cameras, and electronic surveillance devices are valuable corporate tools but the same technology is making employees more sensitive to privacy concerns. Although employers have the right to increase productivity, take precautions against theft, security breaches, access to and use of sexually oriented materials, harassment, safety hazards, and illegal activities, employees also have rights. They have the right to work in an environment of trust, integrity, respect, and dignity. Monitoring is "the modern method of exerting control and power over labor . . . [and] is intrusive and the potential for abuse exists" (Mishra and Crampton, 1998, p. 7). Recent studies have indicated somatic health risks for monitored employees. Many HRD professionals find themselves in the middle of this controversy.

Finding the right mix between what is legal, what is valuable and effective for a company, and what is right is not always easy. It would be nice if we could simply take the attitude that as long as activities like personal use of the Internet do not become a problem, then they will not be treated as such. Unfortunately, not all people are so responsible or mature. But overreacting with heavy-handed surveillance measures can backfire and end up having worse effects on people than no reaction and no monitoring at all. One possible solution is an open and as-needed policy on employee monitoring.

To be successful in addressing organizational, legal, and ethical issues, policies on employee monitoring should be based on standards of integrity, flexible, based on teams and groups rather than individuals, and widely disseminated. If employees understand that certain behaviors will not be tolerated and know the penalties for such violations they are less likely to pursue them. And if and when they do, they are more likely to accept the consequences. Being flexible means no across-the-board monitoring. Similar to common practices in random drug screening (another ethical issue), make it clear that monitoring can happen at any time and will definitely happen if standards are violated. If monitoring is based on teams and groups versus individuals there is less chance that it will impact project team morale and the spirit of community by encouraging individual goals and competition. Cultural context should also be considered. For example, in high-context cultures where teamwork is highly valued, monitoring might offend employees. Finally, the standards and policies must be made clear to all employees. More than a memo, employees need training and educating for awareness of and full comprehension of the standards of behavior as well as the specific processes concerning employee monitoring.

Following a Process Enhances Ethical Decisionmaking. Although many ethical decisionmaking procedures exist, the five-step model for ethical thought and action by Gellerman, Frankel, and Ladenson (1990) is applicable to many of the kinds of decisions HRD professionals are asked to make. The first step, problem analysis, suggests that the HRD professional ask questions about which ethics are violated and whether the violation is ethically justifiable. It also queries which values are in conflict and what priorities exist among the values. The second step involves analyzing the ethical situation (context) to clarify the facts and assumptions and formulate desired results and outcomes. The second step also includes choosing the best option, analyzing consequences, and identifying which ethics are violated and if the violation is justifiable. Step three is making the decision, step four is taking action, and step five is reflecting on the entire process. Becoming familiar with these and other ethical decisionmaking models helps HRD professionals systematically make better decisions when faced with ethical dilemmas.

How to Keep the Organization Change Ready

A change-ready organization can produce ethical behaviors through constant self-assessment and a focus on adaptability. Being adaptable requires an organization to know its strengths and weaknesses and be responsive to external stimuli. HRD adds to this responsiveness through creation of opportunities for people at all levels to understand and "buy into" the positive aspects of change. HRD can also help by stressing infrastructures that enhance responsive and ethical behaviors such as self-managed teams and cross-cultural team building, processes known to enhance the development of a change-ready organization.

Change is synonymous with and dependent on organizational culture and leadership. Existing beliefs, behaviors, and assumptions that support change need to be nurtured and developed. To accomplish a change-ready culture, HRD leaders must first understand the existing culture. An understanding of the culture provides a baseline for development of organization change programs and processes. But mere knowledge is not enough; leaders must also inspire change. Change cannot be inspired in others when leaders are themselves uninspired. Leaders need to be change ready themselves, to be accepting of change and inspire others to accept change. As O'Toole suggested, the "*sine qua non* of effective leadership is the ability to overcome resistance to change among followers" (1995, p. 158).

To work to keep a company change ready and inspire others, HRD professionals should model effective change leadership and model the behaviors of a change agent. According to Gilley, Quatro, Hoekstra, Whittle, and Maycunich (2001), a change agent should be able to influence others and discover and mobilize human energy. To be effective a change agent needs many of the same competencies required by successful HRD professionals, namely organizational knowledge, employee relations, partnership building, learning enhancement, performance management, and facilitation skills. In addition, guiding sustainable change requires heart—servantship, stewardship, value accountability, emotional empathy, and humility (Gilley, Quatro, Hoekstra, Whittle, and Maycunich, 2001). Therefore, the change agent may be more successful by assuming a transformational, servant, or ethical leadership role than one that is more transactional in nature.

How to Emphasize Ethics in HRD

To make ethics an imperative, HRD professionals should adopt and use ethical and socially responsible models, codes of ethics, ethics committees and ethics officers, and other methods and functions. They should advance the role of ethics and responsibility in HRD and identify and rebuke unethical behaviors at the same time as they enhance application of and rewards for ethical behaviors on the job.

Creating and using more sustainable HRD models that reinforce ethics and social responsibility encourage positive outcomes and organizational accountability. Models that fail to address ethical and socially responsible outcomes limit our ability to create ethical, socially responsive, and sustainable organizations. "The problem is that most applied processes and theoretical models used in HRD and PI, such as the common instructional systems development (ISD) model, do not address nor define outcomes *per se*. They are noticeably silent on the impact at both the societal [ethical] and environmental levels" (Hatcher, 2000a, pp. 18–19). Without a focus on ethical and socially responsible outcomes, we are limited in our ability to add value to our organizations or to enhance our communities or the ecosystem. Models such as the *Social Responsibility Performance Outcomes Model* of HRD (Hatcher, 2000a) illustrated in Chapter 1, expands our needs and outcomes to include community, society, and the environment beyond outcomes at the individual, process, and organizational levels.

Another way to approach the development of ethical and socially responsive outcomes is to address them in organizational and HRD planning. Kaufman identified three levels of planning: micro—concerned with the internal effects of the organization; macro—concerned with what the organization delivers to its external clients; and mega—concerned with the "collective self-sufficiency, self-reliance, and quality of life of the world in which we and our external clients live" (1990, p. 2). He suggested that during planning, organizations relate organizational means with contributions to societally useful ends and to view society as a beneficiary (Kaufman, 1997). I developed a strategic planning model useful for HRD professionals to plan for the future: recognition of the organization's and HRD's constituents and applicable social and environmental issues impacting the organization and HRD; identifying, linking, and prioritizing primary constituents with important and topical social issues; establishing HRD goals that support constituents and social issues; identifying processes, methods, and interventions to meet established goals; and evaluating the planning process (Hatcher, 1997).

HRD conceptual and planning models encourage us to look beyond a bottom-line focus and promote ethical and socially responsible outcomes. They enable us to transform cryptic and seemingly idealistic outcomes such as clean air or an ethical workplace into measurable performance goals. "This transformation allows organizational leaders to view social responsibility in terms of measurable performance and as a value-added strategy" (Hatcher, 1997, p. 27).

Strategies, Programs, and Interventions

The seventeen imperatives under strategies, programs, and interventions are:

1. How to address globalization
2. How to understand technology
3. How to increase involvement in environmentalism and employee health and safety
4. How to increase involvement in community-related health
5. How to share ethical business practices and knowledge
6. How and why to choose a cause to champion
7. How to avoid reductions in workforce
8. How to increase awareness of psychosocial contracts
9. How to encourage philanthropy and employee volunteerism
10. How to acknowledge transcendent values
11. How to develop ethical and socially responsible leaders
12. How to develop strategic plans that include ethics and social responsibility
13. How to increase ethics and social responsibility in implementing HRD
14. How to develop orientation and reorientation training that emphasizes ethics
15. How to address work-life issues
16. How to increase research on ethics and social responsibility in HRD
17. How to foster an ethical and responsible HRD profession.

How to Address Globalization

Sustain the positive and diminish the negative impact of globalization. Create a global HR presence that is equitable and adds value to international organizations by implementing a continual process of balancing country-specific social, political, and cultural needs with those of the organization. Enhance cross-cultural adaptation through more recruitment of managers and executives from different areas, acculturation through cultural awareness training, and carefully planned career opportunities (Kim, 1999).

Prepare global employees through training and education. Build and enhance cultural-specific skills such as language skills and knowledge of customs and culture. Also stress cultural empathy and adaptability in training and education programs. For many organizations, training has been restricted to rather limited orientation sessions and cultural briefings or debriefings for repatriation. Cognitive awareness and narrow understanding, although important, are not the only important attributes of successful global employees (Kim, 1999). For employees to successfully adjust and be able to perform well they must be able to apply cultural-specific skills and knowledge in increasingly complex and extensive interactions with diverse cultures. This requires integrating cross-cultural training with a deeper level of self-awareness and understanding of how one's culture impacts personal beliefs and values and thus behaviors. More experiential methods, mentoring with host-country representatives and limited and monitored cultural emergence methods, require development, administration, and evaluation by HRD professionals.

HRD professionals should also help educate and train educators in public education systems as well as administrators and policymakers in developing countries. Working to improve broad public education systems within diverse cultures helps to raise the skill and education levels of an entire workforce and creates a higher quality of available workers. It also showcases the organization as ethical and socially responsible.

Partner with local or national occupational initiatives and professional organizations. In the West, organizations like Health Occupations Students of America (HOSA) offer supporting organizations access to thousands of future industrial and health occupations workers and the opportunity for organizations to encourage skills specific to an industry. In addition, certifying agencies such as the National Vocational Qualification (NVQ) in the UK offer organizations qualified workers' meeting standards set and approved by industry in over twenty occupational areas. HRD professionals should also seek out applicable nonprofit organizations dedicated to business and industry partnerships. Organizations such as the National Alliance of Business (NAB) in the United States serve as conduits between companies and secondary and postsecondary educational programs to ensure that skills required by business and industry are addressed in occupational educational and training programs. Companies that partner with educational and training initiatives such as the NAB's corporate universities and e-learning initiatives gain knowledge of best practices and develop new HRD-related capabilities.

HRD professionals should remain aware of research, surveys, and reports that address globalization and the role of HRD. Keeping abreast of international training and education initiatives and changes, surveys and research, and other related publications and communications enable HRD professionals to make better decisions and provide up-to-date and knowledgeable information to organizational leadership. For example, *Skills for the Future: A Benchmarking Report on Workplace Training and Education in Europe and the United States,* a survey commissioned by the European Union (EU) and conducted by ASTD, found that globalization was the most fundamental force driving skill creation needs in Europe, whereas in the United States rapid technological change was cited as the most significant force shaping training needs (Wagner, 1999). Surveys provide needed information on a broad-based topic such as global training initiatives, whereas research informs HRD professionals and the field of HRD on solutions to specific problems, new concepts and theories, and serve to fill the gap between theory and practice.

In addition to surveys and reports concerning global training and applied and theoretical research, HRD professionals need to be cognizant of changes in credentials, permits, certifications, and licensures that potentially impact the global workforce. Examples include the J-1 training visa, a visa that enables U.S. employers to hire foreign trainees for up to eighteen months for hard-to-fill positions and the internationally developed Internet and Computing Core Certification (IC3) program, a vendor-independent global certification standard for computer literacy.

How to Understand Technology

HRD has an important role in encouraging and equitably applying sustainable technologies in organizations. Technology brings with it ethical issues such as the fair use of information technologies and computer and Internet access. HRD can ensure that all employees receive equal access to learning new skills or retraining of previously acquired skills when the workforce needs technological skills. Although denial of access or training may be a legal issue, there is no doubt that it is also an ethical issue that can have deleterious effects on some groups of employees. HRD professionals need to remain aware that not only does technology have instrumental value, it can also be used to undermine equality and diversity or encourage an unhealthy social hierarchy.

Investments in technology that are designed to improve communications may be underutilized or even counterproductive in cross-cultural business environments. Gundling (1999) reported that technology such as videoconferencing, although in most cases reducing meeting time and improving communication, have caused added resources to be expended for additional meetings and extra costs within certain cultural contexts. The context in which technology is used, according to Gundling (1999), is the core intercultural issue.

HRD professionals should be aware of the context in which communication technologies are used and make decisions based on contextual knowledge, such as whether cultures are low- or high-context in nature. Web-based training may be less successful in high-context cultures, where a high value is placed on face-to-face interaction, socialization, ritual, and nonverbal cues as it is in Western, low-context cultures where an e-mail is usually an acceptable substitute to an in-person meeting. Building context into training, education, and technical communications should be a high priority for HRD in international companies. Using multiple media streams, assessing people's bona fide technical competence, timing, agreement on language use or modification, facilitation, and evaluation of user performance enhances global communication and training and learning contexts.

How to Increase Involvement in Environmentalism and Employee Health and Safety

Many successful companies are using internal broad-based training and education programs to substantially change the way they do business. A good example of such large-scale training is Six Sigma. Using these training initiatives as a model, broad-based environmentally focused educational programs like Education for Sustainability (ES) are one way for HRD to improve a company's as well as a community's environmental knowledge. ES is part of a U.S. national program to support public education about the environment sponsored by the National Science and Technology Council. Companywide ES training is required to ensure that employees have sufficient knowledge of environmental issues to be able to solve organizational environmental problems.

Whether or not employers use large-scale programs such as Education for Sustainability, it is important to the overall success of corporate sustainability to address the companywide environmental education of employees. A good example of companywide environmental education is Interface, Inc. As stated in Chapter 5, Interface used its knowledge of sustainability to create a strong corporate culture that engages all employees in a continuous dialogue about the environment and the company's social responsibility. According to company founder Ray Anderson, learning to engage the workforce in its entirety is one of the reasons for Interface's success.

How to Increase Involvement in Community-Related Health

Organizations that cooperate with external partners discover benefits and in some cases even assistance in environmental and employee health and safety needs. Partnering with local community representatives, environmental leaders, environmental and social activists, and educational and other community leaders provide organizations opportunities to have dialogue with stakeholders and better understand divergent points of view. Mutually beneficial solutions can be discovered for problems such as workplace violence, employee stress and addictive behaviors, and environmental health that plague both company and community. Research suggests that companies that partner with the community are more successful than those that remain isolated (Hatcher, 2000a).

Leaders in HRD can play a significant role in providing communities with opportunities to learn from and partner with their companies. For example, successful training and education programs that are beneficial to the community or the larger society might be offered or replicated. Using the Grameen Bank example in Chapter 6, organizations can share excellent programs or knowledge with the community through nonprofits or governmental organizations such as local, regional, or state environmental or wildlife preservation groups. Another example is partnering with local schools through employee volunteers to provide expertise in environmentalism, and workplace safety and health or other technical expertise.

Sharing analysis, design, facilitation, instruction, and evaluation skills connected with companywide and highly visible initiatives such as ISO 14000 certifications with the community provides many benefits. It helps community leaders build necessary skills and build trust by placing the company and HRD in visible positions within the community. Sharing organizational and HRD competencies with the community displays professionalism and ethics, showcases the organization and HRD as value-add, and may help to alleviate any misconceptions the community may have about the company. The use of corporate and HRD-related advisory panels, boards, or committees composed of community leaders and other members are another useful way to increase community involvement.

How to Share Ethical Business Practices and Knowledge

Seek excellence in being ethical and socially responsible as vehemently as seeking excellence in manufacturing, quality, marketing, or any other organizational process or function. Become the organization and HRD function of choice for companies seeking to externally or internally baseline ethics and social responsibility.

One method to accomplish excellence in ethics and social responsibility is to establish venues to share lessons learned from successful HRD projects and specific organizational knowledge that community or societal groups need or consider beneficial. For example, a company might partner with a local community college to offer a successful ethics-training program as a noncredit course. Specific knowledge useful to the community or to society such as understanding of systems thinking or environmental management methods could be shared through presentations to professional and philanthropic organizations.

How and Why to Choose a Cause to Champion

Use human, monetary, and other organizational resources to alleviate a particular instance of human suffering or environmental degradation. Dunfee and Hess (2000) suggested that private firms in particular are in unique positions to provide significant relief to people's suffering. More than simple philanthropy, companies like Merck, an international pharmaceutical company, distributed drugs to fight river blindness in Africa. And hundreds of companies responded to the September 11, 2001, terrorists' attacks on the New York World Trade Centers and the Pentagon. Companies like Merck chose to alleviate a catastrophic condition with little foreseeable profit or return on investment—other than the return that they did something morally significant and right.

Supporting the idea of stakeholder health versus stockholder wealth, what Dunfee and Hess (2000) called direct corporate humanitarian investment is based primarily on manifest morality within economic systems. That is, justification for expenditures is based on the supposition that alleviating misery in one place tends to alleviate suffering in general and thus improves humanity and the environment in general. A healthier humanity/environment benefits all concerned in the long run. For companies with ethics and social responsibility as core competencies and values, HRD can play a leadership role in helping to analyze, design, implement, and assess direct humanitarian investment.

How to Avoid Reductions in Workforce

For companies facing the economic necessity to reduce the labor force, there are alternatives to blanket layoffs that HRD can spearhead. When companies face financial hard times and look to labor rates and salaries for costs relief, HRD can provide alternatives to harsh measures like layoffs. Innovative practices such as furloughs with partial pay, unpaid extended vacations and other time off without pay schemes, and voluntary pay cuts and reductions in salary or benefits are becoming more commonplace as companies struggle through tough but not necessarily fatal times. Companies such as Motorola, Tektronix, and Hewlett-Packard are using innovative compensation and time-off schemes to bolster sagging profits without losing employees or employee loyalties. Employers report that most employees recognize the necessity and accept the loss in pay with little overt reduction in commitment.

How to Increase Awareness of Psychological Contracts

Psychological contracts between employers and employees have the potential to harm or help a company's bottom line or enhance core competencies. Important information on employee's perceived contracts with a company can be obtained as part of companywide employee surveys, needs assessment or other front-end analyses, or more informally through conversations or in meetings. Questions regarding a psychological contract might include: What did the company promise you two years ago? What do they promise you today? What did you owe in return two years ago? What do you owe them today? Asking a variety of employees from long-term to new hires these and related questions sheds light on differences in expectations among employees.

Employees view HRD as an "authority figure," conveying commitments and making promises, what Rousseau (1995) called a contract maker. When training or education are promised, or when employees join a company because of implied opportunities to learn the newest skills, HRD is responsible for upholding the organization's end of the contract with employees. And when promises are not kept, even when circumstances seem realistic and understood by everyone concerned, not only is a social and psychological contract broken, so too is an ethical contract. When HRD makes statements in marketing brochures or training materials that they use "state-of-the-art" training processes or are "experts in instructional design," an obligation exists. If obligations are not met, employees see HRD as a contract breaker, and worse, as not living up to ethical standards.

Employees may also view HRD professionals as contract agents. Even when employees have official and visible supervisors or managers, they may continue to consider HRD professionals as agents. This is especially pertinent in organizations with a strong HRD presence and a clear focus on employee training and development. Expectations in a development-focused organization are established that require HRD to be even more cognizant of its ethical responsibilities. For example, providing new employees with realistic job previews makes job responsibilities clear and can alleviate misconceptions concerning career opportunities. Maintaining opportunities for employees to observe and identify ethical and socially responsible situations and problems through ongoing simulations and case studies builds awareness skills and acceptable behaviors. And developing performance appraisals that specify expectations regarding ethical performance, what interventions are available, and how such performance is measured provides employees with a psychological and ethical contract. By looking at HRD practices in terms of ethical contracts, we can examine the messages conveyed by various activities and functions (Rousseau, 1995).

Because culture determines much of what we know as ethics, psychological and ethical contracts in different cultures pose complex problems for HRD professionals. For example, the expectation of continuous employment tied to successful performance in Japanese society poses problems for Western organizations that might view employment through a more legalistic, "at-will" lens. The establishment of international or universal codes of ethics that include inputs from all participating cultures may help alleviate some of the complexity in meeting ethical contracts. Industry and professional organizations may be a possible source of more universal and culturally nonspecific codes of ethics.

How to Encourage Philanthropy and Employee Volunteerism

Philanthropy can serve pure self-interest or be the cornerstone of a truly socially responsible organization. Although empirical evidence relating philanthropy to increases in profits is inconclusive, there is reasonable evidence of a positive correlation between charitable activities and corporate success. Currently, many firms link philanthropy with corporate branding and marketing. HRD can play a role in encouraging the kind of philanthropy supported by employees and all stakeholders in three ways: Linking philanthropic and organizational missions and objectives, thus ensuring a good mix between the company and the recipient of charitable funds or volunteer resources; sourcing community-based or cause-based organizations through needs assessments, social auditing, and other analysis processes; and serving as a liaison between the company and the nonprofit recipient of resources. Finding the right organization to receive charitable resources is an important aspect of successful corporate philanthropy.

Employees need a choice in where corporate funds and especially their own volunteer time goes. Companies should offer options to employees to ensure equity and motivation. A nonprofit organization with environmental causes like Earthshare is an option to common nonprofits like United Way. Earthshare is the leading federation of top nonprofit environmental and conservation organizations, and prompts public education and charitable giving in workplace payroll deduction campaigns.

Organizations such as Patagonia, SAS, Inc., and Sun Microsystems support local communities and larger social causes through employee volunteers. Some companies do not limit their volunteer spirit by simply encouraging employees to volunteer their time, they offer paid leave and compensate employees for their time away from the office to help others. A few companies even go so far as to offer paid sabbaticals for selected employees to work on long-term social projects, in some cases a full year. Supporting employee volunteerism for social causes is tied to work-family issues that research has shown to be related to turnover and other productivity-starving human resource problems. Linking employee volunteerism as a component of philanthropy with a human resources variable that influences productivity and profits encourages HRD professionals to view volunteerism as a reasonable intervention for performance problems.

How to Acknowledge Transcendent Values

People are seeking more meaning in their lives and in their work. Finding fulfillment in work through a spiritual process is highly related to ethical organizations. High performance, creative, entrepreneurial, and fast-moving companies are imbued with the quality of human spirit; they are considered spirited organizations. Researchers such as Csikszentmihalyi (1990) and Whitney (1997) refer to spirit as meaning in organizations, that having purpose and intention, vision and common values create organizational meaning. Research by Mitroff and Denton (1999) found that meaning in work means realizing one's full potential as a person, being associated with a good or ethical organization, having interesting work, making money, having good colleagues, serving humankind, service to future generations, and service to community. Defining spirituality in the workplace includes an understanding of how people are interconnected to others, the cosmos, and their higher selves and how these connections are manifested at work. Research has found that organizations viewed as more spiritual get more from employees, and vice versa. But to move workers from an ethic of entitlement, from asking "What's in it for me?" to asking "What can I do to make a difference?" requires open communication at all levels, cooperation based on trust and honesty, a worker's sense of ownership in work, creativity, and innovation, and incentives for integrity. HRD professionals are in a good position to nurture if not lead organizational meaning of work and spirituality initiatives. For example, building stories related to organizational or individual spirit into orientation sessions and training helps to re-create what is meaningful to key members and to the organization.

For some people, however, spirituality has no place in the workplace. They believe that it is beyond the scope of training and the responsibility of HRD. For them, the idea of separation of church and state extends to the work site. Others believe it offers an opportunity to address the fact that people bring their whole selves (mind, body, emotion, and spirit) to their work (Chalofsky, 2000), whether organizations acknowledge it or not. Because of this divergence, some caution should be exercised when addressing the issue of spirituality; some employees may interpret it as religion. Members of alternative faiths may perceive a lack of respect, misinterpretation, or even discrimination when spirituality is discussed.

Although not applicable to all workplaces, the United States has issued guidelines for federal employees regarding religion in the workplace that can be used as a framework for spirituality. The guidelines include: respect of expression of religion in private work areas not open to the public; expression of religious views are acceptable as long as they are not harassing to other workers; using authority (supervision or management) to coerce people to change behaviors regarding religion or requiring participation is not permitted; and protection from harassment through derogatory or inflammatory remarks, unwelcome proselytization, or exclusion of employees from work activities or groups because of membership in or choosing not to participate in a religion or spirituality. HRD professionals can use guidelines such as these when encouraging spirituality and other transcendent values in the workplace.

Allowing and encouraging transcendent values in the workplace can be accomplished through HRD-related activities. Training for new employees might include stories of how people in the organization found success through a mix of skills, knowledge, and transcendent values, or establishing a forum where people can discuss questions and concerns about integrity, values, and spirit. "The absence of such a forum is the cause of the moral stress felt by people in organizations" (Hawley, 1993, p. 159). Additionally, developing and implementing management development and executive education and training around ethical and transformational leadership models helps to build a work environment where spirituality and transcendent values are encouraged.

How to Develop Ethical and Socially Responsible Leaders

Values-based and ethical leadership can be learned. Being ethical and socially responsible is typically not innate. It is based on a mix of personal values, skills, knowledge, and attitudes that can be developed through training and education. HRD professionals involved in management development and executive education programs have the responsibility and opportunity to create educational experiences for people to develop ethical behaviors and socially responsive attitudes.

Good training and educational programs start with a solid theoretical framework. Transformational and ethical leadership serve as the basis for effective leadership training and education. The tenets of transformational and ethical leadership described in Chapters 4 and 5 are a good starting point for analysts and curriculum developers. These tenets become the basis of a sound instructional curriculum or other interventions designed to build ethical leadership skills, knowledge, and attitudes.

How to Develop Strategic Plans that Include Ethics and Social Responsibility

When corporate leaders create original or revise existing strategic plans, HRD professionals can provide expertise in creating business goals and strategies with the potential to enhance ethical and socially responsive outcomes. With an increased understanding of global, economic, technological, and environmental issues, HRD professionals are in a better position to consult with top management in establishing organizational objectives that set the tone for ethics and social responsibility and decide on strategies to meet objectives. For example, a goal to increase production of a product that uses a lot of energy and labor to produce might be reconsidered when the total costs over time and life of the product to people and the environment is figured into costs and expected returns. Or the introduction of a new manufacturing process that requires employees to work in an uncomfortable environment and possibly unsafe conditions may require more detailed analyses. Along with others involved in risk assessment, HRD professionals might assess the possible risks and long-term financial costs of potential employee turnover, long- and short-term health costs, and possible negative impacts on employee motivation, job satisfaction, a healthy work environment, and corporate reputation. Reviewing existing strategic plans with a critical eye toward ethical and socially responsible implications can also impact a company's reputation and profits. Researchers have proven that companies with better reputations have better financial performance (Nakra, 2000; Saxton, 1998).

HRD professionals can help a company's reputation by generally encouraging ethical and socially responsible actions as recommended in this chapter. But more than a general encouragement, they can specifically encourage the use of or implement customer satisfaction indices, social responsibility and ethics surveys, and the use of new kinds of software capable of applying the same processes used for quality management to corporate reputation management (an example is Ki4 software, available from Entegra).

HRD professionals should serve as internal consultants reviewing each strategic objective against ethics codes or standards as well as facilitating discussions about the ethical and socially responsible implications of each objective or goal. For example, an organization had a strategic objective to increase employee satisfaction. Since the company had no ethics standards of its own, the HRD manager suggested that the strategic goal be weighed against the *AHRD Standards on Ethics and Integrity*.

How to Increase Ethics and Social Responsibility in Implementing HRD

Marketing, selection, hiring, training, rewards and incentives, pay, leadership, performance improvement, organization development, change management, evaluation, and employee education are ethics-laden activities. Potential ethical dilemmas, opportunities, or both to enhance ethical and socially responsible behaviors should be examined in each activity and in all HRD-related methods and processes. Look for opportunities for people to learn about and use ethics in their everyday work activities. Encourage analysts, curriculum developers, instructional technologists, trainers, evaluators, and other HRD professionals to be aware of and consider ethics and social responsibility as they analyze, design, develop, implement, and evaluate interventions and interact with employees at all levels.

Report social performance as part of a needs assessment. For example, instead of limiting a needs assessment to the workforce, also include the community. Using an environmental scanning technique, query the community on what it needs from the company and how HRD can address their needs. A needs assessment that is inclusive of the community and the ecosystem might uncover issues around environmental compliance that are important to both the community and the organization but were previously unidentified or considered unimportant. Also include social-ethical auditing as part of assessment and evaluation plans.

Whether doing front-end analysis or evaluating interventions or programs, social-ethical and environmental auditing techniques can add value and help a company baseline its ethics and social and environmental responsibility. Social auditing and accounting is an internal or external process that analyzes how an organization stacks up against a predetermined set of social and ethical criterion. Audits look at organizational performance with regard to commitments to workplace conditions, employment opportunities, and investments in human resources; environmental, safety, and health controls and compliance, fairness and honesty in dealings with suppliers and customers, customer service standards, community investments and charitable involvement, business practices in developing countries, and other criterion. Used in conjunction with preexisting environmental compliance measures such as ISO 14000 or OSHA and EPA regulations, social and ethics accounting as part of a needs assessment or evaluation places HRD in a good position to enhance a company's ethics and social and environmental sustainability. HRD professionals can educate themselves in social and ethical accounting through organizations such as those listed in Appendix F and organizations dedicated to environmental compliance and reporting such as the International Organization for Standardization (ISO) and the EPA.

Use process analysis models that identify how an organization's processes impact sustainability and enhance corporate learning and education programs to include ethics and social and environmental responsibility. The interface between people and processes pose unique ethical dilemmas, thus looking for potential ethical dilemmas when performing a process analysis improves overall performance. Look for opportunities to encourage ethics and social responsibility in all corporate learning and educational activities. This is especially important for large-scale quality improvement programs such as ISO certification and Six Sigma. Encouraging the ethical and socially responsible aspects of such programs enhances their viability with the workforce and increases chances for success.

Processes such as future searches (Weisbord and Janoff, 1995) and open space technology (Owen, 1992) because of their openness and focus on social transformation, are also good tools to enhance communication among varied stakeholders, including community and socioeconomic groups interested in the company.

Use of communication tools also requires that HRD professionals be aware of different communication styles. The ways different cultural groups use language is an important start. For example, some cultures use language primarily to express thoughts, feelings, and ideas as clearly and logically as possible, whereas others use language as a way to maintain social harmony. Hall (1976) identified these two cultural communications as low context and high context, respectively, with Western cultures falling somewhere toward low context.

Helping groups and individuals to communicate also requires skills in helping people and groups dialogue with one another. Dialogue is a reflective learning process. Based on the work of Bohm (1985), dialogue is based on the principle that conception and implementation are linked with a core of common meaning.

Entering into dialogue with enlightened employees, customers, and external stakeholders such as representatives of environmental groups provides an organization with the opportunity to better understand divergent viewpoints and begin to build partnerships. HRD professionals can learn from communicating with people who transcend traditional business views of the world and have broader concerns about the impact of corporations on people and the environment.

How to Develop Orientation and Reorientation Training that Emphasizes Ethics

It is appropriate and necessary for employees to give and receive commitments during their initial phases of employment. This is also the time they learn acceptable and unacceptable behaviors and observe the extent to which the organization is really serious about ethics and social responsibility. The messages that HRD professionals, trainers, and instructional designers send in orientation training set the organizational cultural stage for new employees.

Messages in training that include overt written or spoken statements like "People with integrity will be rewarded," and references to an organization's history or stories about a company's reputation for doing good, according to Rousseau, "have the potential to actively manage the meaning people ascribe to an organization's actions and expressed intentions" (1995, p. 36). Expressions of organizational policies on ethics and standards of behavior in personnel manuals or employee handbooks can serve as touchstones for employees seeking social and psychological relationships with the organization. In addition to overt statements and written policy statements, newcomers also observe how people are treated. Observed inequities or disparate treatment or even an innocent statement or action can influence a newcomer in regard to the organization's intentions toward them and organizational ethics in general. Statements made in training about the importance of ethical behaviors and how a company fixed bad behaviors in the past may be overshadowed by a newcomer's observations of trainers discussing their contempt of an upcoming union negotiation or the like. Such actions, although innocent enough, may lead to misinterpretation and significantly damage the new employee's psychological contract with the company. Explaining the purpose of the action or the statement helps to manage the meaning for new employees. The messages given in orientation training should be taken seriously; they may be more revealing than the company intends (Filipczak, Ganzel, Gordon, and Lee, 1998).

Downsizing, reengineering, or other organizational changes as well as cultural training for global assignments require ongoing reorientation of employees. Incumbent workers need reorienting to set the stage for upcoming change processes or to facilitate positive attitudes and alleviate the trauma experienced from current business changes. Thompson (1992) reported that understanding inevitable fluctuations in the business world and reorienting people to a new organizational structure help reduce resentment and loss of productivity. Like orientation training, successful reorientation requires a focus on ethics and social responsibility. If an organization's values and attitudes toward ethics and social responsiveness change, employees must be aware of these changes and understand their consequences.

How to Address Work-Life Issues

Work-family human resource activities not only enhance quality of work life for employees but also have been shown to impact organizational performance (Perry-Smith and Blum, 2000). HRD professionals play an important role in enhancing work-life programs in organizations by showing value-add through relating work-life issues with organizational strategic goals and when possible and reasonable to do so, calculating and reporting a return on investment.

Employees are looking for firms who recognize that they have lives and responsibilities outside of work, and companies are responding. Recent surveys suggest that many companies are offering a varied scope of work-family benefits such as flexible work schedules, part-time employment (known as downshifting), and job sharing; dependent-care spending accounts, childcare benefits, and on-site or near-site child care centers; elder-care programs, adoption services, and financial security assistance, including financial planning and scholarships; continuing education and training, opportunities for personal and professional growth, educational reimbursement, and career counseling. These and other work-life benefits are related to turnover, absenteeism, employee morale, recruitment, commitment and job satisfaction, and loss of productivity and downtime stemming from stress and personal business. As the workforce changes and grows more diverse, work-life benefits such as flexible work hours and time away from work for personal volunteering may prove to be a competitive advantage that HRD can help a company systematically develop, implement, and evaluate.

How to Increase Research on Ethics and Social Responsibility in HRD

More research is needed to answer questions about how HRD impacts organizational ethics and social responsibility, the extent of HRD's participation in ethics and social and environmental responsibility programs in organizations, and the extent that codes of ethics in HRD influence research and practice, to name but a few. Empirical evidence through research serves to move ethics and social responsibility in HRD out of the realm of "atheoretical good ideas" into a recognized and important research agenda for the field of HRD. Since the vast majority of publications on ethics and social responsibility in HRD in recognized research journals have been conceptual in nature, the time has come for scholars and practitioners to further their understanding by conducting and publishing empirical research. In addition to conducting research, scholars should encourage and mentor student research, dissertations, and theses on ethics, social responsibility, and related issues in HRD.

To advance the ethics and social responsibility research agenda professional organizations and associations need to emphasize ethics and social responsibility in their publications and in the research they support. HRD-related journals are encouraged to publish more ethics-related research. For example, the Academy of Human Resource Development published an issue of *Advances in Developing Human Resources,* vol. 3, no. 1, "Ethics and Integrity in HRD: Case Studies in Research and Practice" (Aragon and Hatcher, 2001).

How to Foster an Ethical and Responsible HRD Profession

The field of HRD will grow as a profession only through the growth of its professionals. To be a professional requires that we strive to act in accordance with a distinctive set of ideals and standards of conduct. Thus, to become a normative group, professionals must begin with common aspirations and values of the individual.

HRD professionals have certain responsibilities, not only to the profession and the larger community, but also to themselves. Even communitarians subscribe to the notion of a core self, that personal identity is necessary to develop social relationships. Thus, development of social networks such as a profession must be associated with a sense of self-awareness. "Self-awareness is the ability to understand one's values and beliefs and to know why one behaves in a particular manner" (Gilley, Quatro, Hoekstra, Whittle, and Maycunich, 2001, p. 13). It also helps us to know why we do things the way we do and when our values are in question. Without such self-understanding, personal integrity and thus professional ethics are difficult to maintain.

Wiley (2000) suggested that there is a relationship between personal ethical behaviors and professional codes of ethics, that a code does impact one's behavior. Thus, we must ensure that professional organizations dedicated to the profession of HRD are based on standards of ethics and integrity and encourage ethical and responsible research and practice. HRD-related codes such as the *AHRD Standards on Ethics and Integrity* typically include obligations to employers, clients, colleagues, the profession, and society. Support of HRD-related professional organizations that mirror ethical and socially responsive behaviors encourages such behaviors in the organizations that HRD professionals serve.

But having a code of ethics is not enough to ensure ethical behaviors. Since most HRD-related codes are aspirational in nature, that is, they depend on people's good intentions for compliance, it is hard to judge their success. Some professionals, such as attorneys and physicians, do not depend entirely on members' good intentions for compliance to professional codes of ethics. Instead, noncompliance may result in punitive actions that range from mild reprimand or loss of licensure to severe legal punishments. I am not suggesting that HRD immediately pursue punitive approaches to compliance with codes of ethics, yet it seems rational and valid to establish penalties for specified behaviors within a profession based on the seriousness of their consequences. Why shouldn't the profession of HRD somehow eradicate or censure unethical members?

Additionally, HRD-related professional organizations should pursue self-assessment of the ethical climate within the profession and report findings to constituents and the HRD community at large. Ethical reporting is important to disclose information to constituents and the general public on what the profession of HRD has done and is doing in regard to ethics, environmentalism, and social responsibility. Additionally, through conferences, committee participation, and networking, professional associations such as the Academy of Human Resource Development (AHRD), the American Society for Training and Development (ASTD), the International Society for Performance Improvement (ISPI), International Personnel Management Association (IPMA), Institute of Personnel and Development (IPD) (UK), International Federation of Training and Development Organizations (IFTDO), Asian Region Training and Development Organizations (ARTDO), and the Society for Human Resource Management (SHRM) can serve as learning and socializing agents especially for newcomers to the field of HRD. In addition to professional organizations, educational institutions developing HRD professionals can promote ethics by including ethics as part of the HRD curriculum using ethics standards and case studies such as the *Advances in Developing Human Resources* by Aragon and Hatcher (2001) and *Values and Ethics in Organization and Human Systems Development: Responding to Dilemmas in Professional Life* by Gellerman, Frankel, and Ladenson (1990).

Summary and Conclusions

This concluding chapter offered imperatives that have the potential to place HRD in the forefront of building ethical and socially responsible organizations. Imperatives included establishing a climate of integrity, keeping an organization ready for change, and making ethics an imperative in HRD. These three requirements set the philosophical stage for the next seventeen imperatives; strategies, programs, and interventions that if accomplished can move HRD into a position of leadership in organizational ethics and social responsibility. Each of the imperatives was described and HRD-specific examples for each imperative was given.

For human resource development to become the conscience of an organization requires the kinds of knowledge, skills, attitudes, actions, and commitments illustrated by these imperatives. Because many if not most of these and other similar imperatives require education and training, it is important that HRD continues to do what it does well—provide high quality training and education to people in organizations.

In this book an agenda was developed for ethics and social responsibility as a primary focus for HRD research and practice. Several arguments for and a few against ethics and socially responsible organizations were developed and offered as well as the development of a rationale for why HRD should take a leadership role in ethics and social responsibility and in many ways be the conscience of our organizations. Because the driving forces are external to organizations and basically beyond our immediate control, it was important to better understand them, to isolate their negative and foster their positive influences. Thus globalization, technology, economics, environmentalism, leadership, and other important issues were discussed in enough detail so that we can better understand their influence on both organizations and the profession of HRD.

The agenda also included lessons on values, ethics, social responsibility, human rights, and what HRD can do to positively impact our organizations. Mastering these lessons better prepares us for a future that can sustain responsible organizations, a healthy environment, and HRD professionals.

Some of the general tone of this new agenda will no doubt be criticized. The environmental destruction examples alone are enough to cause bad dreams. But the tone was not all gloom and doom. Many of the examples were optimistic, suggesting a positive future. Somewhere in the middle common ground is a place where our organizations and the profession of HRD possess a deep-seated and unshakable commitment to values and ethics and to creating nurturing and responsible workplaces that are still economically viable. But as Robert Frost said, ". . . I have promises to keep, and miles to go before I sleep." We have many promises to keep and our journey has just started.

The agenda sets the stage for HRD as a profession to rise to its potential, to refocus its attention and efforts and direct the behaviors of its professionals toward higher and more transcendent goals and objectives. Today's consumer-driven, fast-paced, bottom-line world, with its superpowerful organizations and global economics, requires that we make fundamental changes to ourselves and our professions and take care not to repeat the mistakes of the past. The examples used in the agenda provide hope. There are more people like Ray Anderson trying to build companies like Interface, Inc. than we might think. Tremendous efforts are being placed on creating better places to work and a better world in which we can all live. These changes are not all technical or structural; they are not limited to changing an organizational chart, creating a teamed environment, using instructional technologies, or doing different kinds of research. Real, sustainable change requires more, it requires a profound transformation of our intellect and our psyches.

Some people will scoff at this new agenda and others will fight hard to maintain the status quo. But the true change agent does not collapse under status quo demands nor allow "society's fetters" (Hawley, 1993, p. 180). The inner truth, our transcendental values, impel action—even against pressures to remain the same. It is true; HRD does do well for many organizations. We develop training and education, analyze processes, provide solutions to performance problems, and help develop leaders. And we must continue to do so. But the outcomes, the end game of our efforts, must be broadened. Our view of the world must be enhanced so that we truly grasp what an important role we have in creating a future that is better than the present. The only way to do this is through a real and dedicated commitment to ethics and social responsibility.

from Frost's "The Road Not Taken," seems appropriate

I shall be telling this with a sigh
Somewhere ages and ages hence:
Two roads diverged in a wood, and I—
I took the one less traveled by,
And that has made all the difference.

The road our organizations, our profession, and human resource professionals now take will make all the difference. Peace.

Tim Hatcher
February, 2002

Appendix A:
Academy of Human Resource Development Standards on Ethics and Integrity

Contents

For a pdf copy of the AHRD Standards on Ethics and Integrity go to www.AHRD.org.

Appendix B:
A Summary of the Universal
Declaration of Human Rights

A Summary of the Universal Declaration of Human Rights

PREAMBLE
Recognition of the inherent dignity and of the equal and inalienable rights of all members of the human family is the foundation of freedom, justice and peace.

Rebellion against tyranny and oppression; human rights should be protected by the rule of law.

Reaffirm faith in fundamental human rights, the dignity and worth of the human person and the equal rights of men and women; to promote social progress and better standards of life in larger freedom.

THE GENERAL ASSEMBLY proclaims THIS UNIVERSAL DECLARATION OF HUMAN RIGHTS; it shall strive by teaching and education to promote respect for these rights and freedoms and by progressive measures, national and international, to secure their universal and effective recognition and observance.

There are 30 Articles that cover many human rights issues. A summary of a few Articles as examples follows:

Article 1.
All human beings are born free and equal in dignity and rights. They are endowed with reason and conscience and should act towards one another in a spirit of brotherhood.

Article 3.
Everyone has the right to life, liberty and security of person.

Article 4.
No one shall be held in slavery or servitude; slavery and the slave trade shall be prohibited in all their forms.

Article 11.
(1) Everyone charged with a penal offence has the right to be presumed innocent until proved guilty according to law in a public trial at which he has had all the guarantees necessary for his defense.

Article 12.
No one shall be subjected to arbitrary interference with his privacy, family, home or correspondence, nor to attacks upon his honor and reputation. Everyone has the right to the protection of the law against such interference or attacks.

Article 15.
(1) Everyone has the right to a nationality.

Article 17.
(1) Everyone has the right to own property alone as well as in association with others.

Article 18.
Everyone has the right to freedom of thought, conscience and religion; this right includes freedom to change his religion or belief, and freedom, either alone or in community with others and in public or private, to manifest his religion or belief in teaching, practice, worship and observance.

Article 19.
Everyone has the right to freedom of opinion and expression; this right includes freedom to hold opinions without interference and to seek, receive and impart information and ideas through any media and regardless of frontiers.

Article 23.
(1) Everyone has the right to work, to free choice of employment, to just and favorable conditions of work and to protection against unemployment.
(2) Everyone, without any discrimination, has the right to equal pay for equal work.
(3) Everyone who works has the right to just and favorable remuneration ensuring for himself and his family an existence worthy of human dignity, and supplemented, if necessary, by other means of social protection.
(4) Everyone has the right to form and to join trade unions for the protection of his interests.

Article 25.
(1) Everyone has the right to a standard of living adequate for the health and well-being of himself and of his family, including food, clothing, housing and medical care and necessary social services, and the right to security in the event of unemployment, sickness, disability, widowhood, old age or other lack of livelihood in circumstances beyond his control.
(2) Motherhood and childhood are entitled to special care and assistance. All children, whether born in or out of wedlock, shall enjoy the same social protection.

Article 26.
(1) Everyone has the right to education. Education shall be free, at least in the elementary and fundamental stages. Elementary education shall be compulsory. Technical and professional education shall be made generally available and higher education shall be equally accessible to all on the basis of merit.
(2) Education shall be directed to the full development of the human personality and to the strengthening of respect for human rights and fundamental freedoms. It shall promote understanding, tolerance and friendship among all nations, racial or religious groups, and shall further the activities of the United Nations for the maintenance of peace.

Appendix C:
The Amnesty International
Human Rights Principles
for Companies

Human Rights Principles for Companies:

An Introductory Checklist

1. Company policy on human rights.
All companies should adopt an explicit company policy on human rights which includes public support for the Universal Declaration of Human Rights. Companies should establish procedures to ensure that all operations are examined for their potential impact on human rights, and safeguards to ensure that company staff is never complicit in human rights abuses. The company policy should enable discussion with the authorities at local, provincial and national levels of specific cases of human rights violations and the need for safeguards to protect human rights. It should enable the establishment of programs for the effective human rights education and training of all employees within the company and encourage collective action in business associations to promote respect for international human rights standards.

2. Security.
All companies should ensure that any security arrangements protect human rights and are consistent with international standards for law enforcement. Any security personnel employed or contracted should be adequately trained. Procedures should be consistent with the United Nations (UN) Basic Principles on the Use of Force and Firearms by Law Enforcement Officials and the UN Code of Conduct for Law Enforcement Officials. They should include measures to prevent excessive force, as well as torture or cruel, inhuman or degrading treatment. Companies should develop clear rules for calling in or contracting with state security forces and for not hiring security personnel who have been responsible for serious human rights violations. Any complaint about security procedures or personnel should be promptly and independently investigated. Companies which supply military security or police products or services should take stringent steps to prevent those products and services from being misused to commit human rights violations.

3. Community engagement.
All companies should take reasonable steps to ensure that their operations do not have a negative impact on the enjoyment of human rights by the communities' in which they operate. This should include a willingness to meet with community leaders and voluntary organizations to discuss the role of the company within the broader community. Companies should work cooperatively with organizations, which promote human rights.

4. Freedom from discrimination.
All companies should ensure that their policies and practices prevent discrimination based on ethnic origin, sex, color, language, national or social origin, economic status, religion, political or other conscientiously held beliefs, birth or other status. This should include recruitment, promotion, and remuneration, working conditions, customer relations and the practices of contractors, suppliers and partners. It should include measures to deal with sexual or racial harassment, and to prohibit national, racial or religious hatred.

5. Freedom from slavery.
All companies should ensure that their policies and practices prohibit the use of chattel slaves, forced labor, bonded child laborers or coerced prison labor. This should include ensuring that suppliers, partners or contractors do not use such labour.

6. Health and safety.
All companies should ensure that their policies and practices provide for safe and healthy working conditions and products. The company should not engage in or support the use of corporal punishment, mental or physical coercion, or verbal abuse.

7. Freedom of association and the right to collective bargaining.
All companies should ensure that all employees are able to exercise their rights to freedom of expression, peaceful assembly and association, as well as a fair means of collective bargaining without discrimination, including the right to form trade unions and to strike. Companies have a responsibility to ensure such rights for their employees even if such rights are not protected in a particular country's national law. Companies should take steps to ensure that suppliers, partners or contractors do not infringe such rights.

8. Fair working conditions.
All companies should ensure just and favorable conditions of work, reasonable job security and fair and adequate remuneration and benefits. This should include provision for an adequate standard of living for employees and their families. Companies should take steps to ensure that suppliers, partners or contractors do not infringe such rights.

9. Child Labor.
Companies shall not engage in or support the use of child labor as defined by applicable national laws and relevant international standards.

10. Monitoring human rights.
All companies should establish mechanisms to monitor effectively all their operations' compliance with codes of conduct and international human rights standards. Such mechanisms must be credible and all reports must periodically be independently verifiable in a similar way to the auditing of accounts or the quality of products and services. Other stakeholders such as members of local communities in which the company operates and voluntary organizations should have an opportunity to contribute in order to ensure transparency and credibility.

Appendix D:
Environmental Regulations, Programs, and Organizations

The following is a partial listing of common standards, laws, and regulations concerning the environment and environmental safety and health primarily applicable in the U.S. Environmental regulations are followed by guidelines and voluntary programs concerning the environment and environmental safety and health. The third and final section lists organizations that offer assistance, consulting and/or develop and maintain standards pertaining to the environment and environmental safety and health.

Environmental Regulations	
United States Code of Federal Regulations Title 40 (CFR40), Protection of Environment. *The primary U.S. federal law establishing environmental protection.*	The Superfund Amendments and Reauthorization Act (SARA); 42 U.S.C. 9601 (1986) *Amended and strengthened the original Superfund Act through new enforcement standards, focus on human health problems and greater citizen participation.*
Occupational Safety and Health Act (OSHA); 29 U.S.C. 651 (1970) *Regulations to insure employers provide their workers a place of employment free from recognized hazards to safety and health, such as exposure to toxic chemicals, excessive noise levels, or unsanitary conditions.*	Pollution Prevention Act (PPA); 42 U.S.C. 13101 (1990) *Reducing the overall amount of pollution through cost-effective changes in production, operation, and raw materials use.*
Freedom of Information Act (FOIA); U.S.C. 552 (1966) *Provisions for "any person" to make requests for government information.*	Oil Pollution Act 1990 (OPA); 33 U.S.C. 2702 (1990) *Controlling and responding to catastrophic oil spills.*
National Environmental Policy Act of 1969 (NEPA); 42 U.S.C. 4321-4347. *National charter that establishes national policy for protection of the environment.*	Toxic Substances Control Act (TSCA); 15 U.S.C. 2601 (1976). *Labeling requirements for toxic compounds.*
Clean Air Act and Clean Water Acts; 42 U.S.C. 7401 and 33 U.S.C. 1251 (1970 & 1977) *Regulates air and water emissions and sets goals for problem areas such as acid rain and toxic substances.*	Emergency Planning & Community Right to Know Act (EPCRA); 42 U.S.C. 11011 (1986) *Help for communities to protect public health, safety, and the environment from chemical hazards.*
Safe Drinking Water Act (SDWA); 42 U.S.C. 300f (1974) *Protect the quality of drinking water.*	Federal Food, Drug, and Cosmetic Act (FFDCA); 21 U.S.C. 301 *Protection for food and cosmetics.*
Resource Conservation and Recovery Act (RCRA); 42 U.S.C. 321 (1976) *Law to control hazardous wastes from "cradle-to-grave" including the generation, transportation, storage, and disposal of hazardous wastes.*	Endangered Species Act (ESA) 7 U.S.C. 136: 16 U.S.C. 460 (1973) *Conservation of threatened and endangered plants and animals and their habitats. Includes maintenance of the endangered species list.*

Comprehensive Environmental Response, Compensation, and Liability Act (CERCLA or <u>Superfund</u>); 42 U.S.C. 9601 (1980) *Clean up of abandoned or closed hazardous waste sites.*	Federal Insecticide, Fungicide and Rodenticide Act (FIFRA); 7 U.S.C. 135 (1972) *Federal control of pesticide distribution, sale, and use.*
EEC Treaty (1972) and Articles *European Community environmental protection law.*	Single European Act (1987): *EEC treaty for environmental protection* Treaty of Maastricht (1993): *Established equal footing for EU* Treaty of Amsterdam (1999): *Integration of environmental protection in Community policies* Treaty of Nice (2000-present): *Maintained status quo.*

Environmental Programs

EPA: Design for Environment (DfE): *Helping businesses incorporate environmental considerations into the design and redesign of products, processes, and technical and management systems.*	EPA: Environmental Management Systems (EMS): *Help businesses on environmental management and strategies to move beyond compliance.*
Coalition for Environmentally Responsible Economies (CERES): *Corporate environmental guidelines and reporting requirements.*	Consortium on Green Design and Manufacturing (CGDM): *Research and information on environmental design, management, and manufacturing.*
Natural Step *Environmental education organization with useful tools.*	Balanced Scorecard *Provides information on alignment of environmental and strategic initiatives.*

Environmental Organizations

U.S. Environmental Protection Agency (EPA) *The primary organization with responsibility for environmental protection.*	International Organization for Standardization (ISO): *Develops and regulates international quality and environmental management systems through ISO 9000 and 140000 guidelines.*
U.S. Occupational Safety & Health Administration (OSHA) *The primary organization with responsibility for workplace safety and health.*	International Council for Local Environmental Initiatives (ICLEI): *Local governments dedicated to prevention of local, regional, and global environmental problems through local actions.*
International Water Association: *U.K. based organization focused on water quality needs of the international community.*	World Resources Institute (WRI): *Research on solutions to global environmental problems and issues within industry.*

International Institute for Sustainable Development (IISD): *Applied sustainability information and collaborative projects.*	World Business Council for Sustainable Development (WBCSD): *Coalition of over 140 international companies committed to sustainable development and environmental protection.*
United Nations Conference on Trade and Development (UNCTAD): *Trade, environment, and development section of the United Nations.*	United Nations Environment Program (UNEP) *Work on international trade and environment issues.*
World Trade Organization (WTO) *Committees, programs and symposia on global trade and environmental issues.*	Organization for Economic Cooperation and Development (OECD) *Member of the* International Environment Network *providing information and guidance on international and European Union environmental laws and regulations.*
Rocky Mountain Institute *Amory Lovins' organization dedicated to sustainable development of communities and organizations.*	The Business Enterprise Trust *Promotes business social and environmental responsibility.*
Business for Social Responsibility (BSR) *International organization for socially and environmentally friendly businesses.*	Social Venture Network (SVN) *Network of business leaders dedicated to sustainability.*
Greenpeace International *International organization dedicated to protection of the environment and endangered species.*	Council on Economic Priorities (CEP) *Evaluates and rates corporate social responsibility and environmental performance of companies.*
Prince of Wales Business Leaders' Forum *Promotion of sustainable development as a natural part of UK business operations.*	World Resources Institute *Policy research and technical assistance on global environmental issues.*

Appendix E:
Descriptions of
ISO 14000 and SA 8000

ISO 14000 – International Organization for Standardizations (ISO) Environmental Management Systems (EMS)

ISO 14000 is a series of international standards and certification for incorporating environmental aspects into operations and product standards. Similar to the well known ISO 9000 Quality Management System and certifications, ISO 14001 requires audit, documentation, implementation, monitoring and evaluation of an environmental management system (EMS) in accordance with defined internationally recognized standards.

ISO's home page is www.iso.ch/iso/en/isoonline

SA 8000 – Social Accountability 8000

Social Accountability 8000 is a set of standards and a certification process created in 1997 by Social Accountability International, founded as the Council on Economic Priorities Accreditation Agency. The standard, modeled after the ISO 9000 quality management systems standard, was developed in response to the growing concern about labor conditions around the word. Based on international conventions of the International Labor Organization (ILO) and related human rights documents, including the United Nations Universal Declaration of Human Rights and UN Rights of the Child, SA8000 is a consensus standard specifying minimum requirements in nine core areas that in many organizations fall under the rubric of human resources: Child Labor, Forced labor, Health and Safety, Freedom of association and right to collective bargaining, Discrimination, Disciplinary practices, Working hours, Compensation, and Management Systems. The focus of SA 8000 is on management systems and documentation proving system effectiveness and continuous improvement. SA8000's acceptance is growing because companies recognize the benefits of the system to workers, management and the bottom line. The standard seeks to professionalize corporate social responsibility and recognize companies that are good citizens. SA8000 homepage is www.cepaa.org

Appendix F:
Social and Ethical Reporting and Consulting Organizations

Social and ethical reporting and consulting organizations	
AccountAbility	The site of the Institute of Social and Ethical Accountability. Promotes audits, best practices and development of standards for social and environmental reporting.
Business for Social Responsibility	BSR is a membership organization offering assistance and consulting to companies seeking to improve their social and ethical accountability.
Corporate Watch	Corporate Watch reports on social and environmental impact of globalization.
Council on Economic Priorities	Research organization dedicated to analysis of the social and environmental records of corporations.
The Caux Round Table	Business leaders providing social responsibility principles and standards for businesses.
The Conference Board	The Conference Board provides research and information dissemination on ethics and business practice issues.
Council for Ethics in Economics	Custom consulting, case studies and educational programs.
EthicsScan	Canada-based research and consultancy organization monitoring environmental and social performance of 1500 Canadian companies.
Fairtrade Foundation	Help for third world producers to receive a fair share of their trade. Administers the Fairtrade Mark.
International Society of Business, Economics and Ethics	Information, conferences, and consultations to international business.
Ethics Officer Association	Ethics Officer Association is a U.S. based professional organization for leaders of corporate ethics and compliance programs. Conducts research, conferences, and professional development programs.
Ethics Resource Center	Builds coalitions, conducts research and education and performs consulting and technical assistance.

(*continues*)

(continued)

European Business Ethics Network	Conferences, publications and discussion lists for EU businesses.
Institute for Global Ethics	IGE provides assessments, training and other consulting services.
PricewaterhouseCoopers PwC Reputation Assurance	Strategic consulting services to help companies manage reputation through measurement and reporting.
Social Venture Network	Consulting and standards development for corporate social responsibility.
World Business Council for Sustainable Development	WBCSD is development and administration of the Charter for Sustainable Development outlining principles for social responsibility for international businesses.

References

Akaah, I. "The Influence of Organizational Rank and Role on Marketing Professionals' Ethical Judgments." *Journal of Business Ethics* 15 (1996): 605–613.

Albinger, H. S., and S. J. Freeman. "Corporate Social Performance and Attractiveness as an Employer to Different Job Seeking Populations." *Journal of Business Ethics* 28 (2000): 243–253.

Allen, J., and D. Davis. "Assessing Some Determinant Effects of Ethical Consulting Behavior: The Case of Personal and Professional Values." *Journal of Business Ethics* 12 (1993): 449–458.

Anderson, L. M., and T. S. Bateman. "Individual Environmental Initiative: Championing Natural Environmental Issues in U.S. Business Organizations." *Academy of Management Journal* 43 (2000): 548–570.

Anderson, R. *Mid-Course Correction: Toward a Sustainable Enterprise, the Interface Model.* White River Junction, VT.: Chealsea Green Publishing, 1998.

Anderson, S., and J. Cavanagh. *Top 200: The Rise of Corporate Global Power.* Washington, D.C.: Institute for Policy Studies, 2000.

Apple, M. W. "Between Neoliberalism and Neoconservatism: Education and Conservatism in a Global Context." In *Globalization and Education: Critical Perspectives,* ed. N. C. Burbules and C. A. Torres, pp. 57–78. New York: Routledge, 2000.

Aragon, S., and T. G. Hatcher (Eds.) "Ethics and Integrity in HRD: Case Studies in Research and Practice." *Advances in Developing Human Resources* 3, no. 1 (2001).

Bansal, P., and K. Roth. "Why Companies Go Green: A Model of Ecological Responsiveness." *Academy of Management Journal* 43 (2000): 717–736.

Barker, R. A. "How Can We Train Leaders If We Do Not Know What Leadership Is?" *Human Relations* 50 (1997): 343–362.

Bass, B. M. *Leadership and Performance Beyond Expectations.* New York: Free Press, 1985.

Bass, B. M., and B. J. Avolio. "Transformational Leadership and Organizational Culture. *Public Administration Quarterly* 17 (1993): 112–122.

Bates, R., H. C. Chen, and T. Hatcher. "Value Priorities of HRD Scholars, Practitioners, and Students." Unpublished manuscript, 2002.

Bates, R., T. Hatcher, E. Holton, and N. Chalofsky. "Redefining Human Resource Development: An Integration of the Learning, Performance, and Spirituality of Work Perspectives." Proceedings of the Academy of Human Resource Development Annual Research Conference. Tulsa, Okla., February 28–March 4, 2001.

Beck, D., and C. Cowan. *Spiral Dynamics: Mastering Values, Leadership, and Change.* Cambridge, Mass.: Blackwell, 1995.

Beliveau, B., M. Cotrill, and H. M. O'Neill. "Predicting Corporate Social Responsiveness: A Model Drawn from Three Perspectives." *Journal of Business Ethics* 13 (1994): 731–738.

Berry, T. "The Viable Human." In *Deep Ecology for the Twenty-First Century,* ed. G. Sessions, pp. 8–18. Boston: Shambhala, 1995.

Blank, W., J. R. Weitzel, and S. G. Green. "A Test of the Situational Leadership Theory." *Personnel Psychology* 43 (1990): 579–598.

Bloom, B., et al. "Taxonomy of Educational Objectives." Handbook I: Cognitive Domain. New York: McKay, 1956.

Blumenstyk, G. "Conflict of Interest Fears Rise as Universities Chase Industry Support." *Chronicle of Higher Education* 44 (1998): A41–A44.

Bohm, D. *Unfolding Meaning.* Loveland, Colo.: Foundation House, 1985.

Bowen, H. R. *Social Responsibilities of the Businessman.* New York: Harper and Row, 1953.

Briskin, A. *The Stirring of Soul in the Workplace.* San Francisco: Berrett-Koehler, 1998.

Brown, R. T. "Behavioral Teratology/Toxicology: How Do We Know What We Know?" *Archives of Clinical Neuropsychology* 16 (2000): 389–402.

Brown, W. S. "Ontological Security, Existential Anxiety and Workplace Privacy." *Journal of Business Ethics* 23 (2000): 61–65.

Burbules, N. C., and C. A. Torres, eds. *Globalization and Education: Critical Perspectives.* New York: Routledge, 2000.

Burk, M. "Ideology and Morality in Economic Theory." In *Ethics and Economic Affairs,* ed. A. Lewis and K. E. Wärneryd, pp. 313–334. London: Routledge, 1994.

Burns, J. M. *Leadership.* New York: HarperCollins, 1978.

_____. *Leadership and Performance Beyond Expectations.* New York: Free Press, 1985.

Burns, J. Z., and F. L. Otte. "Implications of Leader-Member Exchange Theory and Research for Human Resource Development Research." *Human Resource Development Quarterly* 10 (1999): 225–238.

Capra, F. *The Web of Life: A New Scientific Understanding of Living Systems.* New York: Anchor Books, 1996.

Carroll, A. B. "A Three-Dimensional Conceptual Model of Corporate Social Performance." *Academy of Management Review* 4 (1979): 497–505.

_____. "Social Issues in Management Research: Experts' Views, Analysis, and Commentary." *Business and Society* 33 (1994): 36–56.

_____. "Corporate Social Responsibility." *Business and Society* 38 (1999): 268–295.

_____. "Ethical Challenges for Business in the New Millennium: Corporate Social Responsibility and Models of Management Morality." *Business Ethics Quarterly* 10 (2000): 33–42.

Center for Business Ethics. "Instilling Ethical Values in Large Organizations." *Journal of Business Ethics* 11 (1992): 863–867.

Chalofsky, N. "The Meaning of the Meaning of Work: A Literature Review Analysis." In *Academy of Human Resource Development 2000 Conference Proceedings,* ed. K. P. Kuchinke, pp. 94–100. Baton Rouge, La.: Academy of Human Resource Development, 2000.

Chalofsky, N., and C. Lincoln. *Up the HRD Ladder: A Guide for Professional Growth.* Cambridge, Mass.: Perseus Books, 1983.

Ciulla, J. B., ed. *Ethics, the Heart of Leadership.* Westport, Conn.: Quorum Books, 1998.

Clarkson, M. B. "A Stakeholder Framework for Analyzing and Evaluating Corporate Social Performance." *Academy of Management Review 20* (1995): 92–117.

Cobb, C., T. Halstead, and J. Rowe. "If the GDP Is Up, Why Is America Down? [Electronic version] *Atlantic Monthly* 10 (1995): 1–27.

Cochran, P. L., and R. A. Wood. "Corporate Social Responsibility and Financial Performance." *Academy of Management Journal 27* (1984): 42–56.

Cole, D., M. J. Sirgy, and M. M. Bird. "How Do Managers Make Teleological Evaluations in Ethical Dilemmas?" *Journal of Business Ethics 26* (2000): 259–269.

Collins, D. "The Quest to Improve the Human Condition: The First 1,500 Articles Published in the Journal of Business Ethics." *Journal of Business Ethics* 26, no. 1 (2000): 1–73.

Conger, J. A., and R. N. Kanungo, eds. *Charismatic Leadership: The Elusive Factor in Organizational Effectiveness.* San Francisco: Jossey-Bass, 1988.

Costanza, R., ed. *Ecological Economics: The Science and Management of Sustainability.* New York: Columbia University Press, 1991.

Csikszentmihalyi, M. *Flow: The Psychology of Optimal Experience.* New York: Harper-Perennial, 1990.

Curtis, J. "Body Shop Plans to Scale Down Its Political Activity." *Marketing* (July 26, 2001): 3.

Dalla Costa, J. *The Ethical Imperative: Why Moral Leadership Is Good Business.* Reading, Mass.: Perseus Books, 1998.

Daly, H. E. *Steady-State Economics.* San Francisco: Freeman, 1977.

_____. *Steady-State Economics,* 2d ed. Washington, D.C.: Island Press, 1991.

Dean, P. J. "A Selected Review of the Underpinnings of Ethics for Human Performance Technology Professionals—Part One: Key Ethical Theories and Research." *Performance Improvement Quarterly* 6, no. 4 (1993): 3–32.

Dechant, K., and B. Altman. "Environmental Leadership: From Compliance to Competitive Advantage." *Academy of Management Executive* 8 (1994): 7–28.

Delaney, J. T., and D. Stockell. "Do Company Ethics Training Programs Make a Difference? An Empirical Analysis." *Journal of Business Ethics* 11 (1992): 719–727.

Des Jardins, J. R. *Environmental Ethics: An Introduction to Environmental Philosophy.* Belmont, Calif.: Wadsworth Publishing, 1993.

Dess, G. G., J. C. Picken, and D. W. Lyon "Transformational Leadership: Lessons from U.S. Experience." *Long Range Planning* 31 (1998): 722–731.

Devall, B., and G. Sessions. *Deep Ecology: Living As If Nature Mattered*. Layton, Utah: Peregrine Smith Books, 1985.

Donaldson, L. *American Anti-Management Theories of Organization*. Cambridge, England: Cambridge University Press, 1995.

Donaldson, T. *Corporations and Morality*. Englewood Cliffs, N.J.: Prentice-Hall, 1982.

_____. "Making Stakeholder Theory Whole." *Academy of Management Review* 24 (1999): 237–241.

Donaldson, T., and L. Preston. "The Stakeholder Theory of the Corporation: Concepts, Evidence, and Implications." *Academy of Management Review* 20 (1995): 65–91.

Donaldson, T., and P. H. Werhane. *Ethical Issues in Business: A Philosophical Approach* 3d ed. Englewood Cliffs, N.J.: Prentice-Hall, 1988.

Douglas, J. D. *Freedom and Tyranny: Social Problems in a Technological Society*. New York: Alfred A. Knopf, 1970.

Driscoll, D. M., and W. M. Hoffman. "HR Plays a Central Role in Ethics Programs." *Workforce* 77 (1998): 121–123.

Drucker, P. F. *The Practice of Management*. London: Pan Books, 1968.

_____. *Post-Capitalist Society*. New York: HarperCollins, 1993.

Druskat, V. "Gender and Leadership Style: Transformational and Transactional Leadership in the Roman Catholic Church." *Leadership Quarterly* 5 (1994): 99–119.

Dunfee, T. W., and D. Hess. "The Legitimacy of Direct Corporate Humanitarian Investment." *Business Ethics Quarterly* 10 (2000): 95–110.

Egri, C. P., and S. Herman. "Leadership in the North American Environmental Sector: Values, Leadership Styles, and Contexts of Environmental Leaders and Their Organizations." *Academy of Management Journal* 43 (2000): 571–604.

Elkington, J. *Cannibals with Forks: The Triple Bottom Line of 21st Century Business*. North Kingston, Great Britain: New Society Publishers, 1998.

Ellul, J. *The Technological Society*. New York: Alfred A. Knopf, 1964.

Engardio, P., and R. Miller. "What's at Stake: How Terrorism Threatens the Global Economy." *Business Week* (October 22, 2001): 34–37.

Estes, R. *Tyranny of the Bottom Line: Why Corporations Make Good People Do Bad Things*. San Francisco: Berrett-Koehler, 1996.

Ethics Resource Center. *National Business Ethics Survey 2000*. Washington, D.C.: Ethics Resource Center, 2000.

Fiedler, F. E. *A Theory of Leadership Effectiveness*. New York: McGraw-Hill, 1967.

Fieser, J. "Do Businesses Have Moral Obligations Beyond What the Law Requires?" *Journal of Business Ethics* 15 (1996): 457–468.

Filipczak, B., R. Ganzel, J. Gordon, and C. Lee. "Your New Cubicle in Hades, Inc." *Training* 35 (1998): 12–13.

Fombrun, C., and M. Shanley. "What's in a Name? Reputation Building and Corporate Strategy." *Academy of Management Journal* 33 (1990): 233–258.

Fox, M. *The Reinvention of Work: A New Vision of Livelihood for our Time*. San Francisco: HarperSanFrancisco, 1994.

Frederick, W. C. "The Growing Concern Over Business Responsibility." *California Management Review* 2 (1960): 54–61.

_____. "Moving to CSR4: What to Pack for the Trip." *Business and Society* 37 (1998): 40–59.

Freeman, R. E. *Strategic Management: A Stakeholder Approach.* Boston: Pitman, 1984.

Friedman, T. L. *The Lexus and the Olive Tree.* New York: Anchor Books, 2000.

Gaudine, A., and L. Thorne. "Emotion and Ethical Decision-Making in Organizations." *Journal of Business Ethics* 31 (2001): 175–187.

Gellerman, W., M. S. Frankel, and R. F. Ladenson. *Values and Ethics in Organization and Human Systems Development: Responding to Dilemmas in Professional Life.* San Francisco: Jossey-Bass, 1990.

Gilley, J. W., S. A. Quatro, E. Hoekstra, D. D. Whittle, and A. Maycunich. *The Manager as Change Agent.* Cambridge, Mass.: Perseus Publishing, 2001.

Goldsmith, E. "Global Trade and the Environment." In *The Case Against the Global Economy: And a Turn Toward the Local,* ed. J. Mander and E. Goldsmith, pp. 78–91. San Francisco: Sierra Club Books, 1996.

Goodson, J. R., G. W. McGee, and J. F. Cashman. "Situational Leadership Theory: A Test of Leadership Prescriptions." *Group and Organizational Studies* 14 (1989): 446–462.

Graves, C. "Levels of Existence: An Open System Theory of Values." *Journal of Humanistic Psychology* 10 (1970): 131–154.

Greening, D. W., and D. B. Turban. "Corporate Social Performance as a Competitive Advantage in Attracting a Quality Workforce." *Business and Society* 39 (2000): 254–280.

Greenleaf, R. K. *Servant Leadership.* New York: Paulist Press, 1977.

Griffon, J. J., and J. F. Mahon. "The Corporate Social Performance and Corporate Financial Performance Debate: Twenty-five Years of Incomparable Research." *Business and Society* 36 (1997): 5–31.

Gundling, E. "How to Communicate Globally." *Training and Development* 53 (1999): 28–31.

Halberstam, J. *Work: Making a Living and Making a Life.* New York: Perigee Books, 2000.

Hall, E. *Beyond Culture.* New York: Anchor Books, 1976.

Halstead, T., and C. Cobb. "The Need for New Measurements of Progress." In *The Case Against the Global Economy: And a Turn Toward the Local,* ed. J. Mander and E. Goldsmith, pp. 197–206. San Francisco: Sierra Club Books, 1996.

Hamelink, C. J. *The Ethics of Cyberspace.* London: Sage, 2000.

Hansen, C. D., and A. K. Brooks. "A Review of Cross-Cultural Research on Human Resource Development." *Human Resource Development Quarterly* 5 (1994): 55–74.

Haque, M. S. "Threats to Public Workplace Democracy." *Peace Review* 12 (2000): 237–241.

Harman, W., and J. Horman. *Creative Work: The Constructive Role of Business in a Transforming Society.* Indianapolis, Ind.: Knowledge Systems, 1990.

Harman, W., and M. Porter. *The New Business of Business: Sharing Responsibility for a Positive Global Future.* San Francisco: Berrett-Koehler, 1997.

Hartog, D. D., R. J. House, P. J. Hanges, and S. A. Ruiz-Quintanilla. "Culture Specific and Cross-Culturally Generalizable Implicit Leadership Theories: Are Attributes of

Charismatic/Transformational Leadership Universally Endorsed?" *Leadership Quarterly* 10 (1999): 219–256.

Harung, H. S., D. P. Heaton, and C. N. Alexander. "A Unified Theory of Leadership: Experiences of Higher States of Consciousness in World-Class Leaders." *Leadership and Organization Development Journal* 16 (1995): 44–58.

Hatcher, T. G. "Improving Ethical Performance: The Personal Ethics Process." *Performance and Instruction* 32 (1993): 21–28.

_____. "Improving Corporate Social Performance: A Strategic Planning Approach." *Performance Improvement* 36, no. 9 (1997): 23–27.

_____. "An Alternative View of Human Resource Development." In *Beyond Tradition: Preparing HRD Educators for Tomorrow's Workforce,* ed. R. R. Stewart and H. Hall, pp. 33–54. Columbia, Mo.: University Council for Occupational and Human Resource Development Education, 1998.

_____. "How Multiple Interventions Influenced Employee Turnover: A Case Study." *Human Resource Development Quarterly* 10 (1999): 365–382.

_____. "The Social Responsibility Performance Outcomes Model: Building Socially Responsible Companies Through Performance Improvement Outcomes." *Performance Improvement* 39 (2000a): 18–22.

_____. "A Study of the Influence of the Theoretical Foundations of Human Resource Development on Research and Practice." Proceedings of the 2000 AHRD International Conference. Research Triangle, N.C., 2000b.

_____. "The Social Responsibility Outcomes Model: How We Can Build Socially Responsible Companies." Proceedings of the 2001 International Society for Performance Improvement International Conference. San Francisco, April 8–12, 2001.

Hatcher, T. G., and S. Aragon. "Rationale for and Development of a Standard on Ethics and Integrity for International HRD Research and Practice." *Human Resource Development International* 3 (2000a): 207–219.

_____. "A Code of Ethics and Integrity for HRD Research and Practice." *Human Resource Development Quarterly* 11 (2000b): 179–186.

Hawken, P. *The Ecology of Commerce: A Declaration of Sustainability.* New York: HarperCollins, 1993.

Hawken, P., A. Lovins, and L. H. Lovins. *Natural Capitalism: Creating the Next Industrial Revolution.* Boston: Little, Brown and Company, 1999.

Hawley, J. *Reawakening the Spirit in Work.* New York: Fireside Books, 1993.

Hersey, P., and K. H. Blanchard. "Life-Cycle Theory of Leadership." *Training and Development Journal* 23 (1969): 26–34.

Hersey, P., K. H. Blanchard, and D. E. Johnson. *Management of Organizational Behavior.* 8th ed. Englewood Cliffs, N.J.: Prentice-Hall, 2000.

Hofstede, G. *Culture's Consequences: International Differences in Work-Related Values.* Beverly Hills, Calif.: Sage, 1980.

Honeycutt, E. D., J. A. Siguaw, and T. G. Hunt. "Business Ethics and Job Related Constructs." *Journal of Business Ethics* 14 (1995): 235–248.

Howard, R. *Brave New Workplace.* New York: Elizabeth Sifton Books, 1985.

Hultman, K., and B. Gellerman. *Balancing Individual and Organizational Values.* San Francisco: Jossey-Bass, 2002.

Hunt, S. D., and S. A. Vitell. "A General Theory of Marketing Ethics." *Journal of Macromarketing* 8 (1986): 5–16.

Husted, B. W. "A Contingency Theory of Corporate Social Performance." *Business and Society* 39 (2000): 24–49.

Ingelhart, R., M. Basaòez, and A. Moreno. *Human Values and Beliefs: A Cross-Cultural Sourcebook*. Ann Arbor: University of Michigan Press, 2001.

"Internet Use Surveillance Rising." *HR Focus* 78 (2001): 8.

Jacobs, R. "Human Resource Development as an Interdisciplinary Body of Knowledge." *Human Resource Development Quarterly* 1, no. 1 (1990): 65–71.

Jones, H. B. "The Ethical Leader: An Ascetic Construct." *Journal of Business Ethics* 14 (1995): 867–882.

Jones, J. M. "American Workers Most Satisfied with Workplace Safety, Relations with Co-Workers." Gallup Organization Poll Analyses, September 7, 2001. URL: http:://www.gallup.com/poll/releases/pr01104.asp.

Jones, R. H. *Reductionism: Analysis and Fullness of Reality*. Cranbury, N.J.: Associated University Presses, 2000.

Jones, T. M. "Ethical Decision Making by Individuals in Organizations: An Issue-Contingent Model. *Academy of Management Review* 16 (1991): 366–395.

Jones, T. M., and A. C. Wicks. "Convergent Stakeholder Theory." *Academy of Management Review* 24 (1999): 206–221.

Jordan, D. J. "Leadership: The State of the Research." *Parks and Recreation* 33 (1998): 32–39.

Jung, D. I., and B. J. Avolio. "Effects of Leadership Style and Followers' Cultural Orientation on Performance in Group and Individual Task Conditions." *Academy of Management Journal* 42 (1999): 208–218.

Kanungo, R. N., and M. Mendonca. *The Ethical Dimensions of Leadership*. Thousand Oaks, Calif.: Sage, 1996.

Kaufman, R. "Strategic Planning and Thinking: Alternative Views." *Performance and Instruction* 29 (1990): 1–7.

———. *Strategic Planning Plus: An Organizational Guide*. Newbury Park, Calif.: Sage, 1992.

———. "A New Reality for Organizational Success: Two Bottom Lines." *Performance Improvement* 36, no. 8 (1997): 3.

Kaufman, R., and R. Watkins. "Getting Serious About Results and Payoffs: We Are What We Say, Do, and Deliver." *Performance Improvement* 38 (2000): 23–32.

Keeley, M. "The Trouble with Transformational Leadership: Toward a Federalist Ethic for Organizations." In *Ethics, the Heart of Leadership*, ed. J. B. Ciulla, pp. 111–144. Westport, Conn.: Quorum Books, 1998.

Kellert, S. R. *The Value of Life: Biological Biodiversity and Human Society*. Washington, D.C.: Island Press, 1996.

Khor, M. "Global Economy and the Third World." In *The Case Against the Global Economy: And a Turn Toward the Local*, ed. J. Mander and E. Goldsmith, pp. 47–59. San Francisco: Sierra Club Books, 1996.

Kim, P. S. "Globalization of Human Resource Management: A Cross-Cultural Perspective for the Public Sector." *Public Personnel Management* 28 (1999): 227–243.

Klein, S. "Marketing Norms Measurement: An International Validation and Comparison." *Journal of Business Ethics* 18 (1999): 65–72.

Kohlberg, L. "The Development of Modes of Moral Thinking and Choice in the Years Ten to Sixteen." Ph.D. diss., University of Chicago, 1958.

Korten, D. C. *When Corporations Rule the World*. San Francisco: Berrett-Koehler, 1995.

———. "The Mythic Victory of Market Capitalism." In *The Case Against the Global Economy: And a Turn Toward the Local,* ed. J. Mander and E. Goldsmith, pp. 183–191. San Francisco: Sierra Club Books, 1996.

Kouzes, J. M., and B. Z. Posner. "Ethical Leaders: An Essay About Being in Love." *Journal of Business Ethics* 11 (1992): 479–491.

Kuchinke, K. P. "Leadership and Culture: Work-Related Values and Leadership Styles Among One Company's U.S. and German Telecommunications Employees." *Human Resource Development Quarterly* 10, no. 2 (1999): 135–154.

Langlois, C. C., and B. B. Schlegelmilch. "Do Corporate Codes of Ethics Reflect National Character? Evidence from Europe and the United States." *Journal of International Business Studies* 21 (1990): 519–540.

Little, A. W. "Globalisation, Qualifications and Livelihoods: Towards a Research Agenda." *Assessment in Education* 7 (2000): 299–312.

Longaberger, D. *Longaberger: An American Success Story*. New York: HarperBusiness, 2001.

Lowe, K. B., K. G. Kroeck, and N. Sivasubramaniam. "Effectiveness Correlates of Transformational and Transactional Leadership: A Meta-analytic Review of the MLQ Literature." *Leadership Quarterly* 7 (1996): 385–425.

Lydenburg, S. D. "Can Corporate Social Responsibility Be Legislated?" *Business and Society Review* 96 (1996): 38–41.

Maclagan, P. *Management and Morality: A Developmental Perspective*. London: Sage, 1998.

Maher, K. J. "Gender-Related Stereotypes of Transformational and Transactional Leadership." *Sex Roles* 37 (1997): 209–225.

Mander, J. "Technologies of Globalization." In *The Case Against the Global Economy: And a Turn Toward the Local,* ed. J. Mander and E. Goldsmith, pp. 344–359. San Francisco: Sierra Club Books, 1996.

Mander, J., and E. Goldsmith, eds. *The Case Against the Global Economy: And a Turn Toward the Local*. San Francisco: Sierra Club Books, 1996.

Marsick, V. J. "Altering the Paradigm for Theory Building and Research in Human Resource Development." *Human Resource Development Quarterly* 1, no. 1 (1990): 5–24.

Marx, T. G. "Corporate Social Performance Reporting." *Public Relations Quarterly* 37 (1992–1993): 38–45.

Maznevski, M., J. J. Distefano, C. B. Gomez, N. G. Noorderhaven, and P-C. Wu. "Cultural Dimensions at the Individual Level of Analysis: The Cultural Orientations Framework." Unpublished manuscript, 2000.

Maznevski, M., and M. F. Peterson. "Societal Values, Social Interpretation, and Multinational Teams." In *Cross-Cultural Work Groups,* ed. C. S. Granrose and S. Oskamp, pp. 61–89. Thousand Oaks, Calif.: Sage, 1997.

McLagan, P. A. *Models for HRD Practice*. Alexandrea, Va.: American Society for Training and Development, 1989.

McLean, G. N. "Ethical Dilemmas and the Many Hats of HRD." *Human Resource Development Quarterly* 12, no. 3 (2001a): 219–221.

_____. "Human Resource Development as a Factor in the Inevitable Move to Globalization." In *Academy of Human Resource Development 2001 Conference Proceedings,* ed. O. A. Aliaga, pp. 356–363. Baton Rouge, La.: Academy of Human Resource Development, 2001b.

McOmber, J. B. "Technological Autonomy and Three Definitions of Technology." *Journal of Communication* 49 (1999): 137–153.

Merchant, C. "Partnership Ethics: Business and the Environment." In *Environmental Challenges to Business,* ed. J. Reichart and P. H. Werhane, Ruffin Series No. 2, pp. 7–18. Bowling Green, Ohio: Society for Business Ethics, 2000.

Micklethwait, J., and A. Wooldridge. *A Future Perfect: The Challenge and Hidden Promise of Globalization*. New York: Crown Business, 2000.

Mishra, J. M., and S. M. Crampton. "Employee Monitoring: Privacy in the Workplace?" *S.A.M. Advanced Management Journal* 63 (1998): 4–14.

Mitroff, I. I., and E. A. Denton. "A Study of Spirituality in the Workplace." *Sloan Management Review* 40 (1999): 83–92.

Moller, L., and P. Mallin. "Evaluation Practices of Instructional Designers and Organizational Supporters and Barriers." *Performance Improvement Quarterly* 9 (1996): 82–92.

Morrow, R. A., and C. A. Torres. "The State, Globalization, and Educational Policy." In *Globalization and Education: Critical Perspectives,* ed. N. C. Burbules and C. A. Torres, pp. 27–56. New York: Routledge, 2000.

Nader, R., and L. Wallach. "GATT, NAFTA, and the Subversion of the Democratic Process." In *The Case Against the Global Economy: And a Turn Toward the Local,* ed. J. Mander and E. Goldsmith, pp. 92–107. San Francisco: Sierra Club Books, 1996.

Nakra, P. "Corporate Reputation Management: 'CRM' with a Strategic Twist." *Public Relations Quarterly* 45 (2000): 35–42.

Needleman, H. L. "Deficits in Psychologic and Classroom Performance of Children with Elevated Dentine Lead Levels." *New England Journal of Medicine* 300 (1979): 13.

Nelkin, D. "Information Technologies Could Threaten Privacy, Freedom, and Democracy." In *Computers, Ethics, and Society,* 2d ed., ed. M. D. Ermann, M. B. Williams, and M. S. Shauf, pp. 20–25. New York: Oxford University Press, 1997.

Neufeldt, V., ed. *Webster's New World Dictionary*. New York: Pocket Books, 1995.

Norris, W. R., and R. P. Vecchio. "Situational Leadership: A Replication." *Group and Organizational Management* 17 (1992): 331–343.

Nyaw, M-K., and I. Ng. "A Comparative Analysis of Ethical Beliefs: A Four Country Study." *Journal of Business Ethics* 13 (1994): 543–555.

O'Toole, J. *Leading Change: The Argument for Values-Based Leadership*. New York: Ballentine Books, 1995.

Owen, H. *Open Space Technology: A User's Guide*. Potomac, Md.: Abbott Publishing, 1992.

Paden, W. E. *Interpreting the Sacred: Ways of Viewing Religion.* Boston: Beacon Press, 1992.

Passmore, D. L. "Ways of Seeing: Disciplinary Bases of Research in HRD." In *Human Resource Development Research Handbook,* ed. R. A. Swanson and E. F. Holton, pp. 199–214. San Francisco: Berrett-Koehler, 1996.

Pava, M. L., and J. Krausz. *Corporate Social Responsibility and Financial Performance.* Westport, Conn.: Greenwood Publishers,1995.

Peet, R. *Theories of Development.* New York: Guilford Press, 1999.

Perry-Smith, J. E., and T. C. Blum. "Work-Family Human Resource Bundles and Perceived Organizational Performance." *Academy of Management Journal* 43 (2000): 1107–1117.

Pfeffer, J. *Competitive Advantage Through People: Unleashing the Power of the Workforce.* Boston: Harvard Business School Press, 1994.

Portugal, E., and G. Yukl. "Perspectives on Environmental Leadership." *Leadership Quarterly* 5 (1994): 271–276.

Postman, N. *Technopoly: The Surrender of Culture to Technology.* New York: Alfred A. Knopf, 1993.

Quarter, J. *Beyond the Bottom Line: Socially Innovative Business Owners.* Westport, Conn.: Quorum Books, 2000.

Ray, P. H., and S. R. Anderson. *The Cultural Creatives: How 50 Million People Are Changing the World.* New York: Harmony Books, 2000.

"Redefining Progress." *Redefining Progress Press Release,* December 6, 2001. URL: http://www.rprogress.org/media/releases.

Reder, A. *In Pursuit of Principle and Profit: Business Success Through Social Responsibility.* New York: Jeremy P. Tarcher/Putnam, 1994.

Reich, R. B. *The Work of Nations: Preparing Ourselves for 21ˢᵗ Century Capitalism.* New York: Vintage, 1991.

Rest, J. "Background Theory and Research." In *Moral Development in the Professions,* ed. J. Rest and D. Narvaez, pp. 33–62. Hillsdale, N.J.: Erlbaum and Associates, 1994.

Rifkin, J. *The Age of Access: The New Culture of Hypercapitalism, Where All of Life Is a Paid-for Experience.* New York: Jeremy P. Tarcher/Putnam, 2000.

Riordan, C. M., R. D. Gatewood, and J. B. Bill. "Corporate Image: Employee Reactions and Implications for Managing Corporate Social Performance." *Journal of Business Ethics* 16 (1997): 401–412.

Rokeach, M. *The Nature of Human Values.* New York: Free Press, 1973.

Rosenthal, S. B., and R. A. Buchholz. "The Empirical-Normative Split in Business Ethics: A Pragmatic Alternative." *Business Ethics Quarterly* 10, no. 2 (2000): 399–408.

Rost, J. C. *Leadership for the Twenty-First Century.* New York: Praeger, 1991.

Roszak, T. "Where Psyche Meets Gaia." In *Ecopsychology: Restoring the Earth, Healing the Mind,* ed. T. Roszak, M. E. Gomes, and A. D. Kanner, pp. 1–20. San Francisco: Sierra Club Books, 1995.

Roszak, T., M. E. Gomes, and A. D. Kanner, eds. *Ecopsychology: Restoring the Earth, Healing the Mind.* San Francisco: Sierra Club Books, 1995.

Rothwell, W. J. *ASTD Models for Human Performance: Roles, Competencies, and Outputs.* 2d ed. Alexandria, Va.: American Society for Training and Development, 1999.

Rousseau, D. M. *Psychological Contracts in Organizations: Understanding Written and Unwritten Agreements.* Thousand Oaks, Calif.: Sage, 1995.

Rowley, T., and S. Berman. "A Brand New Brand of Corporate Social Performance." *Business and Society* 39 (2000): 397–418.

Ruggiero, V. R. *Thinking Critically About Ethical Issues.* 4th ed. Mountain View, Calif.: Mayfield Publishing, 1997.

Rugman, A. *The End of Globalization: Why Global Strategy Is a Myth and How to Profit from the Realities of Regional Markets.* New York: AMACOM, 2001.

Rummler, G. A. and Brache, A. P. *Improving Performance: How to Manage the White Space on the Organization Chart,* Second Ed. San Francisco: Jossey-Bass, 1995.

Russ-Eft, D. "Leaders Behaving Badly: How to Block Innovation in Organizations. In *Academy of Human Resource Development 1998 Conference Proceedings,* ed. R. J. Torraco, pp. 210–215. Baton Rouge, La.: Academy of Human Resource Development, 1998.

Russ-Eft, D., J. Burns, P. Dean, T. Hatcher, F. Otte, and H. Preskill. *Standards on Ethics and Integrity. The Academy of Human Resource Development.* Baton Rouge, La.: Academy of Human Resource Development, 1999.

Sachs, W. "Global Ecology and the Shadow of Development." In *Deep Ecology for the Twenty-First Century,* ed. G. Sessions, pp. 428–443. Boston: Shambhala, 1995.

Salopek, J. J. "Do the Right Thing." *Training and Development* (July 2001): 39–44.

Salt, B., R. M. Cervero, and A. Herod. "Workers' Education and Neoliberal Globalization: An Adequate Response to Transnational Corporations." *Adult Education Quarterly* 51 (2000): 9–23.

Santos, M. A. *The Environmental Crisis.* Westport, Conn.: Greenwood Press, 1999.

Saunders, P. *Capitalism.* Minneapolis: University of Minnesota Press, 1995.

Saxton, K. "Understanding and Evaluating Reputation." *Reputation Management* (May/June 1998): 19.

Schein, E. H. *Organizational Culture and Leadership.* 2d ed. San Francisco: Jossey-Bass, 1998.

Schumacher, E. F. *Small Is Beautiful: Economics as if People Mattered.* New York: Harper and Row, 1973.

_____. *A Guide for the Perplexed.* New York: Harper and Row, 1977.

_____. *Good Work.* New York: Harper and Row, 1979.

Schwarz, M. "The Nature of the Relationship Between Corporate Codes of Ethics and Behavior." *Journal of Business Ethics* 32 (2001): 247–262.

Senge, P.. *The Fifth Discipline: The Art and Practice of the Learning Organization.* New York: Doubleday, 1990.

_____. "Leading Learning Organizations." *Training and Development* 50 (1996): 36–37.

_____. "Rethinking Control and Complexity." In *Rethinking the Future,* ed. R. Gibson, pp. 132–166. London: Nicholas Brealey, 1997.

Senge, P., R. Carstedt, and L. Porter. "Innovating Our Way to the Next Industrial Revolution." *MIT Sloan Management Review* 42, (2001): 24–38.

Sessions, G., ed. *Deep Ecology for the Twenty-First Century*. Boston and London: Shambhala, 1995.

Sethi, S. P. "Dimensions of Corporate Social Performance: An Analytic Framework." *California Management Review* 17 (spring 1975): 58–64.

Shade, L. R. "A Gendered Perspective on Access to the Information Infrastructure." *Information Society* 14 (1998): 33–44.

Shareef, R. "Ecovision: A Leadership Theory for Innovative Organizations." *Organizational Dynamics* 20 (1991): 50–63.

Sharkey, L. D. "Changing Organizational Culture Through Leadership Development: A Case in Leadership Transformation." *Organization Development Journal* 17 (1999): 29–42.

Sheldrake, R. *The Rebirth of Nature: The Greening of Science and God*. Rochester, Vt.: Park Street Press, 1991.

Shrader-Frechette, K. S. *Environmental Ethics*. 2d. ed. London: Rowman and Littlefield, 1998.

Shrivastava, P. "Ecocentric Management for a Risk Society." In *Green Management: A Reader*, ed. P. McDonagh and A. Prothero, pp.22–39. London: Dryden Press, 1997.

_____. "Ecocentering Strategic Management." In *Environmental Challenges to Business, Ruffin Series No.2*, ed. J. Reichart and P. H. Werhane, pp. 23–44. Bowling Green, Ohio: Society for Business Ethics, 2000.

Sims, R. S. "Changing an Organization's Culture Under New Leadership." *Journal of Business Ethics* 25 (2000): 65–78.

Singer, P. "Ethics Across the Species Boundary." In *Global Ethics and Environment*, ed. N. Low, pp. 146–157. London: Routledge, 1999.

Smith, P. L., and E. E. Oakley. "Gender Related Differences in Ethical and Social Values of Business Students: Implications for Management." *Journal of Business Ethics* 16 (1997): 37–45.

Stead, R., and J. G. Stead. *Management for a Small Planet*. 2d ed. Thousand Oaks, Calif.: Sage, 1996.

_____. "Earth: A Spiritual Stakeholder." In *Environmental Challenges to Business, Ruffin Series No. 2*, ed. J. Reichart and P. H. Werhane, pp. 231–253. Bowling Green, Ohio: Society for Business Ethics, 2000.

Swanson, R. A. "Foundations of Performance Improvement and Implications for Practice." In *Performance Improvement Theory and Practice*, Advances in Human Resource Development Monograph No. 1, ed. R. A. Swanson (series ed.) and R. J. Torraco (vol. ed.), pp. 1–25. San Francisco: Berrett-Koehler, 1999.

Taylor, H. "Three Factors Appear to Have Big Impact on Job Satisfaction." Harris Poll #74, November 4, 2001. URL: http://www.harrisinteractive.com/harris_poll/index.asp.

Thompson, C. M. "Reorientation Eases the Pain and Loss of Downsizing." *HR Focus* 69 (1992): 11–13.

Thurow, L. C. *The Future of Capitalism: How Today's Economic Forces Shape Tomorrow's World.* New York: William Morrow and Company, 1996.

Vecchio, R. P. "Situational Leadership Theory: An Examination of a Prescriptive Theory." *Journal of Applied Psychology* 72 (1987): 444–451.

Velasquez, M. "Globalization and the Failure of Ethics." *Business Ethics Quarterly* 10 (2000): 343–352.

Victor, B., and C. U. Stephens. "Business Ethics: A Synthesis of Normative Philosophy and Empirical Social Science." *Business Ethics Quarterly* 4 (1994): 145–155.

Wagner, S. "Globalization Drives Training in Europe." *Training and Development* 53 (1999): 59–61.

Waldman, D. A., G. G. Ramírez, R. J. House, and P. Puranam. "Does Leadership Matter? CEO Leadership Attributes and Profitability Under Conditions of Perceived Environmental Uncertainty." *Academy of Management Journal* 44 (2001): 134–143.

Wartick, S. L., and D. J. Wood. *International Business and Society.* Oxford: Blackwell Publishers Ltd., 1998.

Watkins, K. E. "A Common Body of Knowledge Is Nonsense in a Field in Search of Itself." *Human Resource Development Quarterly* 1, no. 2 (1990): 181–186.

Watkins, R., D. Leigh, and R. Kaufman. "A Scientific Dialogue: A Performance Accomplishment Code of Professional Conduct." *Performance Improvement* 38 (2000): 17–22.

Weaver, G. R., L. K. Trevino, and P. L. Cochran. "Corporate Ethics Practices in the Mid-1990s: An Empirical Study of the Fortune 1000." *Journal of Business Ethics* 18 (1999): 283–294.

Weber, M. "The Sociology of Charismatic Authority." Republished in translation (1946) in *From Max Weber: Essays in Sociology,* ed. and trans. H. H. Gerth and C. W. Mills, pp. 245–252. New York: Oxford University Press, 1921.

Weisbord, M., and S. Janoff. *Future Search: Finding Common Ground for Action in Organizations.* San Francisco: Berrett-Koehler, 1995.

Welles, E. O. "Ben's Big Flop." *Inc.* 20 (1998): 40–57.

Wellins, R., and W. Byham. "The leadership gap." *Training* 38 (March 2001): 98–106.

Wheatley, M. J. *Leadership and the New Science: Learning About Organization from an Orderly Universe.* San Francisco: Berrett-Koelher, 1992.

Whitcomb, L. L., C. B. Erdener, and C. Li. "Business Ethical Values in China and the U.S." *Journal of Business Ethics* 17 (1998): 839–852.

Whitney, D. "Spirituality as an Organizing Principle." In *The New Business of Business: Sharing Responsibility for a Positive Global Future,* ed. W. Harman and M. Porter, pp.191–200. San Francisco: Berrett-Koehler, 1997.

Wilber, K. *A Theory of Everything: An Integral Vision for Business, Politics, Science, and Spirituality.* Boston: Shambahala, 2000.

Wiley, C. "Ethical Standards for Human Resource Management Professionals: A Comparative Analysis of Five Major Codes." *Journal of Business Ethics* 25 (2000): 93–114.

Williams, M. B. "Ethical Issues in Computing: Work, Privacy, and Justice." In *Computers, Ethics, and Society,* 2d ed., ed. M. D. Ermann, M. B. Williams, and M. S. Shauf, pp. 3–19. New York: Oxford University Press, 1997.

Wilson, E. O. *Consilience: The Unity of Knowledge*. New York: Knopf, 1998.

Winner, L. *Autonomous Technology: Technics-Out-of-Control as a Theme in Political Thought*. Cambridge, Mass.: MIT Press, 1977.

Wishard, W. V. D. "The Cultural Context of a Sustainable Future." In *The New Business of Business: Sharing Responsibility for a Positive Global Future,* ed. W. Harman and M. Porter, pp.15–24. San Francisco: Berrett-Koehler, 1997.

Wood, D. J. "Corporate Social Performance Revisited." *Academy of Management Review* 16 (1991a): 691–718.

———. "Toward Improving Corporate Social Performance." *Business Horizons* 3 (1991b): 66–73.

———. "The Fortune Database as a CSP Measure." *Business and Society* 34 (1995): 197–198.

Woodall, J. "HRD in a Values-Driven Business: The Body Shop International plc. Jim McNeish interviewed by Jean Woodall." *Human Resource Development International* 2 (1999): 283–288.

Yukl, G. A. *Leadership in Organizations.* 2d ed. Englewood Cliffs, N.J.: Prentice-Hall, 1989.

Yukl, G. A., and D. D. Van Fleet. "Theory and Research on Leadership and Organizations." In *Handbook of Industrial and Organizational Psychology,* ed. M. D. Dunnette and L. M. Hough, pp. 1–51. Palo Alto, Calif.: Consulting Psychologists Press, 1992.

Zuboff, S. *In the Age of the Smart Machine: The Future of Work and Power.* New York: Basic Books, 1988.

Index